T0212008

Agile Software Engineering Skills

Julian Michael Bass

Agile
Software
Engineering
Skills

 Springer

Julian Michael Bass
University of Salford
Salford, UK

ISBN 978-3-031-05468-6   ISBN 978-3-031-05469-3   (eBook)
https://doi.org/10.1007/978-3-031-05469-3

This Springer imprint is published by the registered company Springer Nature Switzerland AG
The registered company address is: Gewerbestrasse 11, 6330 Cham, Switzerland

For Bizunesh, Alfie, Rosa and Jill.
In memory of Kibe, Alfie and Beryl.

Preface

The skills you learn from this book will help establish your career in software development. You can learn skills for working in self-organising teams, developing software increments and facilitating agile processes. I see a continuing need for an introductory book that draws together this wide range of modern technical, collaboration and software process skills.

The book is aimed at early career software development practitioners. You might be in work or a student and want to work with others and create beautiful computer programs. Working with people is challenging. For some, more challenging than for others. Learning to work in a team, with other people who share all our own frailties, idiosyncrasies and foibles is an important part of life. The hands-on approach in this book will help equip you for success in a software development team.

Book Structure

Agile methods comprise three sets of related ideas: roles, artefacts and ceremonies. Consequently, this book comprises three parts, dedicated to *People*, *Product* and *Process*.

Part I, which focuses on *People*, describes project roles and the skills you need to perform each role. This includes members of self-organising teams, scrum masters, product owners and activities for managing other stakeholders.

I talk about the skills needed to create *Product* artefacts in Part II. You can learn the skills you need to create agile requirements, architectures, designs as well as development and security artefacts.

The agile development *Process*, you can use to coordinate your work with others, is described in Part III. I introduce the skills you need to facilitate an incremental process and to use software tools for version control and automated testing. These processes can improve product quality and tools automate aspects of your development process.

I discuss some more advanced topics in Part IV. These topics include large projects comprising multiple cooperating teams, automating deployment, cloud software services and evolving live systems.

IEEE/ACM Computing Curriculum Competencies

This book addresses, at least in part, significant competencies in the IEEE/ACM Computing Curricula Task Force 2020. Competencies comprise knowledge, skills, dispositions and tasks. Knowledge in the form of factual understanding is a prerequisite for professional practice. The skills are how we apply knowledge to successfully perform professional activities. Dispositions are the attitudes and character we display when performing professional activities. Finally, tasks frame the application of knowledge, skills and dispositions. Some specific competencies addressed include:

- Computer Science Draft Competencies

  - SDF-Software Development Fundamentals
  - SE-Software Engineering
  - SP-Social Issues and Professional Practice

- Software Engineering Draft Competencies

  - Software Requirements
  - Software Design
  - Software Construction
  - Software Process and Life Cycle

- Information Systems Draft Competencies

  - Analysing trade-offs
  - Designing and implementing information systems solutions
  - Leadership and collaboration

- Information Technology Competencies

  - ITE-SWF Software Fundamentals

- Master's in Information Systems Draft Competencies

  - Systems Development and Deployment [SDAD]

The focus on competencies, in the book, also draws on the Skills for the Information Age framework which provides advice for practitioners across the computing and information technology sectors. The skills in this book link together topics from university courses in programming, databases and data structures through an approach informed by practice.

Exercises

You can't learn new skills just by reading about them. You have to read, practice, evaluate, reflect and read some more. By *practice*, I mean *apply* and then *put into practice*. Each chapter has exercises. These exercises are important to help you acquire the skills you need. Some exercises are performed alone; for some, you will need to work in a group. Performing the exercises is, perhaps, the most important part of the book.

Hints, tips and further advice about tackling the exercises are presented at the end of each chapter. I recommend you plan your approach to each exercise (but do not look at the hints or tips). Then, actually conduct or perform the exercise (but, still, do not look at the hints or tips). Reflect on what happened. What went well? What could have gone better? Make some notes about what happened. Now. Only now, look at the hints, tips and advice at the chapter end.

> **Using the Book Parts**
> The book Parts are pretty much stand-alone. So, if you want, you could start with Part II on *Product*. Or, you could start with Part III on *Process*. If you have become familiar with the first three parts, then you can look at Part IV on more advanced topics.

How to Use This Book

You could start at the beginning and read through to the end. But, you don't have to. You should read the Introduction in Chap. 1, first. But then you have a choice, depending on your interests and current skills. You could just carry on to Chap. 2 in Part I on *People*. Or, perhaps you could start with Chap. 7 in Part II on *Product*. Or maybe, you could start with Chap. 13 on *Process* in Part III.

Descriptions at the start of each book part give a brief overview of the contents. Chapter abstracts help you gain a more detailed sense of the overall flow of the book. Reading the book part introductions and chapter abstracts would be a *top-down* approach, which focuses on the holistic structure or organisation of the book. You could use the *top-down* approach to plan which book parts and chapters you would like to explore first.

Alternatively, you could dive straight into one of the chapters that interests you. This is a *bottom-up* approach. The *bottom-up* approach favours starting by getting into the detail of one interesting issue. I recommend that you work through the exercises provided in each chapter. The chapter summaries will help you review and reflect on the skills you have learned.

Once you do decide to read a chapter, I recommend a simple five-step approach:

1. Read the chapter text first, taking notes in your learning journal as you go.
2. Perform the exercises (practice the new skills) at the end of each chapter, taking notes in your learning journal as you go.
3. Review the guidance, hints and tips on each exercise presented at the end of each chapter while making comments and corrections in your learning journal.
4. Review your learning journal and reflect on your new skills.
5. Make plans for the next stage of your skills development effort.

Hence, I advise that you use each chapter as part of a learning cycle. Learn the new skills. Apply and use the new skills as you go through the chapters. Reflect on your learning. Plan what skills you want to learn next.

You will use freely available open-source software tools. This lowers your cost of entry and helps you understand what benefits you might get from purchasing (sometimes expensive) commercial tools later.

Acquire Skills with the Exercises
There are nearly 100 exercises in this book. Use the exercises to try out and apply the skills you need for agile software development.

Some exercises are technical tasks you can try on your own. Some are exercises in group facilitation or team working. For these exercises, you will need friends or colleagues to help.

Hints, tips and advice on the exercises are provided at the end of each chapter, which will help you develop and enhance those skills. Make sure you try each exercise before you look at any advice or solution provided.

Learning Journal

You should try to make your learning explicit and deliberate. One way to do this is by using a learning journal. I suggest you create a journal for each of the three main parts of the book: *People*, *Product* and *Process*. Use the learning journal to capture your newly acquired skills and experiences, as well as to reflect on your own learning process.

Tabby Cat Project

The *Tabby Cat* project integrates and applies the skills from each chapter into a single case study. The *Tabby Cat* project was provided by *Red Ocelot Ltd.*, a software start-up company associated with the University of Salford. You can think of this as a worked example. The project is to build software for displaying activity on a source code repository. You can read each *Tabby Cat* project chapter when you finish reading each Part. Or, you could read the chapters as a sequence from Chap. 6 and then Chaps. 12 and 17.

Student Group Projects and Hackathons

This book is also to support undergraduate software engineering and computing student group projects. Students I've taught, on the *HackCamp* at University of Salford, or the *Software Hut* at University of Bangor, need to gain a range of collaboration, technical and build process skills for success. I wrote this book, in part, to satisfy these needs and because I found it difficult to find a single source elsewhere.

Prior Knowledge

You should already have the skills to implement software solutions to simple classroom problems. I assume you know how to code. Or I should say, I make no attempt to teach you how to code. By which I mean, you should have already learned the basics of one or two programming languages, at least for a semester or two.

You will be able to create the syntax of variables, operators, statements and flow control, in your chosen language. I assume you can create object-oriented classes, and their run-time instances, that interact with each other and encapsulate data. You can probably already use data structures, such as collections, and maybe you have learned how to build a simple database-driven website.

This book is about applying the programming skills you have to your first few projects. If you don't have these skills, you can use this book alongside learning basic programming. Either way, this book will help you acquire the collaboration and agile process skills you need for success.

Manchester, UK   Julian Michael Bass
March 2022

Acknowledgements

Thanks to all my former HackCamp students at the University of Salford and Software Hut students at the University of Bangor. Several commercial partners have shown dedicated support to HackCamp, including Kim Massaro, KRM, Andy Haxby Competa, Mo Tagari, AJ Bell as well as Lester Dias and Kuldeep Padhiar from Manchester Branch, BCS, the Chartered Institute for IT.

I'm also grateful to many collaborators and colleagues, including Prof Sunil Vadera, Dr Tarek Gaber, Prof Richard Heeks, Prof Rob Aspin, Prof Ian Allison, Prof John McCall, Prof Robert Davison, Dr Robert Gittins and Dr Reza Latif Shabgahi. I learned about all the important principles of systems engineering from Prof Peter Fleming and Dr Stuart Bennett at the University of Sheffield.

Thanks also to current and former PhD students: Dr Abubakar Dahiru, Dr Azmi Omar, Dr Charles Ochei, Dr Abdullah Salameh, Dr Scarlet Rahy, Adekunbi Adewojo, Ruth Macarthy, Abdulhamid Ardo, Ben Monaghan and Tom Bolton. Some ideas in the book draw on the many thought-provoking meetings I've had, over the years, with these researchers. Several book chapters are enriched with evidence from their empirical research investigating software practitioners from around the world.

I was privileged to learn much from talented technical architects and consultants working at Chordiant Software. I benefited from the opportunity to work with Add Energy Ltd. and learned much from these activities. At Add Energy, with Hossein Ghavimi and Peter Adam, we co-created a scrum-based software innovation process, and I advised on the development of their AimHi, AssetC and AssetVoice products. Thanks also to Taha Mansouri who worked in collaboration with the team at Invisible Systems Ltd.

I am indebted to my colleagues in Red Ocelot Ltd., which is our software start-up company formed in association with the University of Salford. Red Ocelot is focused on digital solutions for technical debt. Ben Monaghan kindly implemented the *Tabby Cat* project and contributed text to Chap. 12.

Thanks to Amr Hamed who suggested including a case study and provided thoughtful feedback on several chapters. I also want to thank Salford students, including Liam Sutton, who provided specific feedback on earlier drafts of chapters from this book.

Contents

Chapter 1
Introduction and Principles

Abstract This book is divided into three main parts: *people*, *product* and *process*. Each of those parts is summarised by a case study chapter, the *Tabby Cat* project, which runs through an agile software development process. This chapter explains the book structure and introduces some key principles of agile software engineering.

1.1 Agile Software Skills

Software is everywhere. Whichever way we look, there is software we depend on. Transportation, food production, logistics, entertainment and utilities like electricity and water supply all depend on software. But, there is good software and bad software. And, my word, there is plenty of bad software! Business information systems that intelligent people can hardly use. Expensive software development projects that falter and fail. Security breaches that compromise our personal data. We can no longer afford to create bad software. Lots of us need to learn how to create good software. And fast!

This book provides a practical, hands-on, guide to the skills you need to work as part of a team on an agile software development project. It is inspired by the needs of early career practitioners who are new (or newish) to making software with colleagues. We need the ability to create working software in a team and fulfil a client's needs. The skills described here will equip you for success in your first few projects. This book gets you in the game.

The skills you learn here have got people paid work placements (internships) and employment. These topics will give you good things to talk about in job interviews. You will have a chance to learn the skills you need to build more sophisticated software applications. I will show you how to apply some of the latest ideas from agile, lean and Kanban, DevOps (continuous integration and continuous delivery), version control, automated testing and cloud deployment, albeit, at an introductory level.

Software development can be viewed from three perspectives: *people*, *product* and *process*. Hence, the book has been organised around these three key themes, with one book Part devoted to each.

J. M. Bass, *Agile Software Engineering Skills*,
https://doi.org/10.1007/978-3-031-05469-3_1

1.1.1 People

When you first learn to program a computer, most of your learning will take place alone. You will acquire technical skills you need to create a software *product*. But, here's the thing: Building software systems is something people do in teams. Software engineering is a *team sport*. As systems grow larger, few people can wait the time it would take for one person to actually build the thing. Either you enlist the help of some friends or you work as part a commercial team to build a product. In this book, you will learn how to collaborate with colleagues to create working software. Figure 1.1 illustrates the organisation on chapters in the parts of the book.

So, Part I of the book is about *people*. You will have an opportunity to gain personal, teamwork and organisational skills for working with *people*. Skills for self-organising teams are in Chap. 2. We also need people in roles around our self-organising teams that aid, support and enable our software development. The skills used in these roles are discussed in Chap. 3. The teams and their facilitators need to manage a range of other interested parties, called stakeholders. Stakeholders could be customers, executives or outsiders to the development process. The skills you need for managing stakeholders are in Chap. 4. The behaviour and consequences of the technology sector are increasingly attracting the attention of regulators. Whistle-blowers, from within technology corporations, have revealed examples of their employers' anti-competitive practices and consumer harms. The issues of ethics are discussed in Chap. 5.

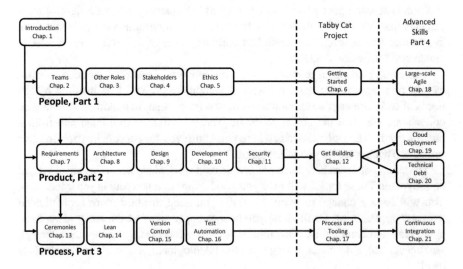

Fig. 1.1 Alternative chapter sequences

1.1.2 Product

The technical skills you need, to build *Products* and systems from working code, are discussed in Part II of the book, as shown in Fig. 1.1. When you start work building a product, you need to know what it is supposed to do. You can learn about the skills and techniques for recording and managing requirements in Chap. 7. Maybe someone (such as a boss, client or some other stakeholder) is going to tell you what software you are supposed to create. But often what you are told is not detailed enough or sufficiently clear for you to go ahead and get working. In this case, we need to embark on a process of requirements discovery.

In the rest of Part II, you can learn about creating software product from requirements. We use feature-driven development. A *feature* is a function that the software must perform. Features provide end-to-end functionality, including front-end (user experience) and back-end (logic and storage) code.

The scope of a product is the number of features, or requirements, your software is to provide. We can increase the scope of our project by building new software features that fulfil more requirements. We can reduce our planned scope by lowering the number of features we aim to create. A *feature* is some client-valued function that the software must perform. Features include end-to-end functionality, comprising front-end (user experience) and back-end (logic and storage) code. We think about features as a *thin slice* through the layers of a business information system. Normally a feature is small enough that we can implement it in a few days. Individual features can be collected into larger groups of business-related functions, sometimes called feature sets or epics. Designing and building software as a series of features allows us to stay focused on what our users (or clients) actually want. They can give us feature-by-feature feedback, so we all know that what we are producing is what is needed. Feature-driven development also facilitates tracking (a benefit to us and the people providing the funding).

Features are collected into larger groups of business-related functions, forming increments. Hence, we advocate an incremental approach to software development. The idea is that we deliver our software as a series of phases or stages. So, an increment is a code release forming some part of a larger working system.

You can learn about the skills to create a high-level software *architecture* in Chap. 8. Here, you can learn about architectural styles. Next, you learn skills of software *design* in Chap. 9. We explore some common object-oriented design patterns. After that, *implementation* skills are described in Chap. 10. Finally, in Part II, you learn about the skills you need for building *secure* systems in Chap. 11.

1.1.3 Process

To ensure software quality, we need a systematic and repeatable *Process* for software development. The process helps us meet client needs and ensure we can deliver a product on time. You need to learn skills about a software *process*. Our goal is to be able to produce software with an appropriate and predictable level of quality. The software development process skills you need are discussed in Part III of the book, as shown in Fig. 1.1.

Engineers understand that software development is not just the technical process of writing computer code, although that is obviously important and central to what we do. As engineers, we are also concerned with project management and developing wider processes that are needed to support software production.

Our goal is to employ repeatable development processes. We want to know we can perform software production over, and over, again. This is why Part III of the book is focused on the software development *process*. We advocate an iterative approach. An iteration is a cycle of activities we use to create the source code, a little development life cycle of planning, designing, building (code) and testing used to develop the features within an increment. Obviously writing the working software is at the heart of this activity. But our feature quality is going to be suspect, if we have not thought much about the design. Similarly, software that has not been tested, is not finished. Untested software is not likely to be good.

You will have a chance to learn about agile *ceremonies* in Chap. 13. While, in Chap. 14, you can learn the skills you need for using *lean* approaches. Version control skills that allow you to establish a revision history and share each other's source code are covered in Chap. 15. Finally, in Part III, Chap. 16, testing skills are described.

1.1.4   Advanced Skills

The advanced skills Chapters stand alone. Consequently, you can read them as a sequence from Chap. 18 to 21. Alternatively, you can jump ahead to the advanced skills chapters that correspond to each part. Chapter 18 is about *people* and how multiple teams are coordinated on larger projects. Chapters 19 and 20 are about *product* and how to deploy software-as-a-service applications to the cloud and manage evolution in live software products, while Chap. 21 is concerned with *process* and how to automate deployment using DevOps.

Hence, this book explores three main areas of software development skills in the *people* aspects of team working, the technical aspects of software *product* development and how to enable a systematic and repeatable software development *process*.

1.2   Engineering Software

Software development is an engineering discipline. Engineers make systematic use of appropriate theories and methods to solve problems and build solutions within defined organisational and financial constraints. When we think of software

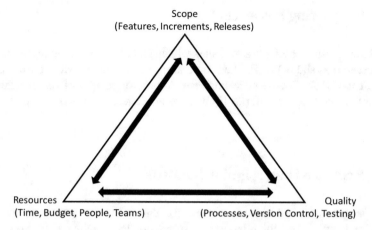

Fig. 1.2 The software triangle

development as an engineering discipline, we recognise the need to consider all aspects of software production, from early stages of conceptualisation and planning right through to enhancing live systems and their eventual retirement.

If we have been assigned to a software team in work or college, we have little control over the resources available. But as the software triangle shown in Fig. 1.2 illustrates, even with fixed resources, we can balance the effort devoted to project scope and software quality. We can't usually increase the number of features we create and increase product quality at the same time, unless we add time or resources. Hence, we have to balance conflicting trade-offs. We have to make a choice between producing additional features or achieving higher quality (assuming fixed resources).

We can improve quality by investing more effort in source code peer reviews and additional software testing, for instance. But in some cases, we have to compromise on quality to get a product to market quickly. On the other hand, our reputation suffers if we produce poor-quality products.

If you increase scope, with fixed resources, the product quality tends to go down. Similarly, if you wish to increase quality, either you must increase resources or reduce project scope. In software development, these conflicting trade-offs are inherent.

1.3 *Tabby Cat* Project

The *Tabby Cat* project is a case study that applies the skills from each chapter [6]. The *Tabby Cat* software is used to display developer activity on a source code repository. *Tabby Cat* is described in Chaps. 6, 12, and 17 and was provided by Red Ocelot Ltd., our own software start-up which itself emerged from our industrial collaboration [9].

1.4 Supporting Resources

The book is supported by a website, which includes instructor resources such as presentation slides [3]. Further, there are several source code repositories that support the book. Source code implementations for several of the exercises are available in GitHub repositories [4] and are referenced in appropriate parts of the book.

1.5 Evidence Underpinning the Book

I have taught software design to commercial clients in Europe, South Asia and North America. Further, the book is based on research conducted with software practitioners and experts from around the world. Over one hundred practitioner interviews have informed this book. This research has been published in international peer-reviewed conferences and journals, notably [1, 2, 5] and more recently [8, 10]. For more details about the research methods employed, see Appendix A.

This research has enabled several industrial collaborations. These collaborations have focused on agile innovation processes and cloud-hosted software service deployment. The collaborations have resulted in the conceptualisation, design and deployment of several software products.

1.6 Software HackCamp

The Software *HackCamp* provides an opportunity for students to work together in a team while tackling a challenge set by a client. The HackCamp has been recognised as a Practice Highlight by BCS, the Chartered Institute for IT [7]. A 2 min video was produced by The University of Salford on the 2020 HackCamp [11]. More details and resources for running your own HackCamp are available from [3].

1.7 Create Yourself a Livelihood

The skills you learn in this book can provide a lifetime of fulfilling and creative work. You could stay local, or travel the world. Your software could aid health and wellbeing. Your solutions could build communities, strengthen inclusion and support diversity.

These skills can get you a job. But these skills, with the right dedication and commitment, can also serve you well if you want to become a freelancer, or a technology entrepreneur.

With these skills, you can build products to create commercial revenue. Of course. But, you can also use software to improve people's livelihoods, wellbeing and life chances. Let's help make the world a better place, one software product at a time.

References

1. Bass, J.M.: How product owner teams scale agile methods to large distributed enterprises. Empir. Softw. Eng. **20**(6), 1525–1557 (2015). https://doi.org/10.1007/s10664-014-9322-z, http://link.springer.com/article/10.1007/s10664-014-9322-z
2. Bass, J.M.: Artefacts and agile method tailoring in large-scale offshore software development programmes. Inf. Softw. Technol. **75**, 1–16 (2016). https://doi.org/10.1016/j.infsof.2016.03.001, http://www.sciencedirect.com/science/article/pii/S0950584916300350
3. Bass, J.M.: http://www.agileskillsbook.com (2022)
4. Bass, J.M.: Julianbass - overview (2022). https://github.com/julianbass
5. Bass, J.M., Haxby, A.: Tailoring product ownership in large-scale agile projects: managing scale, distance, and governance. IEEE Softw. **36**(2), 58–63 (2019). https://doi.org/10.1109/MS.2018.2885524
6. Bass, J., Monaghan, B.: Tabby Cat GitHub Explorer. Red Ocelot Ltd (2022). https://github.com/julianbass/github-explorer
7. BCS, The Chartered Institute for IT: University of Salford – HackCamp (2021). https://www.bcs.org/deliver-and-teach-qualifications/university-accreditation/practice-highlights/university-of-salford-hackcamp/
8. Rahy, S., Bass, J.M.: Managing non-functional requirements in agile software development. IET Softw., 1–13 (2021). https://doi.org/10.1049/sfw2.12037
9. Red Ocelot Ltd: Enhancing digital agility (2022). https://www.redocelot.com
10. Salameh, A., Bass, J.M.: An architecture governance approach for agile development by tailoring the Spotify model. AI Soc. (2021). https://doi.org/10.1007/s00146-021-01240-x
11. The University of Salford: HackCamp 2020: Computer science and software engineering on Vimeo (2020). https://vimeo.com/395147780

Part I
People

Software development is a social activity. Software built at any significant scale requires the involvement of teams. Also, software is built to fulfil people's needs. Hence, Part I of the book focuses on *people*.

Most *people* engaged in agile software development are members of self-organising teams. Chapter 2 addresses the skills you need for success in self-organising teams. You will find out about agile principles of self-organising teams, forming teams and collaboration activities within teams.

So, while Chap. 2 addresses team members, Chap. 3 focuses on the skills needed in other agile roles in software development projects. The *scrum master* is a mentor and facilitator, supporting the team. While the *product owner*, thinks and acts like a customer, prioritising work and approving releases.

Successful software development involves attracting 'outsiders' to support the software development process. I call these outsiders *stakeholders*. Hence, Chap. 4 focuses on the skills needed to manage these stakeholders.

Finally, we need to consider good practice in terms of ethical behaviour, as discussed in Chap. 5. The big tech sector risks becoming toxic because of the negative impacts it can have. We, as a profession, need to think more carefully about how we affect people's lives.

The *Tabby Cat* project is a software for displaying activity on a GitHub repository. *Tabby Cat* uses the GitHub application programming interface (API) to obtain repository data and provides various information display options. In Chap. 6, we apply the skills we have learned in Part I to this case study project.

Other Book Parts

The overall design of this book is around *people*, *product* and *process*. Parts II and III are, more or less, stand-alone. So, if your main interest is in the technical *product*, you could skip to Part II. Also, if the development *process* is your main concern, then you might want to skip ahead to Part III. The skills required for some more advanced agile software engineering topics are described in Part IV.

Chapter 2
Self-Organising Teams

Abstract When groups of people come together to carry out a shared task, they form teams. Small self-organising teams are the core building block of any meaningful software development effort. If we need more people, we use multiple small teams. This chapter describes the skills you need to create self-organising teams. You will learn about agile principles and how to energise and support teams. I discuss the benefits of teams comprising diverse skills and virtual teams where members work remotely.

2.1 Introduction

Agile methods are now the norm for business information system development [4, 5]. Furthermore, most people, working on agile software projects, work in small self-organising teams. In this chapter, I will explain how teams are formed and how we can enhance the performance of these teams. I will explore what distinguishes groups from teams and how team performance can be enhanced.

2.2 Self-Organising Teams

Self-organising teams manage their own achievement of tasks towards a mission or goal set by the client, customer or organisation. The customer defines the goal. The team manages its delivery. The priorities around *what* must be accomplished come from the business domain, while decisions about *how* to achieve the goals come from within the team.

© Springer Nature Switzerland AG 2022
J. M. Bass, *Agile Software Engineering Skills*,
https://doi.org/10.1007/978-3-031-05469-3_2

2.2.1   Attributes of Self-Organising Teams

There are several attributes that define self-organising teams:

1. Autonomy
2. Requisite Variety
3. Learning to Learn
4. Cross-fertilisation
5. Self-evaluation

Self-organising teams have the *autonomy* to manage and assume responsibility for their own tasks and experience minimum outside interference in their day-to-day activities [19]. Only the critical factors that are needed to direct the team are externally defined [15].

Software development teams face dynamic environments, with changing customer requirements and ever-evolving technology stacks. The solutions used on a previous project might not work for this project. Self-organising teams can be more adaptable at handling this changing landscape. Hence, self-organising teams develop a *variety* of approaches to problem-solving, which they can deploy when needed. For example, requirements backlogs and Kanban boards, described in Chap. 10, are used pretty frequently. In contrast, some teams use spikes and pair programming, from Chap. 13, only when needed.

Conventional organisation form teams into organisational units comprising people with the same skill set, as shown in Fig. 2.1a. Self-organising teams, in contrast, are composed of individual members with diverse skills and specialisations, as shown in Fig. 2.1b. Agile software development teams include developers, testers and business analysts. Multidisciplinary teams foster *cross-fertilisation* within and also between teams.

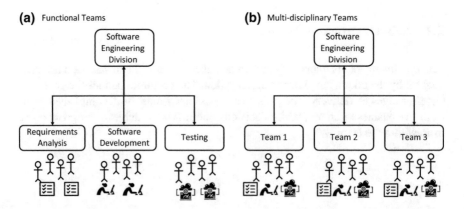

Fig. 2.1 Multidisciplinary teams

Teams *learn to learn* when they change the way they look at problems, review and refine the best work method and reconsider the best outputs to deliver. Agile practices that help teams *learn to learn* include retrospective workshops and stand-up meetings, more on these practices in Chap. 13.

Self-organising teams establish their own goals and keep on *evaluating* themselves such that they are able to devise newer and better ways of achieving those goals [19]. This self-evaluation is often aimed at improving productivity and product quality. We find that productivity and product quality are often conflicting objectives, and achieving the right balance between them requires constant attention.

Diversity in the team is an asset. Teams that develop a single view of the world are at a disadvantage when confronted with a changing environment. More effective is where diverse team members interact amongst themselves leading to better understanding of each other's perspectives [11].

2.3 Groups and Teams

There are several characteristics that define teams [13]. Let's very briefly explore these characteristics:

- Team size
- Skills portfolio
- Common purpose (including shared performance or quality goals)
- Common approach
- Mutual accountability

Teams are small, typically comprising seven plus or minus two members. Larger groups of people have difficulty interacting constructively as a team. Teams are used to bring together group members with complimentary skills, as just discussed in relation to Fig. 2.1. Teams where everyone has exactly the same skills are less effective than teams with a mix of skills.

Teams are created around a common purpose or a shared set of goals. A meaningful purpose establishes aspiration for the team. Often teams are characterised by shared commitment to a set of performance or quality goals. Also, effective teams are committed to a common approach. This is the way they will work together to achieve their shared goals. Finally, team members are jointly accountable for outcomes. A team also shares responsibility for its own successes and failures.

2.3.1 Building Team Performance

There are some techniques we can use to build high performance teams. But, we need to be cautious here. Teams are different and team members are different. Also, of course, the context in which teams work are different from each other.

Consequently, there is no rule book we can follow that automatically creates a high performing team. We know elite teams when we see them. But we cannot magically and turn any group into an outstanding team.

Bearing in mind that caveat: what can we do to help create a highly functioning team? As I mentioned, here are some techniques that can help build team performance [8, 13]:

- Establish urgency and direction.
- Select members based on skills and potential (not personalities).
- Pay attention to first meetings and actions.
- Set rules for acceptable behaviour.
- Focus on few short-term performance tasks and goals.
- Update facts regularly.
- Spend (lots of) time together.
- Exploit positive feedback.

Teams tend to work more effectively if there is a shared sense of direction and an urgency of purpose. The more strongly the team members feel that sense of direction and urgency, the more effective the team is likely to be.

Effective teams select team members based on their skills. In general, teams need technical, problem-solving and interpersonal skills. Some team members need to specialise in each of these three areas. Being more focused on delivery of working code, you might want to make sure you have:

- Front-end, human-computer interaction and user experience skills
- Back-end, web services and database implementation skills
- Testing and evaluation skills
- Deployment skills to place working code on servers accessible by users

Consequently, in a HackCamp or Hackathon setting, it is much better to choose team members based on skills, rather than friendship groups.

Software Company Start-up Team Members
In software company start-ups, there is a trendy saying that your team should comprise a *hacker*, a *hipster* and a *hustler*. The *hacker* is an innovation thought leader and brings strong technical skills. The *hipster* brings graphical design, visual creative and user experience skills, while the *hustler* is a deal-maker and negotiator who can close sales. Okay, so this saying is a bit of cliché, but it illustrates the benefits of a diverse skill set in your teams.

The set-up phase of the group is very important. Early meetings set the tone for performance of the group. A calm yet purposeful and collaborative atmosphere is to be encouraged. Setting the right tone at early stages is healthy and important.

The team needs to gain consensus on working practices and acceptable behaviour. A team in which bad behaviour is permitted is not likely to lead to good success. What is defined as bad behaviour can vary depending on context. Hence, the group needs to establish its own standards, which may involve intercultural negotiation. But, remember diversity of perspectives is often an asset for the team.

The team will benefit from some quick wins. What might they be? Look for opportunities to successfully achieve some early goals or performance enhancements. You need to identify tasks you can complete and improvements you can make with modest effort, short time-scales and measurable success.

We need to ensure that the team benefits from regular updates of information. In self-organising agile team, we use daily coordination meetings, in scrum called stand-ups, to update everyone on status. These information-sharing events encourage commitment to the team from members, because everyone can see what everyone else is doing.

Face-to-face time together can help build trust and mutual confidence. Understanding challenges from the perspective of different members of the team is important to ensure collective ownership of problems.

Feedback to the team needs to reinforce the growth, goals or performance objectives. Early wins can be used to reward yourselves with positive feedback. The concept of 'gold stars' may come from nursery school, but rewards in terms of celebrating successes and giving kudos really help.

2.4 Agile Principles

We will return to the agile principles of iterative and incremental development in Part III, but here we are interested in the principles of sustainable pace and collective code ownership.

2.4.1 Sustainable Pace

There is a school of thought that you can write excellent software by 'pulling an all-nighter'. The contention is that you can solve challenging problems, with logically coherent solutions, in the dead of night or during early hours of the morning (ideally after an energetic and entertaining night out). Let me share with you a naughty secret: I have, in the past, been known to work on software development at unseemly hours.

But honestly, I don't think 'pulling an all-nighter' is a good idea. I certainly don't think it is good idea when your boss, through omission or design, prevails on you to work all night. Okay, so maybe when writing software for self-learning or for your own entertainment, all-night coding might be okay. A hackathon can be a great way to learn and often involves a short and intensive burst of activity. But for professional software development, this is not really the way to go.

This realisation, that all-night coding is not ideal, partly informs the concept of *sustainable pace*. The idea is that software engineering is a creative activity that should be conducted when people are awake, alert and fully focused on the job. This is the idea that creative work needs to be conducted in normal office working hours and not involve long periods of evening or weekend working. The implication is that carefully implemented software development processes enable a sustainable approach to code creation, sustainable over weeks, months and years.

2.4.2 Collective Code Ownership

Code can be written by individuals but, according to the concept of collective code ownership, should be a resource belonging to the whole team. It is argued that we should not put names on the modules of software we write. There should be no impediment to making changes or corrections to code written by others. The team, as a whole, stands or falls by the software created by its members.

2.5 Forming Teams

There are many models of the processes that happen when people come together to work in small groups. Perhaps the most well-known is Tuckman's [20] comprising:

- Forming
- Storming
- Norming
- Performing
- Adjourning stages

This model is obviously a bit of a simplification but has stood the test of time remarkably well. During the forming phase, group members create a team with clear structure, goals, direction and roles so that members begin to build trust. During the storming phase, frustrations and perhaps conflicts build up. The team often needs to refocus on its goals, perhaps breaking larger goals down into smaller, more achievable steps. As the team moves into the norming phase, team members begin to resolve the differences between their initial expectations and the reality of the team's experience. Team members often notice more frequent and more meaningful communication amongst team members and an increased willingness to share ideas or ask for help. During the performing phase, there is significant progress towards team goals, and team members show high commitment to the team's goals. Finally, during the adjourning phase, team members complete their deliverables (final software, test execution, reports and so on), evaluate performance with a particular focus on identifying 'lessons learned' and celebrate the contributions and accomplishments of the team.

2.5.1 Accelerating Team Formation

Given this model of small group development, there are steps we can take that will support this process. During the early stage of coming together as a group, we can undertake several activities to help establish shared goals and build trust. The exercises in Sect. 2.9, at the end of this chapter, can help you during this team-forming stage.

2.5.2 Handling Difference and Conflict

There are three main attributes of techniques for handling disagreements. When negotiating solutions to differences of opinion:

1. Focus on the problem.
2. Avoid focusing on personalities.
3. Seek solutions that maximise benefit to more of the participants [7].

Taking a vote could seem like a good solution, but the majority within the team may not be as well informed as an expert. So discussion and learning, while working towards consensus, is often a better way to reach agreement.

2.5.3 Accelerating Norming

Successful team norming relies on good communication and a shared sense of purpose within the group. Team members are focused on the task at hand, and not on conflict resolution and impediments to efficient working. Exercises 2.4 and 2.5, at the end of this chapter, can help you prepare for this team-norming stage.

Theory X and Theory Y
It has been observed that there are two views of organisations [14]. Theory X describes organisations founded on the idea that people don't want to work and need to be coerced or controlled to create good work. Theory X advocates a hierarchical approach to management structures, where roles are task oriented, repetitive and inflexible.

Theory Y, in contrast, suggests that people want to work to gain self-esteem, recognition and satisfaction. In Theory Y, the role of management is to create a supportive environment in which people can do their best work. There is less emphasis on command and control structures and more focus on facilitating opportunities for collaboration.

2.6 Collaboration Activities Within Self-Organising Teams

We will look at the technical tasks performed by teams in Part II. But, in software development, several collaboration and communication-focused activities within the self-organising team role have been observed [12]. These activities may be performed by different team members or by the same team member at different times. An attribute of more experienced and adept team members could be the ability to perform more of these activities on behalf of the team.

2.6.1 Mentor

We will find out more, in Chap. 3, about the scrum master role. The scrum master helps inculcate the use of agile methods in the team. But other members of self-organising teams must also mentor each other. Perhaps someone new joins the team and needs advice to get started and feel welcome. Perhaps someone already in the team needs to learn a new technology. Mentors guide and support team members, help them become more confident about using agile methods and encourage the ongoing use of agile practices.

2.6.2 Co-ordinator

The co-ordinator acts as a representative of the team to manage customer expectations and co-ordinate customer collaboration with the team. The co-ordinator has to collate team member requests for information from customers (to avoid irritating duplication of questions) and deal with the whole issue of *change request* handling.

2.6.3 Translator

Translators are needed that can make clear the meaning of business language used by customers for the benefit of technical team members. Participants in the self-organising team need to contribute to improved communication between these two domains. Understanding the business domain of the project is the primary role of the product owner, as we will see in Chap. 3. But self-organising teams benefit from gaining this understanding too.

2.6.4 Champion

Champions are team members that advocate for agile methods with senior management within their organisation. We want senior executive support for the self-organising agile team. It is hard for agile to flourish without senior management support. The champion is adept at explaining agile benefits using language and evidence that is convincing for senior executives.

2.6.5 Promoter

The promoter is a proponent of agile methods with customers. The promoter secures customer involvement and collaboration to support the efficient functioning of the self-organising team. Customers play a vital role in identifying and prioritising requirements, while the promoter ensures that the team gets all the support needed from customers.

2.6.6 Terminator

Sometimes, teams find themselves with a member who is not a force for good, someone maybe persistently unproductive or the negative behaviour of this team member can threaten the wellbeing of the rest of the team. Self-organising teams are often happy to take damage limitation steps to cover for a team member who is 'having a bad day'. But if a team member is causing problems over a long period, then more drastic action may be needed. In the most extreme case, members of the self-organising team may engage external stakeholders to get support for removing someone from the team.

2.7   Virtual Teams

Periods of self-isolation during the COVID-19 pandemic showed that online teams can be very effective. Virtual teams are formed, when some or all team members work remotely and communicate using technology. The time, cost and environmental impact of daily travel to work is avoided.

As already argued, multidisciplinary teams have become the norm in software development, as shown in Fig. 2.1b. Consequently, the team employs diverse skills to deliver a specific product, and communities of practice are used to share knowledge and experience about their specific skill set or role.

2.7.1   Principles for Virtual Team Management

Virtual teams have advantages such as avoiding work-related travel—where team members can remain in their preferred home location without the need to co-locate with work colleagues. The digital nature of agile software engineering work means the job activities can travel to the skilled people, rather than skilled people travelling to the work.

However, the absence of informal networking and impromptu opportunities to meet and socialise can lead to challenges. Consequently, we can identify several principles for supporting virtual team working [10].

It is particularly important to ensure there is consensus on clear goals with virtual teams. Sometimes, virtual team members do not have visibility of the range of activities and responsibilities for other team members. Consequently, it is important to be alert for inconsistencies in team member goals.

Communication and collaboration processes need to be more carefully implemented for virtual teams. These processes are needed to expose and resolve misunderstandings and diffuse conflict.

Despite the absence of opportunities for impromptu interaction in virtual teams, creating opportunities for social communication seems important. Communicating as a group on different topics and activities and building awareness of other team members seem to help with goal achievement.

Helping team members build inter-dependence through goal setting and task design also seems to help with the development of successful teams. Trying to help team members understand the strengths each person brings to the work helps overcome disconnectedness.

These activities can be supported by specific training and team kick-off activities to develop the culture of communication across different aspects of team working. While work-focused tasks are most important, these other opportunities to build consensus are also valuable.

2.7.2   Preparation for Team Success

There are a number of steps we can take (or tactics we can adopt), to maximise the chances of team success.

2.7.2.1   Cultural Diversity

Cultural diversity is a feature of globally distributed teams and those in many urban conurbations in the global north. Cultural ambassadors with experience and understanding of the different cultures can support communication at times of stress or tension within the group. Otherwise, cultural awareness and sensitivity are needed for group members to empathise and build trust.

2.7.2.2   Remote Pair Programming

Often specific software development tasks can be performed by individuals within the team. Software to implement a screen, database table or a class can be developed. Many employers like the idea of a 'full-stack' developer that can contribute across the application spectrum (front-end to back-end) and also across the life cycle (from requirements to test). However, some parts of an application are new, complicated or critical in some way, which makes a shared thought process attractive. It is a good idea to identify these difficult tasks during backlog grooming and sprint kick-off activities, as discussed in Chap. 13.

Tactical use of remote pair programming can be useful tool for managing these difficult tasks. Set aside time for pair programming during sprint planning. Each pair programming session needs clear goals and a set agenda before the start. Pair programming also is a good way to on-board new members of a team.

A basic way of doing remote pair programming is to use any video conferencing platform that allows screen sharing (popular favourites at the moment include Microsoft Teams, Skype and Zoom). Customary approaches include:

- Driver/navigator: the driver works on careful implementation of code, while the navigator is doing a real-time code review while thinking about issues such as readability and architecture adherence; swap every 30 min or so.
- Ping-pong: One person writes a test, while the other person then codes against the test criteria. Once the test passes, swap roles.

2.7.3   Launch

The launch phase of a virtual team is particularly important. A *kick-off* phase serves five main purposes [10]:

- Getting acquainted with other team members
- Clarifying the team goals
- Clarifying team member roles and functions
- Discussing efficient communication technologies use
- Developing general teamwork rules

The exercises at the end of this chapter can help you prepare for launching your team.

2.7.4 Performance Management

In virtual teams, performance is achieved through a combination of goal setting, participation and feedback on task fulfilment. Performance feedback, on an individual and group level, should be frequent, concrete and timely. As examples of this, in an agile approach, virtual daily stand-ups using a shared Kanban board show team members group and individual progress towards goals, while customer demonstrations provide frequent, timely and concrete feedback, as described in Chap. 13.

Organisation of the group is focused on moderation, facilitation and supporting communication. Leadership is responsible for information sharing, organisation of meetings and facilitating communication within the team. Team effectiveness is enhanced where the team attains goal clarity and lack of goal conflict and also benefits from good-quality feedback.

It is possible that uninhibited and hostile communication can emerge in virtual teams. This is discouraged through frequent opportunities for synchronous online feedback and development of explicit norms and rules for communication.

Communication media need to be selected based on their fit for the task at hand. Slack [17], for example, has tended to be popular with software developers because it offers synchronous text-based communications, document sharing and long-term, archival, information storage, while videoconferencing is better for problem-solving and creating shared goals. Making astute use of the most appropriate media is important for team success.

It seems high-performing virtual teams also exhibit high quantity of non-job-related communication. By engaging in social processes, virtual teams build cohesion, trust and motivation. One important problem is that it is possible that non-job-related communication is consequence of high performance in the team.

2.8 Communities of Practice

It is useful to be aware of another type of team that exists within the software development ecosystem. These are teams with members that do not contribute to shared work tasks but that nevertheless share ways of working, membership rituals and often shared goals. A community of practice is a voluntary, often rather unstructured, group that supports and facilitates knowledge and experience sharing.

In the agile development culture developed at the music streaming service Spotify, the concept of Guilds is introduced that to some extent formalise the community of practice as part of the development process [18]. The Guilds tend to be organic and emergent. Guilds vary in size, mission, membership and activities.

2.9 Exercises

Start by creating a learning journal for Part I *People*, if you haven't already. Use this learning journal to keep notes on the things you learn. You can also use the learning journal to plan your future skills development activities. What are your priorities? The journal should, eventually, include a section for each book chapter.

It is better not to look at the hints, tips and solutions chapter, at this stage. First actually perform the exercises (but, still, do not look at the hints or tips). Then reflect. Only after that, look at the hints, tips and advice in Sect. 2.10.

Exercise 2.1 (Learning Journal)

2.1 The first exercise is to review the material in each chapter. Write a few notes in your learning journal for this chapter. These could be brief notes, just a few bullet points. Or perhaps you want to create a longer essay.

Exercise 2.2 (Skills Inventory)

2.2 Work with the other members of your team to identify the various sills you have between you. As a group, you should discuss two main areas:

1. What are the types of skills and skill categories available within the group?
2. What metrics or experience levels do you use to assess a skill competency?

Of course, you will want to include on technical skills in your inventory. What technologies have you worked with? What techniques have you learned (across the development lifecycle, perhaps)? What do you know already about agile methods?

Some people might find the following categorisation useful:

1. Software
2. Hardware

(continued)

Exercise 2.2 (continued)

3. Networks
4. Information management or storage
5. Processes

Don't forget to include non-technical skills. Think about your hobbies, interests and pastimes. What skills have you acquired during these other activities? These might loosely be called soft skills (administrative, organisational, social and communication skills, etc.). You might have all sorts of skills that will be useful to your group. It is best not to be shy about the range of skills you have. Something you take for granted might be seen as a huge asset to another member of the group.

In terms of experience levels, you might find the following categorisation useful:

1. Novice (I was taught a University course on this and completed some assignments.)
2. Competent (I've been using this routinely for a couple of years.)
3. Proficient (I have 3–5 years' experience with this.)

Create a spreadsheet or use some other way to collate and capture all the skills in your group. If your group is rather homogeneous, then you might have a lot of similar skills. With luck, your group is more heterogeneous, coming from a wide range of different cultures, experiences and previous backgrounds. A heterogeneous group will likely have a wider range of different skills that you can draw on.

Exercise 2.3 (Personal Learning Timeline)

2.3 A personal learning time line is a graph of your life so far. Time goes on the x-axis of your graph. The y-axis represents your learning. High values are for periods in your life when you learned a lot. Low values are when you did not learn so much. Best to use a large sheet of paper, such as a sheet of flip chart paper.

This exercise provides a vehicle for learning about each other's life story. You will probably learn some surprising things about friends and colleagues. This exercise can help you bond with the other members in your group.

1. Start off by working alone to plan your personal learning time line. Think about the times in your life when you learned a lot. There may be life experiences or events that caused you to learn about yourself as a person. There may be specific projects of experiences where you learned a lot

(continued)

Exercise 2.3 (continued)

technically. What happened? What did you learn? What about the periods in your life where you didn't learn much? Why was that?

2. Draw your personal learning timeline on a sheet of flip chart paper. Think carefully about what you are willing to share with the other members of your group.

3. Now, with the other members of your group, take turns to share your learning time line. Describe the most important periods in your life for learning.

Exercise 2.4 (Group Behaviour Exercise)

2.4 We need to develop a set of ground rules about what sort of behaviours are acceptable in the group. Of course, we want the other group members to treat us with respect. Right? But what does that mean? What is respectful behaviour? Some members of your group might have very different expectations than you.

Things you consider normal may, in fact, be strange or even offensive to others in your group. You should try to find out if there are any culturally sensitive areas for any members of your group. You should also try to find out what has annoyed the other group members about working in teams in the past.

Work as a group to answer the following questions. Depending on the level of experience within the team, you might want to do some online information gathering to explore tools and techniques to answer the different questions. Why not have each group member write a short report on one of the topics? Use this exercise to learn new skills about ways of working in teams.

1. How will we communicate?
2. How will we collaborate?
3. How will we provide feedback?
4. How will we make decisions?
5. How will we handle conflict?
6. How will we prioritise work?
7. How will we measure our work?
8. How will we recognise or celebrate each other's contributions?

The outcome is a set of guidelines for methods of working, acceptable behaviour and conduct within the group. You should list accepted behaviours about how you would like to be treated by other members of the group. You should also list any unacceptable behaviours you found out about in your discussions.

Exercise 2.5 (Creating Shared Goals)

2.5 In this exercise, you will try to establish a sense of common purpose in your group. A well-developed shared mission can help you perform better as a team.

1. Work independently. Each member of the group writes 'what would you like this team to accomplish?' Write a single accomplishment on each sticky note.
2. Now, work as a group. First, identify common themes. These are important; they are shared goals.
3. Order the accomplishments into priorities. Two categories is enough: high priority and low priority.
4. Create a two-by-two matrix (e.g. on a whiteboard). The two axes are shared vs. individual goals and low- vs. high-priority goals.
5. Use the high-priority, shared goals to create a mission statement for your team. Try to create a mission statement that is clear, simple and motivating.

Exercise 2.6 (Learning Journal)

2.6 Reflect on the exercises you have completed, from Chap. 2. Make some notes in your learning journal. Think about what happened during each exercise. How did it go? What went well? What could have gone better?

2.10   Hints, Tips and Advice on Exercises

2.1 *Learning Journal Exercise*

In this chapter, we explored

- Self-organising teams
- Agile principles
- Forming teams
- Collaboration activities within self-organising teams
- Virtual teams

You should aim to write down a few comments about the things you learned in each topic.

2.2 *Skills Inventory Exercise*

There are, at least, three aspects to this exercise. What skills do you have? What level of expertise do you have in each skill? And, how can we guide our own professional development in the future? We need some categories of skills and skill levels. Learning about this will help us identify our own strengths. We can then use the exercise to focus our own professional development and training activities.

The Dreyfus model of skills acquisition has five levels: novice, advanced beginner, competent, proficient and expert [3]. A novice needs close supervision. An advanced beginner is able to achieve some steps using own judgement. Someone competent is able to achieve most steps using own judgement. Someone proficient is able to take full responsibility for own work and coach others. An expert is able to go beyond existing standards. This simple model is probably sufficient for this exercise.

However, in Skills Framework for the Information Age (SFIA), in contrast, there are seven skill levels [16]. SFIA identifies level of experience ranging from entry-level professional through to industry-wide thought leader. The highest level is aimed at senior executives (such as the Chief Technology Officer) of large corporations or Government agencies. These levels are:

1. Follow.
2. Assist.
3. Apply.
4. Enable.
5. Ensure and advise.
6. Initiate and influence.
7. Set strategy, inspire and mobilise.

The levels of responsibility are described in terms of five generic attributes: autonomy, influence, complexity, knowledge and business skills. SFIA provides a detailed breakdown of expectations at each skills level, developed over many years. Consequently, SFIA provides lots of useful information about how to improve your skills.

What about the skill areas themselves? I mentioned that you might want to consider six categories:

1. Software
2. Hardware
3. Networks
4. Information management or storage
5. Processes
6. Soft (transferable) skills

(continued)

But, this might be too tied to specific technologies and not sufficiently focused on the objectives you are trying to achieve. SFIA also has six categories of professional skills, but they are more focused on the goal or purpose:

- Strategy and architecture
- Change and transformation
- Development and implementation
- Delivery and operation
- Skills and quality
- Relationships and engagement

These categories are divided into sub-categories and around 100 different skill areas. For example, the development and implementation category includes:

- Systems development

  - Systems development management
  - Software design
  - Software development
  - Database design
  - Network design
  - Testing

- User experience

  - User experience analysis
  - User experience design
  - User experience evaluation

- Installation and integration

  - Systems integration and build
  - software configuration
  - Systems installation

I like SFIA (and used it in industry to help me create job descriptions) because you can use it to learn about how to develop new aspects of your skill set.

For each category, there is a breakdown of how the skill is applied at the different levels. For example, in the Systems development category and Programming/software development sub-category:

- Level 2 is described as 'Designs, codes, verifies, tests, documents, amends and refactors simple programs/scripts. Applies agreed standards and tools, to achieve a well-engineered result. Reviews own work'.

(continued)

- Level 3 'Designs, codes, verifies, tests, documents, amends and refactors moderately complex programs/scripts. Applies agreed standards and tools, to achieve a well-engineered result. Collaborates in reviews of work with others as appropriate'.
- Level 4 'Designs, codes, verifies, tests, documents, amends and refactors complex programs/scripts and integration software services. Contributes to selection of the software development approach for projects, selecting appropriately from predictive (plan-driven) approaches or adaptive (iterative/agile) approaches. Applies agreed standards and tools, to achieve well-engineered outcomes. Participates in reviews of own work and leads reviews of colleagues' work'. [16].

As you can see from the above example, the levels in SFIA illustrate a growth in experience and influence. The SFIA detailed matrix of skills can also be used to create job descriptions as well as support the personal and professional development of practitioners.

2.3 *Personal Learning Timeline Exercise*

I can't provide a solution to your personal learning timeline exercise, because it's, errh, well, personal to you. This about reflecting on difficult or challenging periods of your life. Think about the lessons you have learned and the skills you have acquired.

For the timeline, draw peaks to represent periods of intense learning. The draw troughs to reflect time when you learned less. The peaks might (or might not) correspond to formal education. You might have peaks for a first unaccompanied camping trip with friends or organising a big family gathering. You might have troughs for boring periods of your life.

You can then share your timeline with the other members of your group. This will give you a framework for learning about each other and your previous experiences. You can use the timeline to learn about the life histories of the other team members.

2.4 *Group Behaviours Exercise*

In groups working together for the first time, there could be different expectations about what constitutes acceptable behaviour. This is particularly important in groups with members from diverse cultural communities.

Think carefully about acceptable behaviours. Discuss your previous experience of behavioural norms: what professional behaviours were accepted and what things did people do or say that caused controversy.

Make a list of unacceptable behaviours. Try to explore areas where members of the group might be offended. This might include working practices, use of language and expectation around meeting attendance and timekeeping.

Finally, make plans for conflict resolution. It is better to consider tactics for making difficult decisions now while things are quite calm and relaxed. Try to prepare a plan for decision-making under pressure and when there are heartfelt disagreements within the group.

2.5 *Creating Shared Goals Exercise*

Research shows that groups are more effective when they have shared goals. You might be able to increase the effectiveness of your group by understanding each other's goals.

Some group members may have very high expectations, in terms of work quality and effort. For other group members, it might be more a question of survival; 'let's just get through this'. You might not be able to change the expectations of other group members, but understanding their perspective might be useful.

Your group performance might be improved if you can get consensus on some aspects of group performance, such as quality of work. Some group members might be happy to accept producing more deliverables than others, if they feel everyone is committed to producing high-quality outputs.

2.6 *Learning Journal Exercise*

Think about how you performed in completing the exercises. Where they easy? Where they challenging? Which areas need some further work? Make some notes on these thoughts in your learning journal.

Make some notes about the quality of your solutions. Try to identify areas where you performed well and those where you might benefit from further reading or other learning.

(continued)

If you are serious about becoming a professional practitioner in the software domain, you need to use your learning journal (or professional diary) to record your activities. The act of writing things down helps you think more clearly about what has happened. As you think more clearly, because of your writing, so you learn more about the skills you are acquiring.

Don't just write a sequence of events; try to reflect on the skills you used. The main purpose is not only to create a timeline (although that can be useful to you later). The purpose is to think about the successes and failure of what happened. Try to list things that went well. Also write things that did not go so well. Then, make notes about what you might do differently next time.

Is your learning journal low tech or high tech? I don't care. You could use a cloud-hosted software tool accessible from any device (like Evernote [6] or Trello [1]). Or, you could use a computer office application such as a word processor. Or, you could buy an expensive pen and nice notebook. Whatever works for you. I don't care. But, write a journal.

Is your learning journal personal or team based? Both! Some of your learning will be personal. Private. Confidential, even. You need to think about your own reaction to the things you are learning. How did you feel during the exercise? What made you happy or uncomfortable? Why was that? Face it, learning is stressful, sometimes. If you don't challenge your own boundaries, you're not really learning anything new. Some, perhaps, more friendly, sociable or amiable people find working with others easy. Enjoyable even. I don't. I find, I can sometimes inadvertently upset people, or they upset me. Professional relationships can be challenging.

You will want to keep this relationship stuff private, partly because nobody cares what we think or because nobody needs to know what nonsense is going on inside our heads and partly because some of your learning will be about working with others, and that needs to be kept to yourself. If you don't write something that should be private, then you're not *really* thinking about your own learning, or you don't yet have a good enough understanding of the boundaries between you and others.

But you also need to learn, as a team, together. You need a group Kanban board (Trello) [1], wiki site or development platform, such as GitHub [9], to record your group decisions. You might like to use an instant messaging and file-sharing platform like Slack [17]. These tools allow you to record group decisions and exchange information with each other. Kanban boards provide a visual overview of the project status. Using a shared wiki platform you can share architecture and design models. Instant messaging allows you to ask, and answer, questions.

2.11   Chapter Summary

Most people engaged in a software project will be members of self-organising teams. So, in this chapter, I have explained some defining characteristics of teams and some techniques to encourage higher performance from teams. I've focused on team life cycle and team formation issues, as well as looking at some research, which shows what collaboration activities self-organising teams in software projects undertake.

Exercises have focused on developing an understanding of the skills available in your team, developing shared goals to improve productivity and establishing good behavioural practices within your team.

In Chap. 3, I will look at the other roles that are defined when using agile software development methods. These roles are important, for supporting self-organising teams that develop software.

References

1. Atlassian: Trello (2019). https://trello.com
2. Coad, P., LeFebvre, E., De Luca, J.: Java Modeling in Color With UML: Enterprise Components and Process. Prentice Hall, Upper Saddle River (1999)
3. Dreyfus, S.E.: Formal models vs. human situational understanding: inherent limitations on the modeling of business expertise. Office Technol. People **1**(2/3), 133–165 (1982). https://doi.org/10.1108/eb022609
4. Dybå, T., Dingsøyr, T.: Empirical studies of agile software development: a systematic review. Inform. Softw. Technol. **50**(9–10), 833–859 (2008). https://doi.org/10.1016/j.infsof.2008.01.006
5. Dybå, T., Dingsøyr, T.: What do we know about agile software development? IEEE Softw. **26**(5), 6–9 (2009). https://doi.org/10.1109/MS.2009.145
6. Evernote Corp.: Best Note Taking App—Organize Your Notes with Evernote (2019). https://evernote.com
7. Fisher, R.: Getting to Yes: Negotiating Agreement Without Giving in, 3rd revised edn. Baker and Taylor, London (2011)
8. Fitzpatrick, B.W., Collins-Sussman, B.: Team Geek: A Software Developer's Guide to Working Well with Others, 1st edn. O'Reilly Media, Sebastopol (2012)
9. GitHub Inc.: Build software better, together (2019). https://github.com
10. Hertel, G., Geister, S., Konradt, U.: Managing virtual teams: a review of current empirical research. Hum. Resour. Manag. Rev. **15**(1), 69–95 (2005). https://doi.org/10.1016/j.hrmr.2005.01.002
11. Hoda, R., Noble, J., Marshall, S.: Developing a grounded theory to explain the practices of self-organising Agile teams. Empirical Softw. Eng. **17**(6), 609–639 (2011). https://doi.org/10.1007/s10664-011-9161-0
12. Hoda, R., Noble, J., Marshall, S.: Self-organizing roles on agile software development teams. IEEE Trans. Softw. Eng. **39**(3), 422–444 (2013). https://doi.org/10.1109/TSE.2012.30
13. Katzenbach, J.R.: The Wisdom of Teams: Creating the High-Performance Organization. McGraw-Hill, London (2005)
14. McGregor, D.: The Human Side of Enterprise. McGraw-Hill, New York (1960)

15. Morgan, G.: Images of Organization, 1st edn. SAGE Publications, Thousand Oaks, California (2006)
16. SFIA Foundation: SFIA (2018). https://www.sfia-online.org/en
17. Slack: Where work happens (2019). https://slack.com/intl/en-gb/
18. Smite, D., Moe, N.B., Levinta, G., Floryan, M.: Spotify guilds: how to succeed with knowledge sharing in large-scale agile organizations. IEEE Softw. **36**(2), 51–57 (2019). https://doi.org/10.1109/MS.2018.2886178
19. Takeuchi, H., Nonaka, I.: The new new product development game. Harv. Bus. Rev. **64**(1), 137–146 (1986)
20. Tuckman, B.W., Jensen, M.A.C.: Stages of small-group development revisited. Group Organ. Stud. **2**(4), 419–427 (1977). https://doi.org/10.1177/105960117700200404

Chapter 3
Agile Roles

Abstract Self-organising teams create software. Scrum masters and product owners provide an environment in which teams can work. The scrum master facilitates team working, mentoring team members and removing impediments. The product owner engages with clients and markets to define and prioritise requirements. This chapter explores the scrum master and product owner roles in detail and the skills needed for them to perform their activities.

3.1 Introduction

In Chap. 2, I discussed self-organising teams and how they work. In this chapter, we will focus on roles outside the self-organising team and introduce the skills you need to perform these roles. The scrum master and product owner support the work of self-organising teams.

3.2 Scrum Master

Scrum masters facilitate the scrum process on behalf of the team, monitor team status and remove impediments [7, 8]. Practitioners consider the role as central to the success of the scrum method [2]. You can learn more about the ceremonies that involve scrum masters later, in Chap. 13.

Research that investigates what scrum masters actually do [2, 6] identifies five coordination activities: process anchor, stand-up facilitator, impediment remover, sprint planner and integration anchor. We can now discuss each of these activities in turn.

© Springer Nature Switzerland AG 2022
J. M. Bass, *Agile Software Engineering Skills*,
https://doi.org/10.1007/978-3-031-05469-3_3

3.2.1 Process Anchor

The process anchor mentors team members in scrum method use. The agile process is described in Chap. 13. The idea is to nurture, encourage and perhaps gently cajole people to learn and use agile methods appropriately. This means understanding how agile methods work, by creating transparency about who is doing what.

The scrum master is not a team leader or supervisor in the conventional sense. The scrum master does not tell people what to do. However, the scrum master has to encourage, sometimes recalcitrant team members, to give their productive best.

Agile teams often like to get into a rhythm, known as a *cadence*. That means everyone knows what to expect when a week starts with sprint planning or ends with a customer demonstration. People can plan their work, and perhaps even their social lives, around this iteration cadence.

3.2.2 Iteration Planner

The iteration planner activity helps select and estimate requirements for implementation. Iteration planning is described in Sect. 13.2. Everyone on the team is involved in iteration planning for half a day, or a day, at the start of each iteration; see Fig. 3.1a. But, the important point to make here is that the scrum master facilitates the iteration planning process.

3.2.3 Stand-up Facilitator

The stand-up facilitator conducts coordination meetings within a team. Facilitating a stand-up involves influencing the conduct of the meeting while saying as little as possible. You can learn more about what happens in a stand-up meeting in Sect. 13.3.

When meeting participants go off topic, you want to guide them gently back to the purpose of the meeting. The whole purpose of the stand-up is to discuss and disseminate the status of the project. Impediments are mentioned, but not discussed in detail. Do not get drawn into trying to resolve impediments during the stand-up itself.

You want to be alert for these and other issues that need to be discussed outside the stand-up meeting and who needs to be involved in those other conversations. It will be your responsibility to organise and facilitate those other meetings. Make sure you only involve those who need to be consulted. A common mistake is to let stand-up meetings go on too long, discussing topics that are not of interests to all the people involved and (from their point of view) wasting their time.

3.2.4   Impediment Remover

The impediment remover eliminates work blockages for team members. Imped-iments are often varieties of missing information or lacking knowledge. So, a scrum master needs to find out who has the elusive knowledge and convey that to the blocked team member. This process of information gathering requirements a combination of networking skills (knowledge of who knows what) and diplomacy (to convince people too busy or self-regarding to part with information).

3.2.5   Integration Anchor

The integration anchor facilitates amalgamation of software elements. The whole point of a software development team is to produce software. Right? Of course it is! So, someone has to glue together all the bits of software being created by the members of the team. From a feature perspective, each piece of code goes through a plan, design, build and test lifecycle as shown in Fig. 3.1b. But the scrum master needs to make sure this code integration happens. This might involve checking up on someone who has taken on the task regarding the integration issue. You can learn more about some software tools you can use to help with this in Part III.

3.3   Product Owner/On-site Customer

The central purpose of product ownership is to communicate a business need to a development team. The development team knows how to design, build, test and deploy systems, and the product owner comes to know what system needs to be built. Extreme programming advocates an on-site customer, a client representative

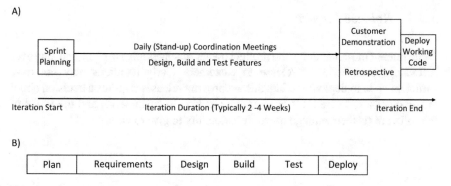

Fig. 3.1   (a) Iteration structure and (b) feature life cycle

that is available to the team on a full-time basis [4]. The product owner role is formally defined in scrum [8]. Product ownership plays a central role in the overall software development process [5].

I now want to look at some of the activities product owners perform as part of their role [3]. Taken together, these activities comprise the product owner role.

3.3.1   Product Grooming

In the product grooming activity, the product owner gathers, or elicits, requirements from business clients in business-to-business contexts. You can learn more about requirements in Chap. 7. The product owner needs to interact with customers in order to gather the requirements. For business-to-consumer applications, the product owner needs to develop detailed awareness of market trends and competitor behaviour.

However, simply compiling a list of requirements is not sufficient; the requirements must also be prioritised according to their value to the business.

3.3.2   Prioritiser

In the prioritiser activity, the product owner ensures that requirements bring maximum value to the business. In each iteration, the product owner decides which requirements from the product backlog are going to be most important for implementation in the next iteration. Sometimes, this involves choosing to prioritise the needs of one customer group or segment over another. Product owners become experienced in assessing and prioritising the needs of different segments of the customer base.

3.3.3   Release Master

In the release master activity, the product owner manages release plans and approves software source code for release to customers. Early iterations may not have sufficient code to deploy; see Fig. 3.2. Approving releases requires a decision about the quality of software (is it good enough to give to customers?) and the scope of the software (is there enough useful functionality to give to customers?).

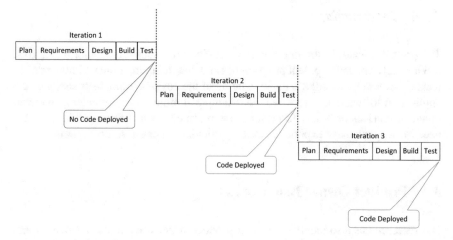

Fig. 3.2 Iterations and source code releases

3.3.4   Communicator

In the communicator activity, the product owner connects onshore and offshore stakeholders in the project team to manage geographical distribution. Geographical distribution is not an ideal attribute for a project team. We would prefer everyone to be located together in the same site. The ease of communication and movement of digital goods means that geographical distribution has become a feature of software development programmes. The product owner, in the communicator activity, uses audio and videoconferencing and online collaboration tools.

3.3.5   Traveller

In the traveller activity, the product owner spends time with geographically remote stakeholders gathering first-hand knowledge of their needs and priorities. For example, a product owner based offshore will sometimes spend time (between 1 and 3 months, depending on the scale of the project) on the client site at the start of the project, becoming familiar with any special features of the client's requirements. The traveller is important for supporting development teams because they are based at the customer site and can get answers to questions.

3.3.6   Intermediary

The product owner, in the intermediary activity, interfaces with senior executives, driving software development programmes and disseminating domain knowledge to teams. Domain knowledge is understanding of the business domain or sector of the application software being created. For example, it might be an application in travel, financial services or retail. To perform the intermediary activities, product owners need to have extensive experience of the particular system business domain.

3.4   Product Owner Behaviours

Our research has also identified a set of product owner behaviours. There are traits that product owners display that are seen as desirable by their line managers. The three main product owner behaviours we identified are to favour face-to-face interactions, understand and focus on real goals and make product owner teams well defined [1].

3.4.1   Favour Face-to-Face Interactions

It is tempting to use digital technologies to overcome geographical distance. Written communication with email and word processing documents can help you deal with geographical, temporal and cultural distances. However, understanding, trust and empathy come from building social capital through face-to-face interactions. It is very important to spend 'face-time' with stakeholders.

3.4.2   Understand and Focus on Real Goals

On successful projects, product owners appear to use influencing skills to keep a wide range of stakeholders targeted on a specific and focused set of goals. Creating a set of clear, transparent and objective test criteria allows teams to demonstrate progress toward project goals. Product owners who are able to stay focused on key project goals even as inevitable challenges and obstacles arise are highly prized.

3.4.3   Make Product Owner Teams Well Defined

As has been suggested, for large projects, the product sponsor, intermediary, technical architect and other members form a product owner team. The process of building the product owner team should be explicit and well defined. Product sponsors should create well-defined processes for product owner team building, induction of new members and succession planning.

3.5   Other Roles: For Larger Projects

We'll look at large-scale projects in more detail in Chap. 18. But, there are a couple of roles it is worth thinking about now: product sponsor and technical architect.

3.5.1   Product Sponsor

The product sponsor is a project funder. In business-to-consumer projects, each individual customer is a project funder. However, in a business-to-business project, or an internal project in a large organisation, there is an individual that signs off funding for a project. Depending on the size of organisation, this individual may be a company chief officer (chief technical officer, chief financial officer or something) or perhaps some other senior executive.

You may not see much of the project funder, if you have one. They may be busy with other responsibilities. But, trust me, the project funder is important. Ultimately, they are the persons that the team needs to satisfy. So, listen carefully to what they say. Try to understand the problem being solved, from their point of view. Aim to see things from their perspective. That way, you stand a better chance of coming up with a solution that works for them.

3.5.2   Technical Architect

In smaller systems, architecture is often straightforward. You choose an appropriate architectural style and stick to it. You end up with a clear and simple high-level design. A design everyone can adopt, without much dissent.

On larger systems, high-level design or architecture becomes much more sophisticated. Different subsystems may have contrasting architectural styles. The choice of architectural style may be more controversial and less obvious. An experienced technology leader might be required to have the gravitas to carry the team towards a coherent approach. Hence, the overall system architecture can be much more finely balanced and complex.

3.6   Exercises

These exercises will help you practise the agile roles discussed in this chapter. Don't look at the hints, tips and solutions chapter, at this stage. First actually do the exercises, then look at the advice in Sect. 3.7.

Exercise 3.1 (Learning Journal)

3.1 As explained in Exercise 2.1, it is a good idea to create a learning journal. Consequently, for the first exercise in this chapter, write a few notes in your learning journal for this chapter. What were the most important things that you learned or found interesting? A few bullet points will be sufficient.

Exercise 3.2 (Iteration Planning Exercise)

3.2 In this exercise, scrum masters and agile coaches practise facilitating an iteration planning process. The iteration planning process is described in Sect. 13.2. Team members will collaborate to create technical tasks for each high-priority requirement. Estimate each requirement. Decide how many (and which) requirements you can accommodate in the next iteration. Make sure someone in the team has chosen tasks to work on. There is more detailed guidance on how to conduct sprint planning in Sect. 3.7.

Exercise 3.3 (Coordination Meeting Exercise)

3.3 In this exercise, scrum masters practise facilitating a coordination meeting. Coordination meetings are described in Sect. 13.3. The scrum master makes sure the meeting stays focused on project status. Team members should learn who is working on what. The meetings are often held looking at a (real or virtual) Kanban board. The scrum master ensures the meeting lasts no more than 15 min.

Exercise 3.4 (Customer Demonstration Exercise)

3.4 Practise facilitating a customer demonstration. You can learn more about customer demonstrations in Sect. 13.4. You might want to rehearse the demonstration, so you can advertise the new features of your working software in a positive light. Make sure you record all the feedback you are given. Review all the feedback later, and action any comments you have been given.

Exercise 3.5 (Retrospective Exercise)

3.5 Practise facilitating a retrospective. You can learn more about retrospectives in Sect. 13.4.1. Collect feedback from team members on what went well in the last iteration. Collect feedback on areas for improvement. Try to identify consensus on areas for improvement and create one action point for each.

Exercise 3.6 (Requirements Elicitation Rehearsal Exercise)

3.6 In this exercise, a product owner will rehearse facilitating a fictitious requirements elicitation workshop (focus group). You might want to learn more about requirements by reading Chap. 7. Identify who are going to be your key informants (possibly friends or colleagues, for this exercise). Before the workshop, prepare a logical set of open-ended questions.

The scenario for this fictional exercise is: 'what activities do you do in the morning between waking up and arriving at work, university or college?' The objective of the workshop is to identify 10–15 activities that the members of your focus group perform in the morning (assuming you wake up in the morning). Make sure you have arranged someone to record the answers you are given in the workshop.

During the workshop, lead the discussion through your questions. Ask some open-ended questions to see if there are topics your informant wants to tell you about, which you didn't realise were important. There are some more detailed hints and tips on how to conduct requirements elicitation in Sect. 3.7.

Exercise 3.7 (Requirements Gathering Workshop Exercise)

3.7 In this exercise, a product owner will facilitate a requirements gathering workshop (focus group) for your team. As I mentioned in Exercise 3.6, you can learn more about requirements by reading Chap. 7. Choose a specific epic (large use case or user story) that will be needed as part of your project. Before the workshop, make lists of questions and discussion topics to explore the epic user story. The discussion topics should be areas of uncertainty (or where there is disagreement) in current understanding of the requirements. The objective is to achieve concise, clear and complete understanding of the selected epic.

Exercise 3.8 (Requirements Prioritisation Exercise)

3.8 As a product owner, practise prioritising different user stories. You will need a real (or imagined) product backlog of user stories. Collect closely related user stories into groups. If you have only one group, either your project really is trivially simple or you have not thought about the requirements in sufficient detail. Assuming you have more than one group of requirements, this exercise involves building an imaginary increment based on one group first. What would the product look like at the end of the first increment?

Exercise 3.9 (Learning Journal)

3.9 Reflect on these exercises from this chapter. Think about what happened during each exercise, and make some notes in your learning journal.

3.7 Hints, Tips and Advice on Exercises

3.1 *Learning Journal Exercise*

The focus of this chapter has been on the facilitation activities within the scrum master and product owner roles in scrum.

Reviewing these activities can help you make sure that your team is provided with the support it needs to function effectively.

(continued)

If you notice gaps in the skills available, then you can attempt training or professional development in these areas. A knowledgeable proxy product owner can fill gaps in support activities meant to be performed by your actual product owner.

3.2 *Sprint Planning Exercise*

The sprint planning is a cyclic process comprising four phases:

- Select the highest priority requirement, and decompose it into technical tasks.
- Estimate the effort required to implement each technical task.
- Combine technical task estimates into an estimate for each requirement.
- Ensure that all the technical tasks have been accepted as a work item by someone on the team.

Repeat this cycle for each high-priority requirement, until no further effort for completing technical tasks in the iteration.

Look at the high-priority requirements on your backlog. The prioritisation will have been done by the product owner. For each requirement, create the full set of technical tasks needed for implementation.

As you develop a list of technical tasks for each requirement, you can more accurately estimate the effort needed to implement the requirement. Think about which method you want to use for estimation (story points or T-shirt sizing). Practise and rehearse using your chosen method on a toy example before you use it on a project. The purpose of estimating is to help you monitor an equitable allocation of work to team members and to ensure your team will not be over (or under-)-utilised during the next iteration.

Once estimation is complete, you can choose a specific set of requirements for the next iteration. This might be straightforward. Or, there may be some tasks forced upon you by dependencies. So, you need to implement something that is only needed right now in order to finish something else. Or, you may need to pull up some smaller tasks because you do not have team capacity to undertake another large task. So, as you can see, there are some trade-offs here.

Finally, team members have to choose work tasks. Remember scrum masters don't assign work. But they do need to ensure all tasks are assigned to someone. So some encouragement or cajoling might be needed to get all the tasks taken up by someone.

3.3 *Stand-Up Meeting Exercise*

Remember the stand-up meeting ground rules. Everyone should answer the following three (or four) questions: (1) What have I been doing since the last stand-up? (2) What will I be doing between now and the next stand-up? (3) Are there any impediments preventing me from making progress? And, maybe, (4) am I going to create any blockers that might impede others?

When facilitating, listen carefully to the discussion. If anyone diverts onto other topics, make sure you make a note of the issue and set up a separate meeting for that discussion. Steer people (firmly, but politely) back onto the three questions.

3.4 *Customer Demonstration Exercise*

Here is a bit of a checklist of things you need to remember to do to prepare for the customer demonstration.

- Rehearse and time the demonstration before you show the customer.
- Make sure you have arranged a good venue. Is the customer demonstration online or face to face? If online, rehearse the technology setup. If in a venue, make sure it is booked for your exclusive use.
- Make sure that all the team members and product owner are available and aware of the time and venue.
- At the start, briefly introduce the demonstration purpose, and review the requirements you were supposed to implement (the iteration backlog).
- Demonstrate the features of the software.
- Describe the quality assurance activities performed (code reviews, testing on so on).
- Describe any requirements that you were unable to implement for any reason and any known bugs or issues.

Conduct the customer demonstration. Carefully note any feedback obtained from the product owner (or customer). Check if the product owner requires any further quality assurance actions before release. If not, seek approval for the software release.

3.5 *Retrospective Exercise*

There are several ways of conducting retrospectives, but you might consider using the following steps:

(continued)

- Everyone in the team privately writes three sticky notes: 'things *we should continue* to do'.
- Collect all the sticky notes (which should be anonymous) together on a blank whiteboard (physical or virtual).
- Everyone writes three sticky notes: 'potential *areas for learning* or improvement'.
- Collect all the sticky notes together on a blank whiteboard.
- Spend a few minutes, as a group, reviewing all the sticky notes.
- Try to collect the 'potential *areas for learning* or improvement' into groups or categories. Look for themes.
- Choose the top three 'potential *areas for learning* or improvement'. The top three are likely to be areas of consensus or at least mentioned on more than one sticky note.
- Create one action point for each of the top three 'potential areas for learning or improvement'.

You should encourage implementation of the three action points during the coming iteration. The scrum master should remind the team members about the action points during the iteration, to help learning and improvement.

3.6 *Requirements Gathering Workshop Exercise*

The purpose of the workshop might be simply to gain better understanding of what is needed. Or, the workshop might be designed to resolve differences in opinion within your among project stakeholders, about the meaning of a specific requirement.

We'll find out more about requirements in Chap. 7. We want a discussion about customer needs and the services that the software should provide.

Use the workshop to explore customer acceptance test criteria. How will you, or the customer, know when the epic is complete? Test criteria will help define automated test conditions.

3.9 *Learning Journal Exercise*

Before you look at these hints and tips, think about how you performed in completing the exercises. Where they easy? Where they challenging? Which areas need some further work? Make some notes on these thoughts in your learning journal.

(continued)

After you look at these hints and tips, make some further notes about the quality of your solutions. Try to identify areas where you performed well and those where you might benefit from further reading or other learning.

3.8   Chapter Summary

In this chapter, I have explained the scrum master and product owner roles. I have described how the scrum master facilitates teamwork, mentors team members and removes impediments. We do not advocate having a team leader when using agile methods. In contrast, the scrum master facilitates the self-organising team discussed in Chap. 2.

The product owner, in contrast, defines and prioritises requirements. The product owner reviews demonstrations of working code at the end of each sprint and decides if code quality is sufficient for release to customers. The exercises have focused on facilitating stand-up meetings, customer demonstrations and sprint planning.

Should we do our best to build a good solution? Yes, of course. Should we tell our boss if we are failing to achieve this goal? Well, yes. It might not be pleasant. But we need to be able to communicate good news, bad news and technical decisions. In Chap. 4, we will learn about managing other people that are interested in the software development process, people we call stakeholders.

References

1. Bass, J.M., Haxby, A.: Tailoring product ownership in large-scale agile projects: managing scale, distance, and governance. IEEE Softw. **36**(2), 58–63 (2019). https://doi.org/10.1109/MS.2018. 2885524
2. Bass, J.: Scrum master activities: process tailoring in large enterprise projects. In: 2014 IEEE 9th International Conference on Global Software Engineering (ICGSE), pp. 6–15 (2014). https:// doi.org/10.1109/ICGSE.2014.24
3. Bass, J.M.: How product owner teams scale agile methods to large distributed enterprises. Empirical Softw. Eng. **20**(6), 1525–1557 (2015). https://doi.org/10.1007/s10664-014-9322-z
4. Beck, K., Andres, C.: Extreme Programming Explained, 2nd edn. Addison Wesley, Boston (2004)
5. Hoda, R., Noble, J., Marshall, S.: The impact of inadequate customer involvement on self-organizing agile teams. Inform. Softw. Technol. **53**(5), 521–534 (2011). https://doi.org/10.1016/ j.infsof.2010.10.009
6. Noll, J., Razzak, M.A., Bass, J.M., Beecham, S.: A study of the scrum master's role. In: Product-Focused Software Process Improvement, pp. 307–323. Lecture Notes in Computer Science. Springer, Cham (2017)
7. Schwaber, K., Beedle, M.: Agile Software Development with Scrum, 1st edn. Pearson, Upper Saddle River (2002)
8. Schwaber, K.: Agile Project Management with Scrum, 1st edn. Microsoft Press, Redmond (2004)

Chapter 4
Managing Stakeholders

Abstract This chapter describes relationship management skills. Relationships with customers, clients, bosses, supervisors and other stakeholders interested in the software we create. The chapter will provide some basic techniques for communication with people outside your team. We will explore how to manage software demonstrations and create presentations, reports, online resources and videos.

4.1 Introduction

Your team members, and the solutions you create, will benefit from skills you acquire in managing relationships with other people outside your team. Here, I am thinking about relationships with bosses, clients, academic supervisors or others who have an interest in your work.

Of course, Chap. 2 has explored skills needed to manage relationships within your self-organising team. In addition Chap. 3 discussed scrum master and product owner roles. Here, we consider managing upwards, managing outwards, contracts and communication skills.

4.2 Managing Upwards

Somebody, somewhere is going to be your customer, boss or academic supervisor. It is a good idea to think about who that is and what they want. For a software developer working as part of a team in a large company, you will have a clearly defined line manager, but the customer might seem rather remote. For a freelance software developer, in contrast, there is a customer but no obvious outside boss.

We should learn what the customer wants, either by talking to customers directly or by identifying a surrogate that understands customers well. Usually, as software development specialists, we are trying to solve somebody else's problem. If we don't understand, or worse misunderstand, the problem, then our solution will be poor at

© Springer Nature Switzerland AG 2022

J. M. Bass, *Agile Software Engineering Skills*,

https://doi.org/10.1007/978-3-031-05469-3_4

best. A deep understanding of the problem we are trying to solve will significantly improve our chances of success. In managing upwards, there are four main issues to consider: expectations, crises, successes and unreasonable demands.

4.2.1   Set Expectations

Set realistic expectations about what you are going to achieve. Don't promise to deliver things you can't fulfil. It is better to set expectations low and then over-deliver. Rather that, than setting high expectations and failing to deliver. Identify risky areas, areas where you are uncertain or engage with high degree of novelty. Make public these areas of risk. You never know, some risky things might not be important to your stakeholders. By pointing out they are risky, your client might remove them from the project scope.

4.2.2   Confess to Catastrophe

Hopefully, you will never have a catastrophe. But if something goes wrong, it is better to confess sooner rather than later. The idea is to give your boss, client or other stakeholders as much time as possible to help you plan a recovery strategy. Trying to hide a mistake or misstep is a risky strategy. It is dishonest and you might get found out. Better to work with your stakeholders and try to come up with a way forward.

4.2.3   Share Success

Make sure you share your successes. When you achieve a technical breakthrough, tell people about it. Hopefully, your customer, boss or academic supervisor will be pleased to share your success, by which I mean they will be happy for you. It is important for them to understand amount of work required to achieve that success.

4.2.4   Unreasonable Demands

Fend off unreasonable demands. It might be that your client thinks your team is superhuman or that your team is willing to work 24 h a day, for 7 days a week. Perhaps your client does not know if it is possible to create an entire enterprise resource planning system during a weekend Hackathon.

So, you need to educate and inform. Explain how much work is involved. You need to create a detailed breakdown of each work item involved. Each work item needs its own estimate of effort, see Sect. 13.2. In this way, you can encourage your customer, boss or academic supervisor to prioritise the work items they really care about and de-emphasise those that are less important.

4.3 Managing Outwards

There are lots of other stakeholders that can support your software development activities. In a commercial setting, you might interact with personnel, finance and payroll departments. In an academic setting, you might deal with people from careers, library and the registrar's department. Try to win support for your team from these other stakeholders. Your project will go more smoothly if these stakeholders can be convinced to help you, in spite of their own problems, priorities and pressures. You will want your team to look professional and efficient, so respond to enquiries promptly and with courtesy.

There might also be peer groups, other teams that might be working on similar projects. What can you learn from these other groups? I'm not suggesting that you unscrupulously copy other people's work. But, there might be an approach they are taking that you can apply and learn from.

4.4 Contracts

Contracts are legal agreements between parties. Negotiating large contracts involves specialist legal advisers. Never sign a contract you don't understand. Always get knowledgeable and impartial advice. There are two main categories of contract that govern the procurement of software: *fixed-price, fixed-scope* and *time and materials*.

4.4.1 Contracts and Change Requests

A *fixed-price, fixed-scope* contract, as the name suggests, ensures the financial value is known in advance for a clearly defined set of software requirements to be implemented. Usually a delivery date is specified too. Simplistically, this is the clearest arrangement. The client says 'these are the software features I want', and the software provider says 'this is how long it will take to build and how much it will cost you'. Simple. What could possibly go wrong?

Well, a *fixed-price, fixed-scope* contract requires agreement on a detailed set of requirements. These requirements need to be specified before any code is written. Who writes the requirements specification? The client? The vendor? As a vendor, are you getting paid for developing software according to your interpretation of the requirements? No, of course not. You are getting paid for the client's interpretation of the requirements. So, you had better understand what the client means. Okay, so what if you, as a vendor, write the requirements specification? Fine. But who pays for writing the specification? You? Or, the client?

Finally, as we know, change is going to happen during the project. Things out there in the real world are going to happen. A new browser version will be released. A new operating system release will come along. You manage this process by using change requests. A change request is a documented (and funded) change to the contract specification. Each time the client changes their mind about the specification, you have to estimate and cost all the consequent changes.

So now, instead of creating software, you are running a whole little industry: gathering, estimating, implementing and testing changes to the original specification. But despite the problems with fixed-scope contracts, they remain very popular because of their apparent clarity and simplicity.

4.4.2 Time and Materials Contracts

To overcome some problems with fixed-price, fixed-scope projects, people use *time and materials* contracts to manage client and vendor relationships. Here, there is no fixed-scope specification. Instead, the software development team charges *by the hour*. The client adopts a product owner role, establishing, prioritising and managing requirements. The team creates features requested by the product owner, iteration by iteration.

Time and materials contracts avoid the need to manage change requests. Consequently, effort is focused on developing working code. Good. But it is a bit challenging convincing clients to buy the software. Initially, they will not know what they will get, how much it will cost or when they will get it. This requires considerable trust between the client and vendor. And so, we come full circle, back to fixed-price, fixed-scope contracts.

4.4.3 Outsourcing Contracts

Outsourcing is the generic term for buying products or services from third parties. Corporations often outsource their catering, cleaning and so on. If you are not a technology organisation, it can be attractive to outsource IT provision and software development to a specialist third party. There are large international companies that make a good living from these arrangements.

4.4.4 Offshoring Contracts

It is often said you should outsource to organisations like yours. Similar size, conveniently local. Small companies find it risky to outsource to big companies; they are too expensive, they will 'eat you for breakfast'. And, yet, some organisations find outsourcing attractive, sometimes to far-flung, cheap and often exotic locations. Digital goods and the availability of excellent technical skills and computer networks make this possible.

You can get excellent value for money by *offshoring* your software development needs in this way. But new challenges caused by inconvenient time zones and significant geographical distances can emerge. There is also an environmental cost to the extensive travel involved in building trust through long-distance relationships.

4.4.5 Academic Contracts

There are also contracts in a university or college setting. Some institutions use learning agreements, between students and teaching staff, to help set expectations and establish norms of learning and teaching behaviour. Education institutions also commonly have course, programme or module descriptions for teaching staff and other stakeholders. These course descriptions often include various forms of aims or learning objectives. It is a good idea, of course, to familiarise yourself with the aims and objectives of the courses that you are studying.

4.4.6 Negotiating Contracts

The key to negotiating, actually whether it is within your team or beyond, is to understand everyone involved. We all have our own goals, hopes and fears. So, we need to try to understand the world from the perspective of other people in the negotiation. Good negotiators seem to be able to imagine the needs, wants and goals of others in the negotiation. This means focusing on the interests of everyone involved, not taking positions in the negotiation.

Understanding others does not mean giving in or capitulating. Negotiating only to win on your terms is short-sited and transactional. Better, to search for ways that everyone can move closer to their desired outcome. Successful negotiation comes where everyone benefits. You are looking for imaginative ways in which everyone wins. You want to invent options for mutual gain. This helps you build strong and lasting relationships.

Try to use practical and objective criteria as the basis for negotiations. The criteria should create the basis for a fair settlement. Focus on the search for criteria that enable you to reach a mutually beneficial agreement.

4.5   Communication Quality

There are several ways to improve the quality of our communications. Here, we focus on audience, narrative, language and process.

4.5.1   Audience

For your communication to be effective, you need to understand your audience and their expectations. The vocabulary, terminology and jargon need to be appropriate for them, and, crucially, may not be the same as yours. How much does the audience know about your subject? If they are experts, don't spend too much time on the basics of your topic. If the audience are not specialists in your area, then avoid using technical jargon.

4.5.2   Narrative

Why are you writing a report? To convey an argument. That argument might be: 'I've done enough good quality work that I am entitled to a good grade at University'. Or, it might be: 'I've done a diligent and thorough job of work, so you should give me a promotion or pay rise'. Okay, so maybe you don't want to make those arguments explicit. But you should think carefully about the argument you do want to convey.

The argument should be developed in logical steps and should be supported by evidence. You can sometimes adopt a journalistic device and summarise the main argument at the outset [6].

4.5.3   Language

Use good language skills in your technical communications. Mistakes in grammar and punctuation undermine your effort to make a good argument and present a professional image. You need to ensure you follow conventions in English language usage and punctuation [9]. This is a particular challenge if your communications are not in your first language. Enlisting the help of a native speaker, to proof read your writing, is a good tactic.

4.5.4 *Process*

Productive writers tend to write and then edit their work. Focus, first on getting words on paper. Then, focus on revising and editing [2]. Using analogy to iterative software development, try to achieve cycles of writing activity followed by editing. Write. Edit. Write. Edit. These cycles will help you improve the quality of your writing. You can't write the finished product first time.

4.6 Communication Tools

In professional life, we communicate with others to convey information and ideas, convince financiers to invest resources and sell solutions to customers. We practice various forms of communication for university assessments, such as essays, laboratory reports and dissertations.

4.6.1 *Reports*

Non-fiction writing is partly about writing design concepts such as clarity and simplicity but also a matter of basic principles such as grammar, punctuation and paragraph structure [12].

4.6.1.1 Report Composition

Good scientific writing is truthful, evidence-based, clear and simple. Clear writing is an indicator of clear thinking. It is wise to follow the guidance given by proponents of this writing style [8, 11, 12]. As I have already said, write and then edit your writing.

The paragraph is the basic unit of composition. A paragraph focuses on one topic. Each paragraph benefits from a topic sentence, which summarises the subject. The topic sentence is followed by further expansion. A good paragraph concludes with a summary sentence that reinforces the topic sentence.

Use the active voice. An active voice is more direct, forcible and vigorous than passive writing. This can be controversial. For academic writing, 'use the third person' is often given as advice. But you can see that 'I used an object-oriented design method' is clearer than 'an object-oriented design method was used in this project'. Use active voice where you can.

Make statements positive. Avoid hesitating, evasive and non-committal language. You might say 'the performance did not fluctuate as user numbers seemed to vary'. It is better to say 'performance was constant, despite varying user numbers'.

Remove unnecessary words. Make your writing concise. Making your argument with the fewest possible words leads to strong, direct writing. These composition guidelines are to make life easier for the reader [1, 3]. Don't forget: Write first, to get the ideas down on paper, and then edit your writing to improve composition and clarity.

4.6.1.2   Report Content

As well as a front sheet, and a table of contents, a report of any length will likely need an abstract or executive summary. The abstract summarises the content of the entire report and consequently should be written at the end when you know what the report actually says. A structured abstract comprises context, goal, methods, results and conclusions. The context describes the domain or application area of the report. The abstract then summarises the problem solved or goal of the project. Next, provide a brief overview of the methods or approach you took. Then, summarise your findings or results. Finally, summarise your conclusions.

Next, your report needs an introduction. An introduction has two main purposes. Firstly, provide a brief overview of the motivation or justification for performing the work. Include some evidence supporting the significance of the problem you are solving. Use references to sources and provide a bit more detail than given in the abstract. Secondly, summarise the main outcome, result or conclusion of the report. You might describe the main results from some experiments and discuss their implications. Or, you might provide an overview of the features of a system you have built showing how they solve the problem you confronted.

A report often requires a survey of the literature or field. Present the survey as if it were a funnel. You need to start off with the broader (wider) topics and then gradually focus on the specific area of your project. A weak literature review will describe each source in turn. A stronger literature review will organise a collection of sources into themes and then compare and critically discuss each theme.

Your report needs to describe the approach you took. In medical research, this is referred to as 'methods and materials'. You are supposed to provide enough information that someone could repeat your work and consequently get a similar outcome. Justify your choice of approach to solving the problem.

The main body of the report focuses on the findings of your work. You might be advocating a new approach or justifying a technology choice. Here you can weigh up the advantages and disadvantages of the various options. For a design and build type project, you will have a series of chapters describing the requirements, design, implementation and evaluation phases of development. In a more scientifically oriented project, you might describe the results of a series of experiments you have conducted.

You will then, likely, discuss or analyse your findings. If you have research questions, you can answer them here. If not, you discuss your findings in relation to other published results and describe the implications of your proposals in the context of the problem you are trying to solve.

Finally, the conclusions has three main purposes: summary, conclusions and future work. As reports get bigger, a carefully selected re-statement of ideas becomes an important means of giving emphasis. Never copy and paste within the report. We don't want to read the same sentence or paragraph twice. But, briefly re-stating the context, aims, methods and findings shows that you understand the most important elements of the project. You can then describe the lessons you have learned from the project. What aspects of the project went well? What aspects of the project proved to be more challenging than expected? At a fundamental level, was the method you selected appropriate? It is helpful to discuss anything you would do differently if you were asked to do the whole project over again (but this time with the benefit of hindsight). At the end of your conclusions, include next steps for the project or future work. Your report conclusions are important because you summarise the whole project and describe the implications of your work in the context of the problem you were trying to solve.

4.6.2 Presentations

Presentations play an important role in modern professional life. You might be presenting to win over your team to a new reference architecture for a project. This might involve describing the benefits and features of the new architecture. There is more on reference architectures in Sect. 8.4. You could be trying to explain something, show something or sell something. The format is similar.

4.6.2.1 Presentation Types

There are some circumstances where a presentation can be given without any supporting materials, for example, where the presentation is informal or very short. An example is the agile customer demonstration, discussed further in Sect. 13.4. In a customer demonstration, we focus our attention on demonstrating working code. Usually, however, presentation slides of some kind are used.

4.6.2.2 Presentation Content

Visually appealing imagery can play an important part in engaging with your audience [5]. Choose imagery that is relevant to your topic and that reinforces your argument. For important presentations, you can obtain photographs and diagrams from commercial or open access visual media repositories [10]. Sometimes, a presentation containing only images, and no words, can work well. Your imagery needs to complement and emphasise the narrative you are telling. You want to select imagery that reinforces, rather than distracts from, your message.

Avoid using too many words in your presentation. Do you want the audience to be reading or listening to the presenter? Commercial trainers follow the *five by five* rule. That means no more than *five* rows of text on each slide. Each row of text should have less than *five* words. These days, presentations with even fewer words are common. Use words for emphasis.

4.6.2.3 Presentation Delivery

Your presentation needs to engage your audience. Use eye contact and engage the entire audience. Don't just look at one person all the time. Make your presentation flow smoothly, and present your content confidently. Avoid a halting or hesitant delivery style.

Your audience will be more attentive if they are calm, relaxed and focusing on the presenter. Watch the body language of your audience, and be alert for signs of boredom or distraction. Is the audience being distracted by noise from elsewhere? Is it too hot (or too cold) in the room? Create an atmosphere where the audience is listening.

4.6.2.4 Presentation Rehearsal

For a presentation of any significance, you will want to practice, especially when you present as a team. Make sure you stick to the agreed duration. Check for consistent presentation materials and content, and practice handing over from one presenter to another. Make a plan for when things don't work or go according to plan. When travelling abroad to give presentations, I used to carry paper copies of materials in case projectors or electronics failed.

4.6.3 Blogs and Wikis

Various editable online writing platforms have become popular to support communications in software development teams. Tools and platforms fall in and out of favour. At the time of writing, Slack is popular with development teams because it enables instant messaging, content sharing and archiving [7]. Our research suggests that while Slack is popular within development teams, in contrast, managers, executives and client-facing relationship managers prefer face-to-face interaction, or audio- and videoconferencing infrastructure [4].

Content management systems enable sharing of audio-visual or multimedia content as well as written material. Diagrams, videos and recording of workshops can be hosted online as part of a project repository. Such resources are typically hosted behind firewalls on secure intranets to avoid public disclosure.

4.6.4 Videos

Video and multi-media presentations have become commonplace in professional circles. Video can support sales, provide news and information as well as engage new audiences. The cost of video production has declined, while audiences have also become more accepting of lo-fi or improvised production values.

4.7 Exercises

Working through these exercises will help you acquire skills for managing stakeholders, as discussed in this chapter. First do the exercises, then reflect on what you have learned. Finally, look at the advice in Sect. 4.8.

Exercise 4.1 (Learning Journal)

4.1 As in each chapter, the first exercise is to write a few notes in your learning journal for this chapter. Write about anything you found useful.

Exercise 4.2 (Presentation Review)

4.2 Film yourself making a presentation. This is probably best done on a practice presentation. But, make the rehearsal as realistic as you can. After the presentation, carefully review the video. What can you learn from watching the video that will help you improve your presentation skills?

Exercise 4.3 (Writing Exercise, Free)

4.3 For 10 or 15 min, write about anything that comes into your head.

Exercise 4.4 (Writing Exercise, Focused Free)

4.4 For 10 or 15 min, write anything you can think of, relating to the topic of interest.

Exercise 4.5 (Non-fiction Writing Exercise)

4.5 For 10 or 15 min, write about a skill, or area of expertise, that you have acquired. You should assume that your reader is not knowledgeable in this area, so avoid using jargon. Try to avoid your writing sounding like a dry instruction manual. Break down your skill or expertise into a series of understandable steps. Try to describe as many aspects of this skill as you can.

Exercise 4.6 (Edit Your Writing)

4.6 Take an example of something you have already written. Perhaps a previous report or assignment, or even the previous exercise. Sentence-by-sentence go through your writing removing needless words. Try to make the same arguments or address the same topics, but use fewer words.

Strengthen your paragraph structure. Make sure each paragraph sticks to only one topic. Ensure your paragraph starts with a topic sentence. Try to expand on the topic with each sentence in the paragraph. Can you finish each paragraph with a summary sentence?

Compare your writing before and after the exercise.

Exercise 4.7 (Video Production Exercise)

4.7 For a bit of fun, make a documentary-style video explainer about your team. Your documentary should be 2–4 min long. You are aiming for short and interesting rather than long and dull.

Step 1: Script

Create a script. Answer questions about your team members. Who are you? Where do you come from? What are the passions in your lives? Why have you come together as a team? How do you plan to tackle your project? What will your roles in the team be? Describe the special skills you have. You can interview each other asking and answering questions. Or, perhaps you can do head and shoulders shot facing the camera. Can you walk around talking or stand in front of some iconic location?

Step 1: Storyboard

Create a storyboard, a series of drawings or diagrams showing the locations you plan to use and the action you want to show. You do not have to be an artist. You can use stick figures and written labels to overcome any

(continued)

Exercise 4.7 (continued)

shortcomings in artistic merit. The purpose of the storyboard is to help you think about the story, locations and action you want to show.

Step 2: Shoot Footage

Use any smart phone or DSLR you have available to shoot your video. Make sure your filming locations are safe and that you have appropriate permissions. Try to choose locations that support your story.

Step 3: Soundtrack

Record sound and music to support your video. Make sure you own the copyright of any audio resources you use. You may also want a smart phone to record audio live, or in separate recording sessions (perhaps for voice-overs).

Step 4: Edit

You can use free online clip editing tools to edit your video. Think about pacing. You want to avoid long dull sequences, but too much motion and too many quick cuts from one thing to another will be distracting and difficult to follow.

Step 5: Disseminate

Review the quality of your video. Show it to a few friends or family members. Are you confident the content is appropriate and the quality good enough? You may need to seek approvals (boss or academic supervisor) depending on your context. If you are comfortable that your reputation is going to be enhanced (and not damaged), then post your video to a sharing platform.

Exercise 4.8 (Learning Journal)

4.8 Reflect on the exercises you have completed from this chapter. What went well? What could have gone better? What would you do differently next time? Make a few notes in your learning journal.

4.8 Hints, Tips and Advice on Exercises

As you become a technology professional, you will be increasingly called upon to communicate ideas to different audiences. Use the advice below to further develop your communication skills to manage stakeholders.

4.1 *Learning Journal Exercise*

Stakeholders are people interested in the software development project but not direct participants in the team. We need to develop the skills needed to manage our relationships with these interested parties.

In this chapter, we have considered managing upwards, managing outwards, contracts, communication quality and communication tools. Write a few notes about what you have learned on these topics.

4.2 *Presentation Review*

Look carefully at the video of your presentation. Are you maintaining eye contact with your audience? Are you prone to annoying hand gestures? What are your hands doing? What are you wearing? Are your clothes appropriate for your audience? Do you have any verbal ticks (such as hesitancy or often repeated phrases) that might irritate your audience?

Are you using multimedia aids to support your presentation? Do the sounds or visual aids reinforce the presentation? Do the sounds or visual aids distract? Or, perhaps worse, do the sounds or visual aids undermine the presentation?

How is your body positioned? Are you standing in front of any visual aids? Are you static or moving around? Is any movement supporting the presentation?

Try to learn from watching the video and perhaps repeat the exercise.

4.3 *Free Writing*

Apparently, writing (as in generating written words) and editing (correcting, reformatting, re-phrasing) use different parts of the brain. The idea of free writing is to only use the creative part of the brain that helps you produce written material.

The purpose of this exercise is to generate as many words as you can. Consequently, during the free writing exercise, it is important to focus only on writing words. Some research suggests that free writing is useful to help you overcome writer's block.

Do not stop writing to correct grammar or spelling. Just keep writing. If you can think of anything to write about, just write about that!

Some psychologists suggest that you should start each period of writing with a 10-min free writing session. The idea is to get you in the mood for churning out words. Any words. Just get words down on paper (or, more likely, on screen). See how it works for you. If you like it, do it again.

4.4 *Focused Free Writing*

This approach is development of the free writing in Exercise 4.3 and can also help you overcome writer's block. Use this focused free writing to get you in the mood for generating words.

Don't worry about grammar or spelling. Don't stop to make any corrections. Just write down everything that comes into you head on the chosen topic. Get as many words as you can on paper (or on screen).

In this focused free writing approach, there is a second stage. After the 10- or 15-min writing window, you can review what you have written. Try to extract the aspects of your chosen topic you have covered. Some people call this reverse headlining. Extract bullet points, each representing a different aspect of your topic, from your focused free writing words.

Now, in this second stage, you can edit the random flow of words into some structure. Organise the writing into sections or a timeline, depending on the subject at hand.

As a result of organising your focused free writing, you should start to notice gaps or areas where you can then provide even more detail in the writing. These new areas can even become the topics for your next focused free writing exercise.

4.5 *Non-fiction Writing*

This exercise is designed to help you generate written material about something familiar. You should be as descriptive as possible. For example, if you are writing about a skill, try to answer questions like:

- What is the skill you have learned?
- Why is it useful or important?
- How do you feel when you exercise the skill?
- When did you learn the skill?
- Where do you exercise the skill?
- Who is involved when you rehearse your new skill?

On the other hand, if you are writing about a technology, answer questions like:

- What are the advantages (or strengths) of this technology?
- What are the disadvantages (or weaknesses) of this technology?
- How widely used in the technology?
- How easy is the technology to learn? (Are there plenty of learning resources available?)

(continued)

- How easy is the technology to use?
- Why have you chosen to use this technology? (Justify you choice.)

Trying to answer all these questions in your non-fiction writing can help you develop your descriptive vocabulary skills.

4.6 *Edit Your Writing*

You might start by editing one of your focused free writing exercises, from Exercise 4.4.

Try to apply the following style rules:

- Remove needless words.
- Ensure paragraphs only address one topic.
- Ensure paragraphs start with a topic sentence (and perhaps end with a summary sentence).
- Write in positive terms ('do this' is more powerful in writing than 'don't do that').

Some people suggest you should try to reduce the length of your writing by 10%. This improves focus and makes the writing stronger and more direct. I am confident that applying the writing style guidelines from [8] or [12] will help you improve the clarity of your writing.

4.8 *Learning Journal*

Before you look at these hints and tips, think about how you performed in completing the exercises. Where they easy? Where they challenging? Which areas need some further work? Make some notes on these thoughts in your learning journal.

After you look at these hints and tips, make some further notes about the quality of your solutions. Try to identify areas where you performed well and those where you might benefit from further reading or other learning.

4.9 Chapter Summary

In this chapter, I have explored the relationship between your team and the outside world. In a work environment, you might be trying to satisfy your boss or a client, or, you might be in a university, trying to satisfy academic supervisors. In each case, you want your team to produce the best it is capable of and get the recognition you deserve. This is achieved by managing your relationships with these outside stakeholders. Keep your relationships professional, and keep interested parties informed of your progress towards goals.

Communication skills play an important part of managing relationships with others. Use appropriate means of communication and make sure your communications are right for your audience. Simplicity of message, clarity and presentation quality are key objectives.

References

1. Clark, R.P.: Writing Tools: 50 Essential Strategies for Every Writer. Little Brown Book Group, reprint edn. (2010)
2. Elbow, P.: Writing With Power: Techniques for Mastering the Writing Process, 2nd edn. Oxford University Press, New York (1998)
3. Purdue University: Welcome to the Purdue University Online Writing Lab (OWL) (2019). https://owl.english.purdue.edu/. Accessed 9 Oct 2019
4. Rahy, S., Bass, J.: Information flows at inter-team boundaries in agile information systems development. In: Themistocleous, M., Rupino da Cunha, P. (eds.) Information Systems: EMCIS 2018. Lecture Notes in Business Information Processing, vol. 341, pp. 489–502. Springer, Limassol, Cyprus (2019). https://doi.org/10.1007/978-3-030-11395-7_38
5. Reynolds, G.: Presentation Zen: Simple Ideas on Presentation Design and Delivery, 2nd edn. New Riders, Berkeley (2011)
6. Schimel, J.: Writing Science: How to Write Papers That Get Cited and Proposals That Get Funded. OUP USA, Oxford; New York (2011)
7. Slack: Where work happens (2019). https://slack.com/intl/en-gb/
8. Strunk, William, Jr., White, E. B.: The Elements of Style, 4th edn. Longman, Boston (1999)
9. Truss, L.: Eats, Shoots and Leaves. Fourth Estate, London (2009)
10. Wikimedia Commons: Wikimedia Commons (2019). https://commons.wikimedia.org
11. William Strunk Jr.: The elements of style. http://www.bartleby.com/141/ (1918). Accessed 12 Sept 2014
12. Zinsser, W.: On Writing Well: The Classic Guide to Writing Nonfiction. Harper Collins Publishers, New York, 25th Anniversary edn. (2006)

Chapter 5
Ethics

Abstract Software is getting a bad name. Corporate personal data collection is justified for one purpose but then somehow finds it way into other purposes. Security breaches mean personal data escapes into the public domain. Technology is blamed for spreading fake news that has resulted in mayhem and death. Democracy is undermined. We need to think about our responsibilities as technologists. We are sometimes slow to understand the power of the software we create. We need to focus more carefully on how to create software for good. In this chapter, I will explore some issues to help us decide where to draw the line.

5.1 Introduction

The term *ethics* is about *doing the right thing*. For some people, ethics is about being a professional: being seen to act like a professional, doing good work, being reliable, seeing a project through to successful completion and so on. For other people, ethics is about protecting stakeholder interests and those of the wider public.

In recent years, technology sector influence has grown significantly. We are seeing increasing calls for the technology sector to be held accountable in areas less related to professionalism and more associated with issues like *justice*, *equality* and *fairness*.

5.2 What Went Wrong?

These days, you have to try really quite hard to get sufficiently 'off-grid' to not benefit from somebody's software. Software can bring us benefits in virtually all walks of life. But as software technologies become more pervasive, concerns grow that some aspects are not really serving some stakeholders well or fairly.

© Springer Nature Switzerland AG 2022
J. M. Bass, *Agile Software Engineering Skills*,
https://doi.org/10.1007/978-3-031-05469-3_5

The non-hierarchical and open access ethos of early Internet technologies has set public expectations that Internet services are provided with no financial cost. Many of these services, such as Internet *search*, *mapping* and *social media*, are highly valued by users and becoming difficult to avoid. Of course, these services are not actually free to provide. It's just that the transaction may not be obvious to everyone. The emergence of 'free' services, as John Honeyball, from PC Pro magazine [9], succinctly puts it, means that '*you* are the product' [5]. The 'free' services are actually designed to obtain data about users, for example, so that they can be more effectively targeted by advertisers.

This process has, perhaps surprisingly, created some of the largest commercial organisations ever seen. For some, this has become known as *surveillance capital-ism* [22]. Many of these organisations have been penalised by regulators or legal authorities for their lack of transparency or for monopolistic (anti-trust) behaviour. Some argue that the penalties imposed have been trivial considering the size and revenues of the organisations punished in this way.

5.2.1   Algorithms and Inequality

Researchers have found that search engines reinforce ethnic [12] and gender stereotypes. The near monopoly domination of Internet search engines like Google, which are motivated by sales of online advertising, does not offer a level playing field for ideas, identities and activities. In 2011, a Google search for 'girls' produced innocuous listings relating to fashion and health. In contrast, a search for 'black girls' produced a list dominated by pornographic websites. By 2012, the search algorithm had been changed, and the results listing produced by a search for 'black girls' had changed to something innocuous, whereas a search for 'Asian girls' still produced a listing dominated by pornographic sites.

5.2.2   Platforms and Fake Markets

Platforms have created new markets in sectors such as ride hailing (Uber), temporary overnight accommodation (AirbnB) and even creative work (Amazon MTurk, Upwork, RentACoder and so on). These platforms can provide good experiences for consumers and service providers alike. But there have also been critiques [20]. Work has been commissioned but has gone unpaid. Platform workers have been barred without explanation or recourse to appeal. There have been concerns that platform workers spend a lot of time searching for job that meet their skill set and then creating proposals. The platform workers are then rewarded with relatively small jobs on low rates of pay.

5.2.3   Errors, Faults and Failures

As the public comes to rely on IT ever more, when large systems fail, it attracts attention. IT outages in the financial services sector, for example, have denied millions of customers access to their bank accounts. In some cases, outages have prevented customers from obtaining cash or companies paying salaries to their staff. An IT outage at one major airline grounded flights and stranded around 75,000 passengers.

Outages affecting millions of people can attract significant publicity, adversely affecting company reputations and share prices (the value of the company). Financial regulators have questioned executives, in the banking sector, and senior executives have left their jobs.

The consequences of failure in safety critical applications is even more severe. A fault in the user interface design of a Canadian computer-controlled radiation therapy machine allowed operators to accidentally administer fatal overdoses. Several patients died, and the equipment manufacturer no longer exists.

At the time of writing, anti-stall software has been implicated as being responsible for two commercial airliners killing over 300 people. The Boeing 737 MAX 8 aircraft had software designed to push the aircraft nose down, to reduce the risk of a stall. Evidence to a US congressional hearing revealed this software relied on a single sensor, a so-called, *single-point-of-failure*. Fears have been expressed that sensor failure could cause the anti-stall software to push the aircraft into a dive.

5.2.4   Criminal and Unethical Behaviour

Some unethical behaviour can be viewed as borderline. Such professional lapses can result in disciplinary action by regulators or employers. Such unethical behaviour is narrow in scope and has limited impact on an organisation's customers, consumers, users or reputation.

Criminal action has resulted in jail terms for IT staff members. There are six main categories of unethical behaviour on software engineering projects [15]:

- Lying
- Computer fraud and unauthorised access
- Information theft
- Espionage
- Sabotage
- Subversion of project goals

Lying is almost never admitted to in software engineering projects. In fact, the word is almost always avoided at all costs. However, it has a long tradition in the technology sector. Developers exaggerate progress, project managers 'sanitise' status reporting and sales people advertise software benefiting from features that have yet to be implemented. In some cases, there is a fine line between an optimistic account and reality. Sometimes there appears to be outright fabrication.

Agile methods can help combat various forms of lying by creating a culture of transparency and openness. Estimation effort is targeted on short-term increments rather than attempting to create detailed estimates for far-off features. Poor-quality estimates are quickly exposed, within weeks, rather than months. Daily coordination meetings help ensure transparency on project status. Optimistic assessments of progress are quickly exposed. Finally, time and materials contracts (see Sect. 4.3) make it more attractive to sell the effort needed to create new features, rather than attempt to sell features that don't actually exist.

An important area of public concern is the criminal use of software-intensive infrastructure. Various forms of bank fraud and monetary theft are serious threat. There have been high-profile cases of unauthorised access to various computer systems operated by public, government and even military authorities. Perpetrators can be cyber joyriders, or sometimes there is the suspicion of corporate or governmental actors. Criminal techniques for credit card fraud can include:

- Cracking a server—obtaining card details from databases
- Phishing—enticing victims to hand over credit card details to a fake website
- Spear phishing—targeting high-net-worth individuals to obtain card details
- Pharming—creating a fake website for a well-known financial services provider
- Spyware—malicious software that captures details from victims

Social engineering is the use of various forms of trickery or deception to persuade people to divulge confidential information. Culprits can seek to gather a range of personal information on each data item being used to gather other more sensitive items. An important mitigating strategy is to educate users that IT support staff will never seek passwords.

Information theft can include sensitive corporate intelligence or development artefacts, such as source code. Sensitive information might include client lists, employee records or pricing details, which could give competitors an advantage. Source code or design artefact thefts are also forms of information theft. Actually, like other digital products, the rightful owner still has the original, but the culprit has misappropriated a copy. Good software system security measures can detect unusual usage patterns such as bulk file downloads.

Open-source software takes an alternative approach. In open-source, the software is a consequence of the expertise and process used during creation. Hence, the business model is either based on specialist skills used to create the source code or on providing consulting or support services around the code.

Espionage and industrial espionage is the gathering of confidential material from a foreign country or competitor company. Diplomats have been expelled as a result of allegations of state-sponsored cyber-intelligence gathering. There have been numerous cases of employees moving company and taking corporate intelligence with them. Non-compete contracts are a common tactic that prohibit employees from working in a specific business domain for a period of time.

Sabotage is usually perpetrated by insiders as a form of revenge or retribution. Employees receiving poor performance reviews or not getting the pay rise they feel they deserve have taken matters into their own hands in the past. Sabotage can take the form of data tampering, data destruction and publication of confidential data. Software developers have placed bombs in source code, left the company and then tried to profit from fluctuations in former employer's share price resulting in jail terms. Disgruntled ex-employees have also been sent to prison for publishing confidential data, private personnel data for former colleagues.

Stakeholders who want a project to fail are called subversive stakeholders [15]. Subversive stakeholders are not merely incompetent; they take deliberate actions to undermine the project. There are occasions where conflicts of interest lead to subversive behaviour. This is where one or more stakeholder group is not aligned with the interests of the project sponsor. For example, new software may put jobs at risk and cause people additional workload or loss of control. In these cases, stakeholders may not share a project team's enthusiasm for the new software project.

However, on occasion there seems less justifiable reasons for subversion. It is sometimes open to doubt about the true motives for the subversive's actions. Subversives may act out of a desire to resist change, undermine corporate goals and exact revenge for some perceived former problem, or because of rivalry between colleagues, competition between organisational or business units (for resources or influence). Less commonly, senior management may not be sufficiently committed to shared goals. Entirely malicious subversion seems to be quite rare but is not unknown.

Subversion is best mitigated by good stakeholder analysis, quality communication and support from senior management. An understanding of psychology and organisational theory is helpful to identify potential challenges. Software projects that bring benefits to a wide range of the stakeholders involved and where support is given to those who are disadvantaged are more likely to have a happy outcome.

5.3 Copyright and Patents

Many territories have legal restrictions protecting various forms of intellectual property. It might seem superficially attractive to download free copies of the latest films from a torrent site. However, it becomes less attractive when you made the film and people evade payment for your product.

The same is true for software. If you work hard to create an exciting new software product, you are entitled to expect reasonable payment for your labours. You need to make sure you receive your licence payments; it is often easier to ensure payment by using online software service deployment models.

By the same logic, we have to protect the intellectual property belonging others. We must keep private information shared with us by clients confidential. We take all reasonable precautions about preserving the confidentiality of such information. Keeping privileged information confidential is an important part of being a professional. In many parts of the IT industry, we can be exposed to highly sensitive data. It is our responsibility to ensure that data is kept safe and secure.

5.4   Professional Bodies

There are a choice of professional bodies that support and encourage professionals in the computing, IT and software sectors. These bodies offer services to their members and advocate for the wider discipline. These bodies include:

- Association for Computer Machinery (ACM) [2]
- British Computer Society (BCS), the Chartered Institute for IT [4]
- Institution for Engineering and Technology (IET) [21]
- Institute for Electrical and Electronic Engineering, Computer Society (IEEE CS) [10]

These bodies have members from around the world and often have member groups, such as branches and specialist groups, organised around geographies and technical specialisms, to create opportunities for practitioners to meet, network and exchanges ideas about the field. Many of these bodies organise conferences and journals to publish the latest research in the field.

The International Federation for Information Processing (IFIP) [11] also supports the discipline but is not membership body for practitioners. In contrast, IFIP comprises professional bodies from around the world. So, BCS and ACM, for example, are members of IFIP. IFIP also has working groups covering many technical specialisms along with conferences and journals.

By becoming members of the professional bodies, IT professionals agree to uphold certain standards of practice. Often this involves making commitments around honesty and integrity. A member breaching the standards could be expelled.

5.4.1   BCS Codes of Conduct

BCS, the Chartered Institute for IT, has created a code of conduct for members. The six-page code has a specific section on public interest which states [3]:

"you shall:

- have due regard for public health, privacy, security and wellbeing of others and the environment;
- have due regard for the legitimate rights of third parties;
- conduct your professional activities without discrimination on the grounds of sex, sexual orientation, marital status, nationality, colour, race, ethnic origin, religion, age or disability, or of any other condition or requirement; and
- promote equal access to the benefits of IT and seek to promote the inclusion of all sectors in society wherever opportunities arise..."

This implies a duty of care, by IT professionals, towards the wider public. There are also sections about competency [3]:

You shall:

- only undertake to do work or provide a service that is within your professional competence.
- NOT claim any level of competence that you do not possess.

An important requirement for professionals is the need to keep their skills up to date. As the BCS code puts it [3]: 'you shall develop your professional knowledge, skills and competence on a continuing basis, maintaining awareness of technological developments, procedures, and standards that are relevant to your field'. The BCS and other professional bodies place a responsibility on IT practitioners to keep their knowledge and skills up to date.

5.4.2 ACM Codes of Ethics

The ACM code of Ethics, like that of the BCS, has a commitment to public interest but also makes the case for professional responsibility in handling personal information:

'a computing professional should become conversant in the various definitions and forms of privacy and should understand the rights and responsibilities associated with the collection and use of personal information.'

5.4.3 Problems with Codes of Ethics

At the start of this chapter, I alluded to some of the problems that have heightened public concerns about the software sector: data breaches, service outages, misuse of data and so on. The negative impacts on members of the public I mentioned have happened despite the existence of professional bodies and their professional codes.

There is increased awareness, among professional bodies, of public disapproval of ethical lapses in the technology sector. Several professional bodies now provide help desks or contact points for practitioners facing an ethical dilemma.

5.5 Activism

Software engineers have used various forms of activism to address ethical transgressions. Some employees have organised petitions, to gather support strengthening ethical positions.

For example, in 2018, thousands of Google employees signed a letter 'protesting the company's involvement in a Pentagon program that uses artificial intelligence ... to improve the targeting of drone strikes' [19].

Google employees in 2019 signed a petition opposing provision of cloud services to US Customs and Border Protection (CPB) [13]. The petitioners cite 'human rights abuses at the US Southern border... caging and harming asylum seekers, separating children from parents [and] illegally detaining refugees'.

Some employers have very actively discouraged union membership. But there have been signs of renewed interest in unions, for example, in the gig economy. Delivery drivers in the UK and ride share drivers in the USA have attracted publicity for campaigns to obtain sick pay and paid holidays. Arguably, this activism has led to changes in employment law in California, regarding the definition of an employee and the responsibilities towards contractors.

5.5.1 Whistle-Blowing

Whistle-blowing is the act of exposing ethical wrong-doing with the aim of halting the behaviour. Whistle-blowing needs to be motivated by a commitment to the public good. Whistle-blowers must carefully evaluate the wrongs they seek to expose and choose a suitable outlet.

Whistle-blowing carries risks for the whistle-blower. There is a danger that senior management will be unwilling or unable to tackle the bad behaviour and instead focus on 'shooting the messenger'. Legal authorities, in the current climate, are likely to be supportive of those that expose financial or sexual misconduct.

5.5.2 Unions

Trade unions have not been popular in the technology sector. Trade unions are membership bodies committed to employment protection for their members. They offer legal support for their members in certain employment disputes and can offer a means for employees to work together to address employment-related and wider concerns.

There have been persistent stories about poor working conditions in the technology sector. For example, allegations that Amazon delivery drivers are unable to find time for toilet breaks have led to some public relations controversies [14].

Trade unions have, in recent years, enjoyed some success in tackling unfair practices employed by technology companies. For example, the App Drivers and Couriers Union successfully challenged Uber in the UK Supreme Court [1]. Subsequently, the company announced plans to pay minimum wage, holiday pay and pensions [7]. Trade unions can play an important role in providing employees a voice, a forum to discuss concerns and providing workplace advice.

5.6   Professional Development

Establishing a consistent set of skills standards in the technology sector is desirable to raise standards and enhance the reputation of the field. The UK Engineering Council has defined a set of standards for technicians and engineers, which can be applied in the digital technology sector [8]. The council holds national registers of over 222,000 Engineering Technicians (EngTech), Incorporated Engineers (IEng), Chartered Engineers (CEng) and Information and Communications Technology Technicians (ICTTech). The standards are publicly available and used by professional bodies, whose members wish to obtain certification.

Achieving such certification can improve earnings, provide promotion opportunities, enhance status, offer evidence of expertise and demonstrate commitment to the profession.

Acquiring the knowledge, skills and competencies required to achieve these standards involves cycles of planning, acting and reflecting. More specifically, you need to:

- Identify targets, the skills and competencies you want to learn
- Acquire knowledge
- Rehearse skills
- Reflect
- Repeat

In this way, over time, you can achieve the standards required to attract certification. Any professional development activity starts with a self-assessment of your current capabilities [17].

5.6.1   Initial Professional Development

Initial professional development is required to meet the requirements defined by professional bodies. Master's level educational attainment is typically required to meet the Chartered Engineer requirements. Then, evidence is needed of a sustained level of responsibility within the profession. Details of the syllabus and reading lists are often available online.

For members of the BCS, SFIA Plus provides examples of volunteering and other activities that can be used to gain experience beyond your current role [6]. Identifying and using such opportunities create *stretch tasks* where new competencies can be rehearsed.

5.6.2 Continuing Professional Development

For professionals that achieve chartered status, continuing professional development (CPD) is required to keep skills up to date. Usually, CPD must be recorded to provide evidence of an ongoing commitment to skills enhancement.

5.6.3 Skills Framework for the Information Age

The Skills Framework for the Information Age 'describes the skills and competencies required by professionals in roles involved in information and communication technologies, digital transformation and software engineering' [16].

The framework comprises seven levels, as shown in Table 5.1. Each level, in turn, is defined in terms of responsibilities, autonomy, influence, complexity, knowledge and business skills, as shown in Table 5.2, for Level 1. Consequently, each skill has a rich description of competencies and responsibilities.

Table 5.1 Levels in skills framework for the information age [16]

Levels	Definitions
7	Set strategy, inspire, mobilise
6	Initiate, influence
5	Ensure, advise
4	Enable
3	Apply
2	Assist
1	Follow

Table 5.2 Level 1 dimensions in skills framework for the information age [16]

Autonomy	Works under supervision. User little discretion. Is expected to seek guidance in unexpected situations
Influence	Minimal influence. May work alone or interact with immediate colleagues
Complexity	Performs routine activities in a structured environment. Requires assistance in resolving unexpected problems
Knowledge	Has a basic generic knowledge appropriate to area of work. Applies newly acquired knowledge to develop new skills
Business skills	Has sufficient communication skills for effective dialogue with others. Demonstrates an organised approach to work. Uses basic systems and tools, applications and processes. Contributes to identifying own development opportunities. Follows code of conduct, ethics and organisational standards. Is aware of health and safety issues. Understands and applies basic security practice

5.6.4 Other Training and Development

While professional body certifications and memberships can help with career development, there are a wide range of commercial certifications and massive open online courses (MOOCs) that can help with more specific skills. Some commercial certifications are well respected but are often focused on specific product versions and tend to be expensive. While MOOCs from reputable providers can be of high quality and up to date, the dropout rates are very high due in part to the online delivery format.

5.7 Exercises

Completing these exercises will help you apply the skills in ethics you are acquiring from this chapter. Remember, it is best if you don't look at the hints, tips and solutions chapter, at this stage. I suggest you do the exercises, then look at the advice in Sect. 5.8.

Exercise 5.1 (Learning Journal)

5.1 For this exercise, write in your learning journal about anything you found useful from this chapter.

Exercise 5.2 (Code of Ethics Review Exercise)

5.2 Choose a code of ethics from one of the professional bodies, such as the BCS, the Chartered Institute for IT, the Institute for Electrical and Electronic Engineers, the Association for Computer Machinery or Institution of Engineering and Technology. Review the code of ethics. Sometimes, the codes of ethics have different names, such as a code of conduct (for members). How does the code address responsibilities of IT professionals toward:

- The general public at large?
- Their own ongoing professional and career development?
- The legal and regulatory framework within which they work?

What other kinds of responsibilities are described in the code of ethics?

Exercise 5.3 (Intellectual Property Exercise)

5.3 Presumably you are working on (or planning to work on) a software development project. This project will involve you generating intellectual property. Who does that intellectual property belong to?

If you are a student, find out about your institution's rules on intellectual property. If you are an employee, what rules apply to you? Think about the steps you would need to take to own your intellectual property.

Exercise 5.4 (Stakeholder Analysis Exercise)

5.4 Practice conducting a stakeholder analysis. Choose a project you are currently working on (or that you have worked on before). Identify each project stakeholder. For each stakeholder, identify their specific interests in the project.

Exercise 5.5 (Skills Mapping to SFIA)

5.5 Revisit the output of the team skills inventory you performed in Exercise 2.2. Map the skills you have identified within the team onto the Skills Framework for the Information Age (SFIA) [18]. Now review the other skills categories in SFIA; are there any important skills groups that are missing from your team? What can you do to address any missing skill groups?

Exercise 5.6 (Learning Journal)

5.6 What happened during each exercise from this chapter? What went well? What could have gone better? What did you learn? Make some notes in your learning journal.

Exercise 5.7 (Learning Journal)

5.7   Reflect on the chapters in Part I. Reflect on what you have learned about:

- Self-organising teams
- Roles, such as scrum master and product owner
- Managing stakeholders
- Ethics

Make some notes in your learning journal about each of these topics.

5.8   Hints, Tips and Advice on Exercises

5.1 *Learning Journal Exercise*

In this chapter, we have discussed ethical concerns about 'big tech', copyright and patents, professional bodies, activism and professional development.
    Write some notes on what you have learned about each topic.

5.2 *Code of Ethics, Review*

Briefly, professional bodies like their members to have a positive impact on the public. Professional bodies want their members to avoid bringing their profession into disrepute through any behaviour that negatively affects people outside the profession. While different professions may have higher or lower perceived status in society, the professional bodies themselves want to raise the status of the members where possible.
    At early stages of your career, it can be hard to realise, but your career development is your own concern. Professional bodies often provide groups and resources to support opportunities for professional development, but it is up to members to identify their own needs and take advantage of these opportunities.
    Students have the advantage of a syllabus that has been prepared by their college or university. Hopefully, the syllabus is up to date and has been reviewed (or accredited) by a professional body. Employees in large companies may be able to get advice on opportunities for formal training courses from a training department. Nevertheless, it is up to professionals to

(continued)

identify their own needs and create plans to update existing skills and acquire new knowledge.

Professional bodies will encourage you to become aware of the legal and regulatory framework within which you work. They want their members to stay on the right side of the law to avoid damaging their professional reputation. You should seek out the opportunities professional bodies provide to keep up to date with the legal or regulatory landscape and changes.

5.3 *Intellectual Property*

If you are an employee, the intellectual property will likely belong to your employer. If you are a student, policies can vary from university to university and from country to country about who owns the intellectual property. If you are working as part of a start-up company, spin-up or spin-out, then you might own your intellectual property.

5.4 *Stakeholder Analysis*

When you identify project stakeholders, you might think about:

- Shareholders
- Executive management team
- Line managers
- Employees
- Customers
- The general public
- Government
- Financial institutions
- Non-governmental organisations, activists and pressure groups

Try to think about the specific interests in the project of each of these stakeholder groups.

5.5 *Skills Mapping to SFIA*

You might find some aspects of mapping your skills inventory to SFIA surprising. Your inventory, for instance, might include PHP developer, Java developer and Javascript HTML/CSS developer. In SFIA, these will all map

(continued)

to the developer role. Think about these relationships. Is there a one-to-one relationship between your inventory and SFIA?

Further, I expect there will be roles in SFIA you had not previously considered. There are actually a wide range of technical and business roles in the IT and software sector. Make some notes in your learning journal about two or three unfamiliar job roles in SFIA that would be useful to your project.

5.9 Chapter Summary

Software and digital technologies have been enthusiastically adopted in many walks of life and have the potential to bring significant benefits. However, there are also risks that technology can amplify unfairness, inequality and disadvantage. Marginalised groups can find their undervalued status even further undermined by the introduction of new software systems. The rich and powerful are disproportionately empowered to exploit technology to their advantage. Our responsibility, as software professionals, is to educate ourselves to understand these risks and where possible initiate mitigation.

References

1. ADCU: App drivers & couriers union (2020). https://www.adcu.org.uk/
2. Association for Computing Machinery: Association for Computing Machinery (2019). https://www.acm.org/
3. BCS – The Chartered Institute for IT: BCS code of conduct (2019). https://www.bcs.org/membership/become-a-member/bcs-code-of-conduct/
4. BCS – The Chartered Institute for IT: BCS, The Chartered Institute for IT (2019). https://www.bcs.org/
5. BCS – The Chartered Institute for IT: Surveillance Capitalism – A Panel Discussion – Manchester Branch (2019). https://www.bcs.org/events-calendar/2019/march/surveillance-capitalism-a-panel-discussion-manchester-branch/
6. BCS, The Chartered Institute for IT: SFIAplus – IT skills framework (2021). https://www.bcs.org/membership/sfiaplus-it-skills-framework/
7. Butler, S.: Uber to pay uk drivers minimum wage, holiday pay and pension (2021). http://www.theguardian.com/technology/2021/mar/16/uber-to-pay-uk-drivers-minimum-wage-holiday-pay-and-pension
8. Engineering Council: Engineering council (2020). https://www.engc.org.uk/
9. Future Publishing Ltd.: PC Pro magazine | meet the team (2022). http://subscribe.pcpro.co.uk/meettheteam
10. IEEE Computer Society: IEEE Computer Society (2019). http://www.computer.org/
11. International Federation for Information Processing: IFIP – Home (2019). https://www.ifip.org/
12. Noble, S.U.: Algorithms of Oppression: How Search Engines Reinforce Racism. NYU Press, New York (2018)

13. No GCP for CBP: Google must stand against human rights abuses: #NoGCPfor-CBP (2019). https://medium.com/@no.gcp.for.cbp/google-must-stand-against-human-rights-abuses-nogcpforcbp-88c60e1fc35e
14. O'Neil, L.: Amazon's denial of workers urinating in bottles puts the pee in PR fiasco (2021). http://www.theguardian.com/lifeandstyle/2021/mar/25/amazon-bottles-pee-tweet-warehouse-workers
15. Rost, J., Glass, R.L.: The Dark Side of Software Engineering: Evil on Computing Projects. John Wiley & Sons, Hoboken (2013)
16. SFIA Foundation: The global skills and competency framework for a digital world (2003). https://sfia-online.org/en
17. SFIA Foundation: Self-assessment guidelines (2003). https://sfia-online.org/en/tools-and-resources/using-sfia/sfia-assessment/self-assessment-guidelines
18. SFIA Foundation: SFIA (2018). https://www.sfia-online.org/en
19. Shane, S., Wakabayashi, D.: 'The Business of War': Google Employees Protest Work for the Pentagon. The New York Times (2018). https://www.nytimes.com/2018/04/04/technology/google-letter-ceo-pentagon-project.html
20. Srnicek, N.: Platform Capitalism. Polity Press, Cambridge (2016)
21. The IET: IET – Home (2019). https://www.theiet.org/
22. Zuboff, P.S.: The Age of Surveillance Capitalism: The Fight for a Human Future at the New Frontier of Power, main edn. Profile Books, London (2019)

Chapter 6
Tabby Cat Project, Getting Started

Abstract In this chapter, we consider forming a team to create the *Tabby Cat* case study project. This project will create an opportunity to apply the ideas from the chapters in Part I of the book. We will apply the self-organising team, scrum master and product owner roles to the *Tabby Cat* project. We will also explore managing stakeholders and professional issues. *Tabby Cat* is software for displaying activity from an online source code repository. You can download information about commits on the repository and display the data using various filters and searches.

6.1 Introduction

This case study allows us to summarise and apply the most important ideas we have covered in Part I. Here, you can learn more about agile roles, the self-organising team, managing stakeholders and professional issues.

This case study is based on software developed by Red Ocelot Ltd. [1]. In Chap. 12, you can learn about the case study requirements, design and implementation.

6.2 Online Repository Activities

Your aim is to form a team and create the *Tabby Cat* product. *Tabby Cat* is a skeleton software service for obtaining and displaying activity on a GitHub repository. *Tabby Cat* can connect to any public GitHub repository and extract data on commits, issues and metrics.

Once the data is extracted from GitHub, a listing can be produced. This listing can help understand the focus of developer activity on the target repository.

© Springer Nature Switzerland AG 2022
J. M. Bass, *Agile Software Engineering Skills*,
https://doi.org/10.1007/978-3-031-05469-3_6

Review Your Learning Journal

I have recommended that you create and update a learning journal when you do the exercises in each chapter (see Exercise 2.1). Now is a good time to reflect on your journal

- Re-read your learning journal from the chapter exercises in Part I of the book.
- Think about what went well when you did the exercises.
- Think about what didn't go so well.
- Make some notes, in your learning journal, about the strengths and weaknesses of your work in these areas.
- Create some actions or set some targets for your future learning.

6.3   Actually Getting Started

Team members can be selected or assigned to you. Even if team members are friends, you will likely want to learn more of their likes and dislikes in terms of project work. I recommend you start by conducting a skills inventory of the members of your group. Consequently, your starting point should be to read Chap. 2 and complete Exercise 2.2.

Now complete Exercise 2.3, to learn more about the other members of your team. It is especially important in diverse teams to develop empathy and trust with other team members. This is best achieved by understanding each other's backgrounds and experiences.

Team Diversity

Software teams with a diverse membership are more likely to perform well. Diversity within the team brings different perspectives and complimentary ideas. Attracting team members with diverse skills should be a high priority.

Next conduct Exercise 2.4. It is wise to establish conventions about how to work together and how to resolve differences. Conflict can arise within your team. You hope team members will be passionate about the work. But, passionate individuals may champion very different approaches that they feel very strongly about. Consequently, conflict can arise on issues where there is no clear and obvious right or wrong answer. In these cases, conflict resolution strategies can be helpful to diffuse confrontation and help the team reach consensus.

Then, conduct Exercise 2.5. Teams that have strong shared sense of common purpose tend to perform best. Try to create consensus within the team on purpose. For example, are student groups trying to a good mark? Or, are some student group members going to be satisfied with a bare pass grade? Such differences in expectations can lead to conflict with the team.

Don't Ignore Team Building Activities

Strongly technical team members may be tempted to skip or scrimp on team building activities. This is a bad idea. Solving technical problems within a group is much harder than working alone, while the potential for a team to achieve fantastic results is also greater. The investment in team building is worthwhile.

6.4   Sprint Zero

There's no such thing as a *Sprint Zero*. But, it is a useful metaphor for starting your first iteration. Sprint zero is where you work together to prepare for software development on the *Tabby Cat* project.

Now is a good time to read Chap. 3, if you haven't already. If you have not been assigned a scrum master, you need to choose one. As you learned in Chap. 3, the scrum master facilitates ceremonies within the team.

First, your team can practise sprint planning, as discussed in Exercise 3.2. The sprint planning process is described in Chap. 13. Then, your scrum master can organise and facilitate daily stand-ups, drawing on Exercise 3.3. You may not have any software to demonstrate at the end of Sprint Zero, so you may not want to run a customer demonstration (if you do, though, you can look at Exercise 3.4). But, you should probably conduct a Sprint Zero retrospective. There is more information about conducting a retrospective in Exercise 3.5.

Next, you need a *product owner*. The product owner could be a real customer or perhaps a supervisor or an academic running your course. If the product owner is not obvious, then you need to create a proxy product owner role. Choose the person with the most knowledge of the *Tabby Cat* project domain.

Finally, work with your product owner to undertake requirements gathering workshops, such as those described in Exercises 3.6 to 3.8. You will learn more about requirements, when you read Chap. 7. Specific requirements for the *Tabby Cat* project are discussed in Chap. 12.

6.5   Subsequent Sprints

Now read Chap. 4, if you haven't already. Someone in your team can focus on working through Exercises 4.2 to 4.6. This person can think about how the team will record important decisions, such as design decisions, and how you will report to stakeholders on your activities.

The *Tabby Cat* project may not have serious ethical dilemmas, but read through Chap. 5 in order to consider ethics issues that might arise. In particular, think about the skills you have in the team. Perform Exercise 5.5, and consider any skills gaps you identify. Is there any training members of the team can undertake to address missing skills?

6.6   Chapter Summary

The *Tabby Cat* project will create a skeleton software system for connecting to a public GitHub repository, extracting source code activities and making a display.

In this chapter, we have explored a range of tactics to help you form a team to work on the *Tabby Cat* project. If you have applied the knowledge and skills described, you will be working as a self-organising team with a scrum master and a product owner. You will also have completed a Sprint Zero and practised running a few team meetings.

In Part II of the book, we will explore the technical skills you need for an agile project. I'll explore *requirements* in Chap. 7, high-level design or *architecture* in Chap. 8, *design* in Chap.9, *development* in Chap. 10 and security in Chap. 11. Discussion of this technical side of the *Tabby Cat* project will continue in Chap. 12.

Reference

1. Red Ocelot Ltd: Enhancing digital agility (2022). https://www.redocelot.com

Part II
Product

While Part I of the book focused on *people*, Part II of the book is about *product*. We have to acquire skills in defining the needs our system intended to fulfil and the techniques for creating a software solution.

First, in Chap. 7, there is a discussion of requirements gathering and management for incremental delivery. You will learn about distinguishing functional and non-functional requirements. Specifically, you will learn about employing use cases and user stories for capturing and discussing requirements.

Next, Chap. 8 explores approaches to high-level architectural styles, such as client-server and layered architectures. You can learn about some of the most important design principles, such as the *SOLID* approach.

Then Chap. 9 considers lower-level system design, most notably object-oriented modelling and how to derive a design from a domain model. You can learn about design patterns, such as object factories and the model-view-controller.

Incremental development issues are discussed in Chap. 10. You can learn about the artefacts development teams create while building software systems. This will cover topics like Kanban boards, backlogs and burndown charts.

In contrast, Chap. 11 looks at security issues and the concept of a secure-by-design agile development process. We'll look at creating abuse user stories to model potential threats and guidance on secure implementations.

In Chap. 12, the ideas from Part II are applied to the *Tabby Cat* case study. I explore the technical skills needed to read activity data from an online software source code repository and display the information with various filter options.

Other Book Parts

As I have emphasised, the overall design of this book is around *people* in Part I, *product* in Part II and *process* in Part III. These parts of the book are stand-alone, more or less. So, if your main interest is in the social aspects of software development, for instance, then you might want to skip back to Part I. On the other hand, if your main interest is creating a systematic software development *process*, then you might want to skip ahead to Part III. Some more advanced topics, such as large-scale agile, cloud deployment and continuous integration, are described in Part IV.

Chapter 7
Requirements

Abstract Our customers, clients, users or bosses give us requirements that define the needs our software must fulfil. We need to understand when to use outline requirements, for longer-term planning, and when we need full detail, for the requirements we are going to implement now. Hence, we adopt an incremental approach to managing requirements. We often analyse requirements using user stories and use cases. User stories are great for helping our customers prioritise and communicate about the software needs. However, developers find use cases useful for learning how to elaborate our requirements in more detail.

7.1 Introduction

Requirements engineering is the process of establishing what services our customers want. Further, we also need to understand the constraints within which our system must operate.

Most requirements elicitation involves asking questions. Sometimes, there is a single individual you can go to, such as a product owner, more on that role in Sect. 3.3. Sometimes, we need to ask a group of people (that might have different opinions). In that case, we run a requirements workshop. In both cases, we need to prepare ourselves. What questions do we want to ask? How will we record the answers? During the workshop, we need to keep the discussion focused and on topic and at the same time entice as much detail as possible from the informants.

Journalists and others try to make sure they get answers to questions by using the following list: *who, what, when, where, why and how?*. In terms of requirements elicitation: Who does something? What do they do? When do they do it? Where are they when they do it? Why do they do it? How do they do it? If we are responsible for developing an entirely new and novel system, however, there may be no one you can ask. In such cases, we have to use our imagination and creativity to create requirements.

There are two main approaches to recording and managing requirements: user stories and use cases. Both have benefits and advantages but also some drawbacks. Hence, it is good to learn about both techniques, even if you end up choosing only

© Springer Nature Switzerland AG 2022
J. M. Bass, *Agile Software Engineering Skills*,
https://doi.org/10.1007/978-3-031-05469-3_7

one to use on your project. You can learn more about use cases in Sect. 7.4 and user stories in Sect. 7.5.

7.2   Types of Requirements

We want to explore requirements from the perspective of the functions a system must perform as well as the constraints under which it must operate. We will also explore how to tackle requirements in an incremental development setting.

7.2.1   Functional Requirements

Functional requirements are statements that describe the services the software should provide. This might involve things like how the software will respond to particular sets of inputs, how data should be transformed and what the software does in particular situations. Obviously, the name *functional requirement* is derived from the functions the software performs.

I will talk more about feature-driven development, in Sect. 9.2; this is about developing one particular service at a time. A feature is some client-valued function that the software must perform. We tend to favour descriptions of functionality from a perspective outside the software. We are usually interested in externally visible behaviour.

7.2.2   Non-functional Requirements

In contrast with functional requirements, non-functional requirements are system-wide quality attributes. Non-functional requirements are not concerned with specific features, but rather cross-cutting qualities of the system as a whole. Non-functional requirements might include the length of time allowed to perform functions, the availability (or uptime) of the system or compliance with legal standards or regulations. Sometimes, it is good to think of non-functional requirements as system constraints. The software is not allowed to operate outside those constraints (such as response times, availability or regulations).

Non-functional requirements often have an impact on the overall design ethos of software. A primary flight control system for a commercial passenger aircraft is not built using the same sort of approach to design as a simple mobile phone game.

You can manage non-functional requirements as artefacts in your agile process [4]. That means creating non-functional requirement user stories and tracking them using your Kanban board-like functional features, as discussed in Chap. 13.

Caution!

Safety-critical or safety-related systems are those which could adversely affect our environment or conceivably injure, harm or even kill people. Some applications areas are obviously safety critical; think of medical, transportation (cars, trains, boats and planes) and nuclear power.

The non-functional requirements of safety-critical applications are beyond the scope of this book. There are several specialist techniques that are required for designing and implementing safety-critical systems. In this book, you can walk through the skills you need to create your first software system, working as part of a team. The skills described here are a necessary but not sufficient set of skills for working on safety critical systems. Specialist safety-critical skills are beyond the scope of these chapters.

7.2.3   Incremental Requirements

We have a dilemma about how to handle requirements on agile projects. On the one hand, we can't build the software without complete and detailed information about what the system is supposed to do. On the other hand, it takes a long time to create a detailed specification of requirements for the whole system, and we find some of the requirements changing as we go along.

So, we need more detail about what we are going to build now, but we can live with less detail now, about what we are going to build later. But, hang on. The non-functional requirements are cross-cutting. Non-functional requirements affect the whole system. So, we need to be very careful here.

We do need full detail about the non-functional requirements at the outset. We need to ensure our initial software designs take into account the constraints under which our system will operate. But it is also true that defining detailed specifications for functions we won't be implementing until later in the project is not necessary (so long as they aren't going to dramatically change our understanding of the constraints on the software).

So, we arrive at a point where we need detail about the non-functional requirements from the start but that we can adopt a, sort of, moving window approach to functional requirements. We can develop an outline, overview or fuzzy description of the functionality of the whole system. Then, for the high-priority features we are going to work on first, we need to obtain all the detail.

7.3   Requirements Quality

I have argued we need to be aware of two types of requirements (functional and non-functional) and treat them differently. At the outset, we only need an overview of all the functional requirements. But, we must acquire a detailed view of the non-functional requirements for the whole system from the start. Further, just to be clear, we also need full details of the functionality we are going to implement now.

7.3.1   Requirements Precision

Imprecise requirements are bad news, when we build software. If requirements are ambiguous, the development team may interpret the requirements differently from users or clients. This means we end up building something that does not really meet the needs of the client. And that is the bad news. We end up building a poor-quality product, poor quality because the software does not meet the need (not poor quality in the sense that there are defects in our code). So, when the time comes to build functionality, we need the detail about what it is meant to do.

In large-scale projects, with multiple cooperating teams, ambiguous require-ments can be interpreted differently by different teams. This can lead to confusion between the teams and even source code defects. This is discussed further in Chap. 18.

7.3.2   Requirements Consistency

Inconsistency in requirements creates big problems for a software development project. If our understanding of requirements in one place is contradicted by a requirement some place else, fear, uncertainty and doubt are sure to follow. We have to go back to finding out which is the correct understanding of the requirements. Or sometimes, they are both correct but under different circumstances. So we need to figure out when each situation is true.

A common challenge is using consistent terminology. When talking about requirements, we have to use the same names for things all the time. Err, consis-tently. Right? If we start using a different name for something, our colleagues may think it is, in fact, a different thing.

7.3.3 *Requirements Completeness*

Finally, another killer for software projects is incomplete requirements. What we really want to avoid is discovering significant new requirements part way through the project. Significant requirements are the ones that dramatically affect the underlying assumptions of the system or the constraints under which the system operates. Usually, this means we don't want to discover an important non-functional requirement when we have already started building the software.

When new functional requirements give us big surprises, part way through a software project, it can also be damaging to a healthy life and happiness. It's fine if we discover our software needs to handle `CustomerAge` as well as `CustomerDateOfBirth`. We can just do a little calculation to get `CustomerAge` from `CustomerDateOfBirth`. No big deal. If on the other hand we find out (part way through our website development project) that customers need to be able to tell us their date of birth using a voice interface, then that might have rather bigger implications. Discovering whole new ways of collecting (inputting) data or disseminating results (outputting data) is never good when a project is already under way. We try to understand all required interfaces the outside world, at an early stage of the project.

When big surprises happen, we need additional time and resources to take care of these new functions. We might need team members with a whole new skill set (at the time of writing building voice or audio activated user interfaces is still not exactly mainstream). We might need to reconsider some design assumptions. Worse, big surprises might mean we need to re-design and re-implement parts of the software that we thought we had already finished. No one looks good in this situation. The development team looks like we don't know what we are doing, and managers rarely enjoy paying for things to be done over and over again. I hope you can detect the tone of understatement here. On large-scale projects, big surprises during the project can be career limiting.

> **! Attention**
>
> We must acquire complete, consistent and detailed non-functional require-
> ments at the start of the project. We also need complete, consistent and
> detailed functional requirements for the software we are going to build over
> the next few weeks. However, at the outset, an outline picture of functional
> requirements for the rest of the software system is sufficient. This is provided
> we understand all the interfaces to the outside world or other systems our
> software must interact with.

7.4   Use Cases

A use case is a user interaction scenario, a situation in which a user wants to achieve something by using our software. The use case provides a description of how someone or something outside the software triggers some response. The user usually has some goal or purpose in mind that is made explicit in the use case.

Use cases have two elements: a use case diagram for the whole system and a detailed use case for each specific interaction scenario. The idea here is that the use case diagram is addressing issues of completeness and to some extent consistency, while individual use case scenarios are addressing consistency (again) and precision or detail in the requirements.

7.4.1   Use Case Diagrams

A use case diagram shows users of the system. We give the users a special name *actors*. The actors are shown as stick figures and are usually organised on the left or right edge of the use case diagram. In Fig. 7.1a, you can see an actor called customer. There are two use cases in Fig. 7.1a: Rent and Return. The oval shapes represent the use cases. The words Rent and Return are actually use case titles. Finally, the connecting lines, in Fig. 7.1a, show us that the Customer actor can perform both use cases Rent and Return.

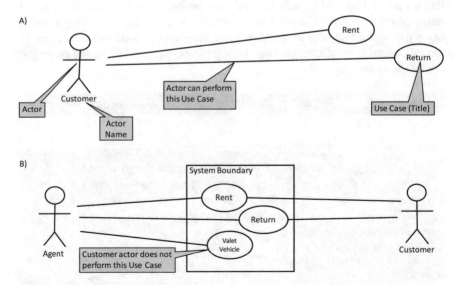

Fig. 7.1 Two simple use case examples. (**a**) Simplified use case diagram. (**b**) Car rental desk use case diagram

The use case shown in Fig. 7.1b is getting slightly more realistic. There are two actors, Agent and Customer, and three use cases, Rent, Return and Valet Vehicle. Notice that there is no connecting line between the Valet Vehicle use case and the Customer. This tells us that the Customer actor, in this illustrative car rental system, is not required to valet their own vehicle when they return it. The use cases that are in scope for a project are often indicated by including a system boundary box on the use case model.

7.4.2 Use Case, Descriptions

Each *Use Case* is described in more detail in tables. The table templates vary from place to place; I show an example in Table 7.1. It is customary to complete the use case table in full.

The use case title is the name of the use case. The name is often quite succinct, but it needs to be unique. Each use case title corresponds to the one shown in the use case diagram, of course.

The primary actors are listed next. A primary actor initiates the use case. As with the use case title, it is important to make sure the actors in the use cases correspond to the actors shown in use case diagram. Sometimes, people add a row to list secondary actors. Secondary actors are required to complete a use case but do not initiate the use case.

The actors are followed by a goal for the use case. The goal describes the purpose of the use case from the user's perspective. What is it that the user is trying to achieve when they perform the use case?

Table 7.1 Example use case template

Use case title	«text for the use case title goes here, corresponds to use case diagram»
Primary actor(s)	«Actor corresponds to use case diagram»
Secondary actor(s)	«If appropriate»
Goal	
Scope	
Preconditions	
Postconditions	
Main success scenario	1.
	2.
	3.
Extensions	1a.
	2a.
	3a.

The scope represents a boundary for the use case. What is included or not included in the use case? Preconditions must be true before the use case runs. Postconditions must be true after the use case has completed.

The main success scenario gives the steps that form an interaction scenario in which nothing goes wrong. Each of the numbered steps reflects a stage in a user interaction with the system.

Finally, the extensions describe the things that can go wrong, or unexpectedly, in each step of the main success scenario. Each numbered step in the extensions corresponds to a numbered step in the main success scenario. Meaning, extension step 2 is a non-successful variation on step 2 in the main success scenario. Extensions must be something the system can actually detect for itself [1]. Also, there is no point in describing an extension the system can't actually handle.

7.5 User Stories

A user story is also written from the perspective of a person who actually uses software. But, whereas use cases are described as being semi-formal, a use case is informal because it is written in simple (natural, non-technical) language. In a way, we can think of a user story as being a handle, or variable name, representing some collection of functions that the software will perform. Let's look at a couple of simple, fictitious, examples:

> User Story 1
> As a *<holidaymaker>*, I want to *<book a flight>*, in order to *<enjoy a holiday>*.

Notice that *User Story 1* has three parts: the user, in this case a *<holidaymaker>*, followed by an action, *<book a flight>*, followed by an objective or purpose to *<enjoy a holiday>*. Actually, there are lots of different templates for user stories, but this is the one I tend to use...

> User Story 2
> As an *<actor>*, I want to *<perform an action>*, in order to *<gain some value>*.

Sometimes, people might be tempted to write a user story like this:

> **User Story 3**
> As a *<user>*, I want to *<book a flight>*, in order to *<get a flight>*.

We try to avoid using the generic name *<user>* in our user stories. Why? Because a *user* is not a specific enough description of the person or thing interacting with our software. We'll explore this idea in more detail in Sect. 7.7, when we talk about personas.

But to make things clearer, let's imagine that our travel booking system in *User Story 1* might also have another user story, like this:

> **User Story 4**
> As a *<business traveller>*, I want to *<book a flight>*, in order to *<have a business trip>*.

In both *User Story 1* and *User Story 4*, someone wants to book a flight. So you might think it would be a simplification to merge them both into *User Story 3*. But perhaps, the *<business traveller>* in *User Story 4* is going to be invoiced through their company, whereas the *<holidaymaker>* in *User Story 1* has to pay online with a credit card. These extra details are not yet obvious from the user stories we've presented. But this illustrates the benefits specific user segments have in our user stories.

So, how do we show these extra details (e.g. card payment or corporate billing) in a user story, then? We often add acceptance test criteria to the user story. We'll discuss the skills you need to perform testing in Chap. 16.

7.6   User Story Mapping

Once you have established a series of user stories, it is a good idea to plan out a user journey through the features [3]. The challenge we are trying to avoid is creating increments with valuable features but that don't provide a useful end-to-end journey for the user. We are going to try and build a matrix of user stories organised according to their order in a user journey and their criticality, as shown in Fig. 7.2.

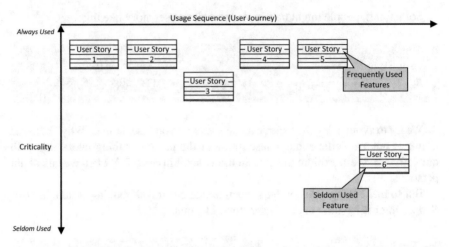

Fig. 7.2 User story mapping (Adapted from [2])

7.7   Personas

Personas are fictional characters that you create to represent user segments or types of actor interacting with you system. The idea is to help you think about using your system from someone else's perspective. Personas arise from your research into typical user behaviour. What are their goals, objectives and motivations in using your system? By developing different personas, you can articulate the different needs user groups have.

The persona comprises a photo or cartoon image to represent this user as an individual. You can then write fictional details about the persona's age, gender, ethnicity, education, lifestyle, interests, values, goals, needs, limitations, desires, attitudes and patterns of behaviour, as appropriate for your application software.

In an online travel booking system, for example, you might distinguish between 'frequent fliers' and 'vacationers'. Frequent fliers tend to be business travellers. This implies solo travel, metropolitan destinations, short-notice trips, late changes of plans and corporate billing. However, we might assume that vacationers are more likely to travel in groups; favour rural, beach or mountain destinations; make fewer more infrequent trips; and accept online credit card payment. We can use personas to tease out more details about these different use groups and their needs.

7.8   Exercises

You should start by creating a learning journal for Part II *Product*, if you haven't already. In the learning journal, keep notes on the things you learn. Use the learning journal to plan your future skills development activities.

Don't forget: it is better not to look at the hints, tips and solutions chapter, at this stage. First, do an exercise. Next, reflect on that exercise. Then, look at the hints, tips and advice in Sect. 7.9.

Exercise 7.1 (Learning Journal)

7.1 The first exercise for each chapter is to review the material and write in your learning journal. Make some brief notes for the material in this chapter.

Exercise 7.2 (Use Case Diagram Exercise 1: Student Record Information System)

7.2 A student record information system is used to manage student progression. Students register for option modules and programmes. Modules have lecturers. Students can transfer from one option module to another within the first 4 weeks of the semester. Modules are assigned to a year with a programme by administrators. Lecturers upload marks for mandatory and option modules which are then ratified by administrators on behalf of exam boards.

Exercise Tasks Your objective is to analyse the scenario above and build a use case model by doing the following tasks:

1. Identify and name the actors of the system.
2. For each actor in the system, identify and name the use cases for the actor.
3. Draw a simple use case diagram for the system.

Exercise 7.3 (Use Case Diagram Exercise 2: Library Information System)

7.3 A library information system is used to manage holdings (comprising books, multi-media recordings, magazines and journals) in both hard copy and online form. Holdings registered in the information system can be searched using titles, keywords and holding type. Senior librarians are responsible for archiving old, damaged and unused holdings as well as purchasing new holdings. Librarians register purchased holdings on the library information systems. Borrowers can borrow and return holdings.

Exercise Tasks Your objective is to analyse the scenario above and build a use case model by doing the following tasks:

1. Identify and name the actors of the system.
2. For each actor in the system, identify and name the use cases for the actor.
3. Draw a simple use case diagram for the system.

Exercise 7.4 (Use Case Diagram Exercise 3: Flight Travel Booking System)

7.4 The Flight Travel Booking System (FTBS) provides online services to travellers for flight and hotel reservations using a reservations transaction handling system such as Amadeus or Sabre. Travellers can search, reserve, book and cancel flights. Traveller cancelations can be performed up to 24 h before departure. Frequent fliers can cancel reservations with no penalty within 6 h of departure.

Exercise Tasks Your objective is to analyse the scenario above and build a use case model by doing the following tasks:

1. Identify and name the actors of the system.
2. For each actor in the system, identify and name the use cases for the actor.
3. Draw a simple use case diagram for the system.

Exercise 7.5 (Use Case Diagram Exercise 4, Advanced: Flight Broker System)

7.5 A travel agent wishes to expand its business by investing in an online flight reservation system. The agency works as a broker for booking and selling flight tickets using a number of airline companies around the world. In order to locate the requested flight, the agency communicates with air companies to retrieve their flight schedules and seat availability.

The agency has two types of clients, individual and corporate clients. Individual clients often request to search for an appropriate flight and compare prices. When searching for a flight, the user may want to sort the results by price, airlines or number of connections.

After choosing the desired flight from the results, they could make initial booking or progress to purchase and payments. Alternatively, they could cancel the search. The system should maintain a database of client accounts through which clients could retrieve all their current bookings and/or past journeys. They may also use the system to cancel or amend a journey; this is dependent on the type of ticket they have purchased. The system should support the following ticket types:

- Full fare ticket, a 1-year open fully refundable and changeable ticket
- Open ticket, a 3-month open ticket which may be changed or refunded subject to 20% administration charge
- Saver ticket, valid for one trip and may not be changed

(continued)

Exercise 7.5 (continued)

Corporate clients enjoy the services of individual clients plus additional ones. They benefit from a 30-day credit facility; the credit amount varies for different clients. A corporate client may purchase tickets using credit or direct payment. If using credit payments, corporate clients may only purchase new tickets if they have not exceeded their credit limit and they do not have any outstanding payments exceeding the 1-month period. They may also use the system to request credit increase. Such request is rejected if the client has outstanding payments exceeding the 1-month period; otherwise, it is forwarded to the agency's staff for processing.

The system may also be used by the agency's staff (agents) to query the system for outstanding bookings pending confirmation or payment. The agents use the information for following up the bookings with clients. The agents may also use the system to retrieve outstanding corporate accounts for following up the settlement of such accounts.

Exercise Tasks Your objective is to analyse the scenario above and build a use case model by doing the following tasks:

1. Identify and name the actors of the system.
2. For each actor in the system, identify and name the use cases for the actor.
3. Draw a detailed use case diagram for the system. Make sure you include actor and use case relationships. You may want to use a software tool to create the use case diagram. A list of UML modelling tools, some of which are open source, is available from [5].

Exercise 7.6 (Use Case Exercise 1: Student Record Information System)

7.6 Use the student record information system scenario in Exercise 7.2.

Exercise Tasks Your objective is to analyse the scenario and write a use case by doing the following tasks:

1. Describe the goal and scope of the use case.
2. Write a series of steps describing the main success scenario.
3. Write extensions describing any error (or exception) scenarios.
4. Identify postconditions for the use case.
5. Can you identify any preconditions for the use case?

Exercise 7.7 (Use Case Exercise 2: Library Information System)

7.7 Use the library information system scenario in Exercise 7.3.
Exercise Tasks Your objective is to analyse the scenario and write a use case by doing the following tasks:

1. Describe the goal and scope of the use case.
2. Write a series of steps describing the main success scenario.
3. Write extensions describing any error (or exception) scenarios.
4. Identify postconditions for the use case.
5. Can you identify any preconditions for the use case?

Exercise 7.8 (Use Case Exercise 3: Flight Travel Booking System)

7.8 Use the Flight Travel Booking System (FTBS) scenario in Exercise 7.4.
Exercise Tasks Your objective is to analyse the scenario and write a use case by doing the following tasks:

1. Describe the goal and scope of the use case.
2. Write a series of steps describing the main success scenario.
3. Write extensions describing any error (or exception) scenarios.
4. Identify postconditions for the use case.
5. Can you identify any preconditions for the use case?

Exercise 7.9 (Use Case Exercise 4, Advanced: Flight Broker System)

7.9 Use the flight broker system scenario from Exercise 7.5.
Exercise Tasks
Your objective is to analyse the scenario above and build a use case model by doing the following tasks:

1. Describe the goal and scope of the use case.
2. Write a series of steps describing the main success scenario.
3. Write extensions describing any error (or exception) scenarios.
4. Identify postconditions for the use case.
5. Can you identify any preconditions for the use case?

Exercise 7.10 (User Story Exercise 1)

7.10 Use the scenarios from Exercise 7.2 to create a set of user stories.

Exercise 7.11 (User Story Exercise 2)

7.11 Use the scenarios from Exercise 7.3 to create a set of user stories.

Exercise 7.12 (User Story Exercise 3)

7.12 Use the scenarios from Exercise 7.4 to create a set of user stories.

Exercise 7.13 (User Story Exercise 4, Advanced)

7.13 *User Story Exercise 2, Advanced* Use the scenario from Exercises 7.5 to create a set of user stories.

Exercise 7.14 (User Story Mapping Exercise)

7.14 Think of all the activities you perform between when you get up in the morning and when you arrive at work or class. For each activity, you create one user story, such as *brush teeth*, *get dressed* or *catch train*. Write each user story on a sticky note (one story per sticky note). These simplified user stories are suitable for this activity. We don't need to use the full template 'As a <user role>, I want to <scenario objective>, In order to <achieve business value>'.

Exercise Tasks You could do this exercise on your own, but it is much better as a group activity. Each group member creates user stories for the morning activities, as described above.

Now share your user stories with the rest of the group. Arrange all the user stories into a logical sequence. You can do this by placing the sticky notes on a white board or sheet of flip chart paper, if there is enough room.

Arrange the sticky notes from left to right. The left-hand side comprises activities conducted earlier. The right-hand side is for activities conducted later. You know, *get dressed* comes before (to the left of) *leave house*. Well,

(continued)

Exercise 7.14 (continued)

get dressed comes before *leave house* for most people, anyway. You can remove or group duplicate (or similar) user stories.

You should be able to make a single row of user stories from earliest activities, such as *wake up* or *switch off alarm* through to latest activities, such as *arrive at work*. Now draw a long horizontal line under the row of user stories.

Now imagine you were running really late. You have to get up and leave home in a big hurry. What are the essential activities you must perform? What activities could you skip if you really had to? Move the optional activities to below the line, leaving the crucial and essential activities above the line.

The row of essential activities you are left with above the line represents a *minimum viable product* (MVP). The MVP is the minimum set of essential activities required to make things work.

Exercise 7.15 (Learning Journal)

7.15 Make some notes in your learning journal about what you learned from the exercises in this chapter.

7.9   Hints, Tips and Advice on Exercises

7.1 *Learning Journal*

In this chapter, we have explored types of requirements, requirements quality, use cases, user stories, user story mapping and personas. Try to write a few comments about the things you have learned in each of these topics.

This book is aimed at early career practitioners, so we have tended to focus on functional requirements. That does not mean we should forget about the challenges presented by non-functional requirements.

7.2 *Use Case Diagram Exercise 1*

See example solution in Fig. 7.3. Yours may not be identical, of course, but hopefully you have more or less the same use cases and actors.

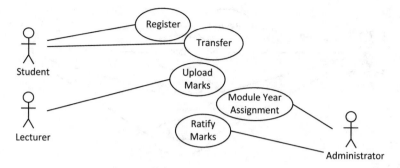

Fig. 7.3 Use case diagram Exercise 1 example solution

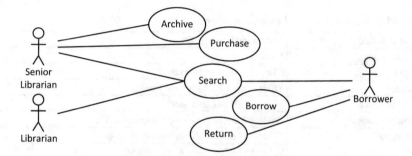

Fig. 7.4 Use case diagram Exercise 2 example solution

7.3 *Use Case Diagram Exercise 2*

See example solution in Fig. 7.4. As in Exercise 1, yours may not be identical, but hopefully, you have more or less the same use cases and actors.

7.4 *Use Case Diagram Exercise 3*

See example solution in Fig. 7.5. Hopefully, your diagram has more or less the same use cases and actors.

7.6 *Use Case Exercise 1*

See example solution in Table 7.2. Hopefully, yours looks pretty similar.

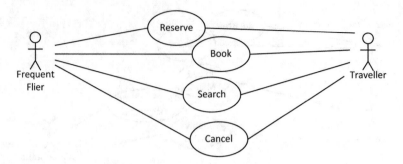

Fig. 7.5 Use case diagram Exercise 3 example solution

Table 7.2 Use case Exercise 1 example solution

Use case title	Option module transfer
Primary actor	Student
Goal	Change selected option module
Scope	Student record information system
Preconditions	First 4 weeks of semester
Postconditions	Student transfer to new option completed
Main success scenario	1. Student selects option module to drop
	2. Student selects new option module
	3. New option module selection approved by timetabling
	4. New option module selection approved by academic programme leader
Extensions	3a. New option module creates timetable clash and hence not approved
	4a. Programme leader does not approve new module selection

7.7 *Use Case Exercise 2*

Yours should look like the example solution in Table 7.3.

7.8 *Use Case Exercise 3*

Again, with luck, yours looks like the example solution in Table 7.4.

Table 7.3 Use case Exercise 2 example solution

Use case title	Holdings purchasing
Primary actor	Senior librarian
Goal	Select and order new holdings
Scope	Library information system
Preconditions	
Postconditions	New holdings ordered from publishers
Main success scenario	1. Review recommendations from subject librarians and academics
	2. Obtain publisher and price information for each recommendation
	3. Check price of recommended holding
	4. Produce purchase order
	5. Send purchase order to publisher of recommended holding
Extensions	2a. Unable to find publisher or price information
	3a. Purchase price exceeds remaining budget, hence unable to purchase

Table 7.4 Use case Exercise 3 example solution

Use case title	Flight booking
Primary actor	Traveller
Goal	Make flight booking
Scope	Flight travel booking system (not including airline reservation systems, such as Amadeus and Sabre)
Preconditions	Flight search complete and on-screen
Postconditions	Itinerary confirmation and e-ticket sent to traveller
Main success scenario	1. Select chosen flight from search results
	2. Produce itinerary based on flight selection
	3. Request seat availability airline reservation system (Amadeus or Sabre depending on airline of flight selected)
	4. Traveller selects seat configuration
	5. Produce final itinerary included seat selection
	6. Traveller confirms final itinerary
	7. Invoke payment gateway (collect online payment)
	8. Send seat reservation to airline reservation system
	9. Confirm airline seat reservation
	10. Send booking confirmation and confirmed itinerary to traveller
Extensions	7a. Payment authorisation declined
	9a. Airline does not confirm seat reservation

7.10 *User Story Exercise 1*

Here are the user stories from the scenario in Exercise 7.2.

- As a `student`, I would like to `Register` for a course, in order to advance my career.
- As a `student`, I would like to `Transfer` from one option module to another, in order to more closely match my interests.
- As a `lecturer`, I would like to `Upload` marks, in order for students to progress through their course.
- As an `administrator`, I would like to `assign modules to years`, in order for students to progress through their course.
- As an `administrator`, I would like to `ratify marks`, in order for students to progress through their course.

7.11 *User Story Exercise 2*

Here are the user stories from the scenario in Exercise 7.3.

- As a `senior librarian`, I would like to `Archive` holdings, in order to make space for new items.
- As a `senior librarian`, I would like to `Purchase` new holdings, in order to offer borrowers the latest materials.
- As a `senior librarian, librarian or borrower`, I would like to `Search` holdings, in order to find materials.
- As a `borrower`, I would like to `borrow` holdings, in order to enjoy materials.
- As a `borrower`, I would like to `return` holdings, in order for others to enjoy the materials.

7.12 *User Story Exercise 3*

Here are the user stories from the scenario in Exercise 7.4.

- As a `frequent flier or traveller`, I would like to `reserve` flights, in order to achieve my travel goals.
- As a `frequent flier or traveller`, I would like to book flights, in order to achieve my travel goals.
- As a `frequent flier or traveller`, I would like to search flights, in order to achieve my travel goals.

(continued)

- As a `frequent flier or traveller`, I would like to `cancel` flights, in order to recover money due to changing plans.

7.10   Chapter Summary

In this chapter, I explored requirements gathering. I distinguished functional requirements (what the system is meant to do, the activities the system performs) from non-functional requirements (which are attributes of the system such as security, reliability, performance, maintainability, scalability, and usability.) I introduced two main approaches to eliciting and managing requirements: use cases and user stories. Use cases provide a way of creating detailed descriptions of people interacting with our software. User stories are simple placeholders that encourage conversations about requirements with non-specialist system stakeholders.

I introduced user story mapping which you can use to link user stories into longer end-to-end goals of using the system. User story mapping can also help you prioritise user stories, when creating a minimum viable product. Personas, in contrast, help you put yourself in the mind-set of your users. Your research identifies different types of users, or users with different goals. Personas help you articulate needs of these different groups.

References

1. Cockburn, A.: Writing Effective Use Cases. Addison-Wesley Professional, Upper Saddle River (2000)
2. Patton, J.: It's all in how you slice it. Better Softw. Mag. **2005**(01) (2005). https://www.stickyminds.com/better-software-magazine/its-all-how-you-slice-it
3. Patton, J.: User Story Mapping: Discover the Whole Story, Build the Right Product, 1st edn. O'Reilly Media, Sebastopol (2014)
4. Rahy, S., Bass, J.M.: Managing non-functional requirements in agile software development. IET Softw., 1–13 (2021). https://doi.org/10.1049/sfw2.12037
5. Wikipedia: List of Unified Modeling Language tools (2019). https://en.wikipedia.org/wiki/List_of_Unified_Modeling_Language_tools. Page Version ID: 909970969

Chapter 8
Architecture

Abstract In this chapter, we explore software structuring skills that help achieve software requirements and manage change. Organising software structure can simplify communications and enable team members to work on different parts of the project at the same time. Software features are independent end-to-end fragments of the functionality of the system. In feature-driven development, end-to-end fragments are worked on by different team members, in parallel. Other structures, or architectures, can also reduce dependencies between one part of the system and another. Structures discussed include client-server, pipe and filter and layered architectures as well as design patterns such as the model-view controller.

8.1 Introduction

Software architecture concerns the overall structure and organisation of the system. On the one hand, architecture is a process, the creative and design activities involved in making an architecture or system structure. In this view, architecture is a set of high-level system design activities.

On the other hand, architecture is one or more outputs or deliverables, a set of architecture design models that describe how the system is organised as a set of communicating components. In this view, architecture is a set of development artefacts, skeleton software systems, drawings or reports used to convey the desired system structuring.

Architectural design happens early in the development process. It overlaps with requirements gathering and often needs to be revisited later during development or production as a refactoring activity. Architectural design requires consultation with stakeholders and is needed to:

- Provide a software infrastructure to meet non-functional requirements
- Enable everyone to clearly picture the overall organisation of the system
- Simplify software development collaboration between more than one person or team

© Springer Nature Switzerland AG 2022
J. M. Bass, *Agile Software Engineering Skills*,
https://doi.org/10.1007/978-3-031-05469-3_8

Moving Beyond Monolithic Software

When we start learning programming, our efforts can tend to towards a monolith. Our code tends to be organised into one centralised location. We might have an overcomplicated main method in a Java program. Or, we might implement one class where the bulk of activity is concentrated.

Working as part of a team brings into sharp relief the limitations of this approach. We need to create a space where different team members can contribute working code without everyone tripping up and falling over each other. Architecture can address this problem. By dividing our system into a set of logical *moving parts*, we can work together more effectively.

The *moving parts* of the system interact through interfaces. We might build part of our system around a set of services that provide data and business-logic functionality to the client side of our system. Once, we create this client-server relationship within our system, we can have one team member focus on the front end and one on the back end and reduce overall system development time.

Making architecture explicit has three main benefits or objectives:

- Stakeholder communication
- System analysis
- Large-scale reuse

As I have hinted, architecture is both a design process and a resultant artefact. The architecture design process needs to involve different stakeholders. We need to obtain advice and support from clients, providers of other software services, service hosting and operations specialists and security specialists in order to design a successful architecture.

Further, the architecture enables analysis to ensure non-functional requirements are achieved. We can stress-test aspects of our architecture or an architectural skeleton of our system. We can gather empirical data to support our design decisions regarding performance and data volumes.

Finally, we need to be able to reuse parts of our system. We always seem to be under pressure to produce more good-quality software with fewer resources. Reuse is always an import goal, because we can, in principle, enhance productivity. We may be able to reproduce the same architecture over multiple product instances.

8.2   Architecture in Agile

A significant effort on architecture prior to starting development work, in agile, has the pejorative name *big design upfront*. Big design upfront has a bad reputation. We invest effort without developing working code. Customers can't realistically give us feedback on our architecture designs. Evaluating architecture, at the design stage, is tricky. Can you detect the tone of understatement there?

8.2.1   Refactoring

Refactoring is where the system is re-structured and re-organised without changing any functionality. Refactoring is a necessary part of incremental development. As new features are added, periodic refactoring enhances code understanding, maintainability and extensibility [4].

It is desirable to invest effort in tidying up the structure of system from time to time. Failure to undertake periodic cleaning results in a code mess few can understand and fewer dare alter. Team members include refactoring tasks in their backlogs of work items to be performed in future development iterations.

8.2.2   Rework

Rework is not the same as refactoring. Rework is repeating the same work over again, in the worst case, because it was poorly done in the first place. Nobody likes rework. Managers hate rework because it is a needless cost. Self-organising team members dislike rework because it is a sign of poor-quality craft.

Experienced teams are often working on applications that are similar to others that they have built before. Hence, architecture tends to be inherited and refined from previous efforts. Obviously, everyone wants to be sure the inherited architecture is good. Hence, some effort to evaluate architecture quality is needed for working or live systems.

But what are we to do if we are learning with an inexperienced team or in a new application domain? We don't have any reliable architecture to inherit from previous efforts. Well, think about the trade-offs. Too much upfront design might be a waste of resources. But, we might end up refactoring the design every iteration. And that could result in excessive rework.

For sure, you mustn't attempt to create a fully articulated, detailed architecture design. If we try to create detailed architecture designs, they may turn out to be useless. We would need to consider features that will not be implemented for months ahead. Things change. Stuff happens. Planned features never get built. The days are gone when we can afford to design architectures for features that are never going to be implemented.

8.2.3   Planned Refactoring

Better that we try to understand what features are going to have a big impact on the architecture. Then, develop an outline architecture, with a release plan, or roadmap for re-architecting when significant feature enhancements are required. That way, those enhancements can be dropped (or replaced) if the features turn out to be superseded.

This *planned refactoring* approach allows the team to consider, externalise and explain the need for architecture re-design at significant stage of the project. Planned refactoring allows you to start delivering working code using a simple architecture to start with. But planned refactoring also requires that you think carefully about the implications of non-functional requirements and features on architecture.

8.2.4 Architectural Abstraction

At one level, architecture is about the structure of individual services, applications and programs. At this level, we are concerned with the internal structure and decomposition of a single program.

At another level, architecture is about sophisticated enterprise systems that comprise systems of systems. Enterprise systems often involve interacting collections of programs harnessed to create some overarching and coordinated set of functions. Typically, enterprise systems are hosted on multiple servers and managed by different service providers.

Hence, we use architecture to simplify and clarify different levels of abstraction. In larger, more sophisticated systems, we use higher-level design styles that define the overall structure of an entire software product and within that use more specific architectural approaches such as design patterns. We will discuss object-oriented design patterns in more detail in Chap.9.

It's All About the Interfaces

Design styles depend on clearly defined interfaces between the components of our system. These architectural styles help us understand and define the way components in our systems interact.

Some interfaces take the form of application programming interfaces (APIs). In an API, the focus is on method naming as well as calling and return parameters. In other design styles, there is more emphasis on data structures during interface design.

As we start to gain experience, we need to create a skeleton architecture and experiment with the interfaces between components. Once our skeleton architecture is working, we can start adding functionality to meet the requirements defined by our client.

8.3   Design Styles

Design styles are reusable structures or overarching organisational approaches that recur in specific application classes. It can save a lot of time and heartache if your application fits into one design style or another. Each design style implies a set of rules or conventions that team members must follow, for the style to work. The common thread between the design styles is dividing the system into a series of subsystems or components, which interact through well-defined interfaces.

Using a design style has several benefits. The overall structure of complex system is simpler to explain and understand if a well-known design style is employed. On-boarding new team members and inducting novice developers is easier when the overarching structure of the system is simple and straightforward. Using a design style is an example of architectural reuse, where multiple system implementations have a shared overall structure.

An important benefit of design styles is in separation of concerns and maintainability. Functionality for one purpose is located in one component. This gives clarity and avoids redundant software source code. Specific components can be replaced, assuming consistent inputs and output data formats, without disrupting the rest of the system. Again, maintainability can be improved if an additional component can be introduced, without disrupting everything else.

In addition, different teams, or team members, can work on specific components in parallel, providing the input and output interfaces have been agreed in advance. Architecture also plays an important role in collaboration between teams on large-scale projects [9]. Carefully designed architecture can dramatically reduce the time required to develop the overall system. In summary, design styles offer benefits in terms of simplicity, reuse, maintainability and separation of concerns [10].

8.3.1   Client-Server

Various configurations of the client-server architectural style have emerged as a ubiquitous approach to accessing software services using Internet technologies, as shown in Fig. 8.1. One or more servers provide services to clients which might include mobile device applications (Mobile Apps) or web browsers.

Hence, functionality is collected into services, which may be delivered from separate servers [8]. We will discuss deploying services to cloud-hosted servers in a bit more detail in Chap. 19. Services can also be replicated on multiple servers to support increased loads. In corporate settings, the client-server approach simplifies the provision of utility services such as printing or email.

Availability of standardised and inexpensive network technologies have made client-server architectural style very popular. In fact, we use the client-server approach in the *Tabby Cat* project in Chap.12. Despite this, there are some drawbacks with the approach. Services are vulnerable to denial of service attacks.

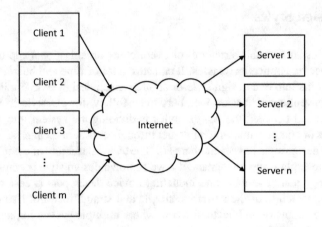

Fig. 8.1 Client-server architectural style

Further, performance is subject to varying network bandwidth and so can be difficult to predict and manage, particularly during peak periods.

8.3.2   Repository Architecture

For some applications, it is fine if the various components manage their own data stores. But in very data-intensive applications, where a consistent view of shared data is required by all components, then a repository architectural style can be attractive. In the repository architecture, components do not interact with each other directly. Rather, all interactions happen through repository data transfers, as shown in Fig. 8.2.

Components do not need to be aware of each other, supporting separation of concerns. Changes to repository data made by one component are available to other components. The centralised storage model simplifies handling of services like backup and data archiving.

A drawback with this approach is that the repository is an obvious single point of failure for the whole system. Any corruption of repository data affects all the components.

You can mitigate risk by creating a distributed repository, with data shared across multiple servers, but that introduces new technical problems such as ensuring consistency of information within the repository. In some technologies, such as Apache Kafka [1], availability is ensured using distributed data structures and redundant layers.

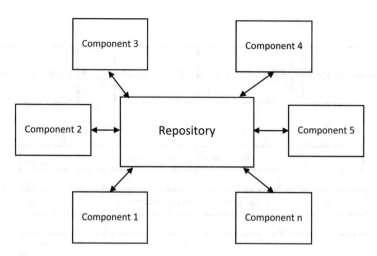

Fig. 8.2 Repository architectural style

8.3.3 Pipe and Filter

The pipe and filter architectural style comprises a chain of transformation components that each process input data to produce some output, as shown in Fig. 8.3a. The chain is often sequential, leading to a batch processing model. More sophisticated implementations can perform transformations in parallel, on different data items, in a more complex data-flow model.

The main challenge is to organise the process into a set of discrete processing stages that is each responsible for a specific transformation. Incremental development is supported, by starting with a few simple transformations. Further processing stages can be added as the software matures. Conventionally, the pipe and filter style used a batch model processing one item at a time. More recently, processing streams tend to be used.

The pipe and filter architectural style does have disadvantages, which include:

1. Unsuitability for interactive systems.
2. Input parsing and output unparsing are required at each stage.
3. Agreed standard input and output data formats are needed.

Despite these shortcomings, pipe and filter architectures are often used in applications such as computer language translators and compilers. You can implement a skeleton pipe and filter architecture in Exercise 8.2. Have a go at the exercise first, but I've put an illustrative solution on GitHub [2].

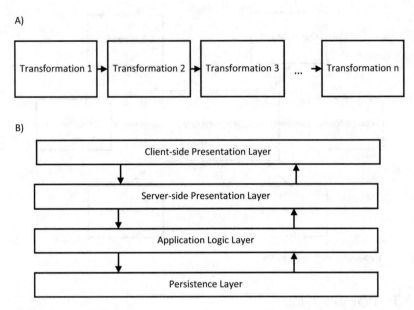

Fig. 8.3 Example architectural styles. (**a**) Pipe and filter architecture. (**b**) Layered architecture

8.3.4 Layered Architecture

When using the layered architectural style, related functionality is grouped into a series of levels, as shown in Fig. 8.3b. Each layer provides an agreed set of services to the layer above. In contrast with the unidirectional pipe and filter architectural style, data flows are bidirectional. Data can flow down through the layers, as well as up. Lower levels provide services to the next layer up, in the system.

The layered architecture requires discipline to ensure that all team members adhere to the model. The maintainability benefits of the layers are lost if service calls jump over a layer and access underlying services. On the other hand, there is a performance cost to passing data through multiple layers for each request. You can implement a skeleton layered architecture in Exercise 8.2.

8.3.5 Clean Architecture

In the clean architecture approach [7], there is a recognition that the application needs protecting from web interfaces and user interface frameworks in much the same way. Consequently, instead of having clients at the top and databases at the bottom, as we do in the n-tier architecture, we form an onion ring perspectives with all the interfaces around the outside, as shown in Fig. 8.4.

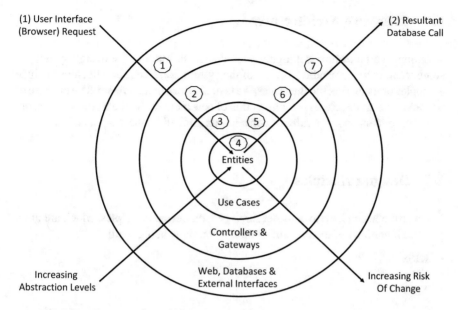

Fig. 8.4 Clean architectural style (Adapted from [7])

Using this model, we have entities in the centre, surrounded by use cases. Then we have a ring for our gateways and controllers. Finally, as I mentioned, the web, databases, devices and other external interfaces form a ring around the outside. The idea is that we may want to swap relational database management system technology in the future. We should not have to re-write the whole application if we want to do that.

Thus, referring to Fig. 8.4, we can imagine a scenario where a user presses a button to request some information stored in a database. When the button is pressed, our user interface (1) calls a controller (2). The controller calls a use case (3) which uses an entity (4) and then (5) calls a database gateway (6). Finally, the gateway calls the database (7) to search for the requested data. The requested data might then be passed back in through the rings to an entity and back out through rings to the user interface.

Entities in the architectural style are abstract enterprise logic. The use cases encapsulate application specific functionality and business rules. The controllers and gateways provide managed interfaces to the outside world such as drivers, databases and the web. This is a useful architectural style for business information systems and will be applied to the *Tabby Cat* project in Chap. 12.

8.4   Reference Architectures

A reference architecture is a highly documented skeleton of the overall system, or some technically demanding aspects of the system. Reference architectures include examples of using specific interfaces, APIs or services in the system. The purpose of the reference architectures is for induction of new members to the team and to ensure everyone understands the rules or conventions implied by the system architecture.

8.5   Design Principles

It is worth pausing here to consider three general design principles, which are good practice regardless of the implementation technology being used:

- KISS
- DRY
- YAGNI

but also two more detailed sets of object-oriented design principles (*GRASP* and *SOLID*) that help to simplify system maintenance.

8.5.1   KISS Principle

KISS is an acronym for Keep It Simple, Stupid. The acronym reminds us to avoid unnecessary complexity in our designs. Our design need contain only enough complexity to achieve our requirements, and no more.

8.5.2   DRY (Do Not Repeat Yourself)

We try to avoid repetition in software development. Repetition means multiple-source code fragments performing a similar task. This becomes a challenge when maintenance is needed, since changes must be made in more than one place. The DRY principle applies to all aspects of our development work and includes scripts, tests, databases as well as source code.

8.5.3 YAGNI (You Aren't Gonna Need It)

Software engineers have the habit of predicting future needs of clients and implementing software features in anticipation of those future requirements. This is not a good practice because sometimes we invest effort in preparing for future features that never come. This results in bloated software source code.

Instead, only functionality needed now must be implemented. This improves productivity against the requirements that have actually been prioritised and also helps keep things simple to accommodate future changes.

8.5.4 GRASP

The *General Responsibility Assignment Software Patterns* (GRASP) principles, proposed by Craig Larman, provide a mental model to help object-oriented design [5]. The GRASP pattern comprises:

- Controller
- Creator
- Indirection
- Information expert
- Low coupling
- High cohesion
- Polymorphism
- Protected variations
- Pure fabrication

The controller is a non-user interface object responsible for handling system events. For example, use cases to `Create Customer` or `Archive Customer` could be performed within a single `Customer Controller` class. The controller class performs appears in the ubiquitous `Model, View, Controller` class and its variants used in web application design.

Creating objects is a common activity in object-oriented systems. In simple systems, constructor methods are used to instantiate objects at runtime. In larger systems, where numerous objects of similar types need to be instantiated at runtime, factory patterns are used. The factory pattern provides a single component for object instantiation (see more in Sect. 9.6.3).

The indirection principle supports reuse and reduces coupling between classes that interact, rather like the way the `Controller` mediates between the `Model` and the `View` in the `Model, View, Controller` pattern. The indirection principle advocates placing an intermediate object between classes that directly interact.

The information expert principle recommends that classes should be assigned responsibility for operations where they have the information needed to fulfil it.

Simply put, classes contain operations that need to be performed on the data they encapsulate.

In general, in object-oriented design, we seek to minimise coupling and maximise cohesion. That is, we want to minimise coupling between classes and maximise cohesion within a class. When we loosely couple different classes, we try to minimise their dependency upon one another. This helps minimise propagation of change through our system, when we make modifications. The contents of cohesive classes are strongly related and highly focused.

Object-oriented programming languages support polymorphism, in which a single interface is used for entities of different types. For example, we can create constructors for our classes, which accept different parameters. The specific constructor executed is assigned automatically at runtime.

We try to improve the maintainability of our system by using stable interfaces around aspects of the system we think are likely to change. Hence, we protect our system from variation. The interface minimises the effect of later changes rippling through our system.

A pure fabrication class, according to the GRASP principles, does not directly correspond to a concept in the problem domain but rather provides a service to other classes in the system.

8.5.5   SOLID

The SOLID acronym was introduced around 2004 by Michael Feathers, to help you remember good principles of object-oriented design [6]. The SOLID principles have some overlap with Larman's GRASP patterns [5]. The SOLID acronym [11] is derived from:

- Single responsibility
- Open-closed
- Liskov substitution
- Interface segregation
- Dependency inversion

The single-responsibility principle dates back to the days of structured programming. Simply put *every class should have only one responsibility*. Consequently, there can only be one reason to change a class. This is another way of expressing high cohesion within a class.

The open-closed principle is a restatement of the *Protected Variations* principles from GRASP, mentioned in Sect. 8.5.4. We want to achieve a design in which classes are open for extension but closed for modification. We can use generalisations, such as inheritance or delegate functions, to extend classes.

The Liskov substitution principle is related to another idea in object-oriented software design, called design by contract. The idea is that children classes, which inherit properties from parents, can be substitutable for parents. For example, if the class Fast Car is a subtype of Car, then a Fast Car object can be used anywhere that Car object is used.

This principle imposes some restrictions on what we can do in child class interfaces, regardless of what the programming language actually allows. For instance, preconditions cannot be strengthened in the subtype, and postconditions cannot be weakened in the subtype.

Interface segregation is one way to achieve high cohesion in user interface design (see *Coupling and Cohesion* in Sect. 8.5.4). User interface software is developed specifically for a client, such that no client is forced to depend on methods it does not use. The interface segregation principle encourages us to develop role-based interfaces. This decouples different clients to simplify software maintenance and evolution.

The dependency inversion principle suggests that our code depends on abstractions not on concrete details [6]. Hence, we introduce *interfaces* or *abstract classes* as a level of indirection between components that would otherwise be rather tightly coupled. This idea is illustrated in Fig. 8.5. In Fig. 8.5, (a) the layers are rather tightly coupled. Changes in one layer ripple through to another. In contrast, if we look at Fig. 8.5, (b) changes to the implementation of the concrete application logic layer, for instance, have less impact on the server-side presentation layer.

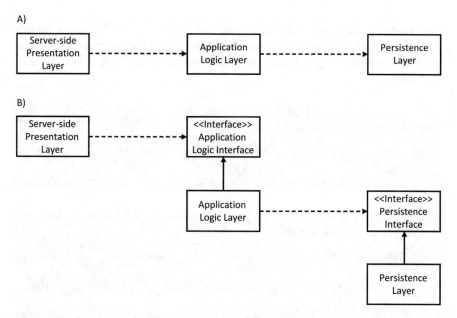

Fig. 8.5 Dependency inversion pattern. (**a**) Conventional layer pattern. (**b**) Dependency inversion pattern

8.6 Architecture Implementation

Once we have selected an architectural style, we can build a reference architecture comprising a simple skeleton of the overall system. We can use the reference architecture to discuss, qualitatively assess and perhaps validate the chosen design style. The skeleton is used to illustrate the interfaces between main components. Usually, in production software, a reference architecture will include source code documentation which discusses conventions, such as naming.

Before we can start designing specific features, we need some overall structure in the system. We need an overall organisation for the system. A novice may start with little or no structure and hope to refactor, through successive increments, until a nice structure emerges. But the danger here is that there won't be time to refactor. So, better to create a simple structure that everyone can use and play along with. Later refactoring may still be necessary. But, some structure at the start is a recipe for success. So, when we start designing features, in Chap. 9, let's assume you have a simple architecture in place already.

8.7 Exercises

Now complete these exercises on the material from Chap. 8. This will help you consolidate your skills in architecture. Remember, don't look at the hints, tips and solutions chapter, just yet. Have a go at the exercises, then look at the advice in Sect. 8.8.

Exercise 8.1 (Learning Journal)

8.1 Write down what you have learned about the material in Chap. 8 for your learning journal.

Exercise 8.2 (Pipes and Filters Exercise)

8.2 For learning and experimental purposes, implement a skeleton pipes and filter design.

Exercise Tasks Use any programming language of your choice. I'm choosing to use Java.

- Create three filter classes that accept a string input and create a string output. The string manipulation can be simple. Let's say each filter

(continued)

Exercise 8.2 (continued)

adds one word to the string. The final output should be `my initial string: one, two and three`.

- You could create a parent class from which the three filter classes could inherit.
- Finally, create a `main` method or unit tester to execute the pipeline. Check the output produces the correct string.
- Now, implement a new version of the second filter class. The final output should now be `my initial string: one, two and three`. Notice that you can revise the string manipulation in the second filter without changing the other filter classes.

This example is sufficiently simple that a pipeline of filter classes is not really required, of course. But the intention is to build something simple to help you understand the principles of this architectural style.

Exercise 8.3 (Layered Architecture Exercise)

8.3 For learning and experimental purposes, implement a skeleton layered architecture design.

Exercise Tasks Use any programming language of your choice. I'm choosing to use Java.

- Create a three-layered architecture that accepts a string input and creates a string output. The string manipulation can be simple. Let's say each layer adds one word to the string. The final output should be `my initial string: one, two and three`.
- You should access each layer using a simple interface.
- Finally, create a `main` method or unit tester to invoke the highest level layer. Each layer should then invoke the next lower level. Check the output produces the correct string.
- Now, implement a new version of the middle layer class. Notice that you can revise the string manipulation in the middle layer without changing the other layer classes.

This example is sufficiently simple that a layered architecture is not really required. But the intention is to build something simple to help you understand the principles of the architectural style.

Exercise 8.4 (Programming Language Choice)

8.4 Choosing a programming language is an aspect of technology stack selection. Write a brief technical report on your choice of programming language.

Exercise 8.5 (Learning Journal)

8.5 Think about the exercises from Chap. 8. Reflect on the exercises you have completed. Make some notes in your learning journal.

8.8   Hints, Tips and Advice on Exercises

8.1 *Learning Journal*

In Chap. 8, we have discussed agile architectures, design styles, technology stack selection (where you have the opportunity to exercise that choice), reference architectures, design principles and architecture implementation.

Take a few minutes to write some notes on what you have learned about each of these topics.

8.2 *Pipes and Filters Exercise*

A very simple illustration of the pipes and filter style is implemented here [2].

8.3 *Layered Architecture Exercise*

A very simple illustration of the layered architecture style is implemented here [3].

8.4 *Programming Language Choice*

Your brief report should, at least, include:

- Advantages (or strengths) of your chosen language
- Disadvantages (or weaknesses) of your chosen language
- Range and suitability of learning resources (tutorials, examples)
- Materials available to support language use (language reference, language enhancement releases)
- Language compatibility (or support) for preferred development environments,
- Summary and recommendations

It is good to learn new programming languages and technologies. However, using a language you already know is often much quicker and more efficient. Learning a new language in a HackCamp or Hackathon setting (with a short time scale and emphasis on solution delivery) adds stress. Better to learn lots about a new language 'offline', and after that, you can apply your new skills in a project setting.

8.9   Chapter Summary

Architectural design is the process of creating a high-level structure or organisation for our system. Defining a simple set of interacting components helps you achieve non-functional requirements. Failure to impose an overarching design style results in monolithic applications, which are difficult to understand or maintain.

Choosing an architectural style can help team members understand the structure of the system. Well-understood component interaction models also make it easy to divide work between multiple developers or teams.

We can often inherit architectural styles from one software product or version to another. This is a valuable form of reuse. Our high-level software organisation is already defined, and everyone can understand the basic model being used. This eases induction of new team members and support for novice developers. Further, navigation around the software source code is simplified.

Each style implies some rules or conventions everyone must follow. This includes appropriate use of folder structures and naming conventions. For example, when using a repository architectural style, components must only communicate with each other through the repository. The approach falls down, if people do not follow these conventions, and system maintenance becomes a nightmare.

In object-oriented system design, there are also several design principles we employ. The *GRASP* and *SOLID* concepts provide checklists of good practices to use in our designs. Becoming familiar with these practices and adopting them in appropriate settings will help improve the quality and maintainability of our software.

We are now ready to move from high-level architectural design to more detailed design concerns.

References

1. Apache Software Foundation: Apache kafka (2017). https://kafka.apache.org/
2. Bass, J.M.: Pipeandfilterexample (Jan 2022). https://github.com/julianbass/PipeAndFilterExample
3. Bass, J.M.: Layeredarchitectureexample (Jan 2022). https://github.com/julianbass/LayeredArchitectureExample
4. Fowler, M., Beck, K., Brant, J., Opdyke, W., Roberts, D.: Refactoring: Improving the Design of Existing Code, 1st edn. Addison Wesley, Reading, MA (Jun 1999)
5. Larman, C.: Applying UML and Patterns: An Introduction to Object-Oriented Analysis and Design and Iterative Development, 3rd edn. Prentice Hall PTR, Upper Saddle River, NJ (2004)
6. Martin, R.: Clean Code: A Handbook of Agile Software Craftsmanship, 1st edn. Prentice Hall, Upper Saddle River, NJ (Aug 2008)
7. Martin, R.C.: Clean Architecture: A Craftsman's Guide to Software Structure and Design, 1st edn. Addison-Wesley (Sep 2017)
8. Richardson, C.: Microservices Patterns: With Examples in Java, 1st edn. Manning (Oct 2018)
9. Salameh, A., Bass, J.M.: An architecture governance approach for agile development by tailoring the Spotify model. AI & SOCIETY (Jun 2021). https://doi.org/10.1007/s00146-021-01240-x
10. Sommerville, I.: Software Engineering, 10th edn. Pearson Education, Harlow (2015)
11. Wikimedia Foundation: (Mar 2021). https://en.wikipedia.org/w/index.php?title=SOLID&oldid=1014595482, page Version ID: 1014595482

Chapter 9
Design

Abstract Having created a high-level structure or adopted an architectural style, in Chap. 8, we can now create some designs to meet our requirements. We will create class diagrams and object sequence diagrams to understand how our software will be structured and how the moving parts interact during runtime. We will also implement some design patterns to solve well-established problems that recur in objective-oriented systems. We will run through some examples and exercises.

9.1 Introduction

As part of our software development process, we've established requirements using the skills in Chap. 7. Then, once we have developed a high-level structure or selected an architectural style, as discussed in Chap. 8, we can build a reference architecture comprising a simple skeleton of the overall system. We can use the reference architecture to discuss, qualitatively assess and perhaps validate the chosen design style. Now, we can start designing specific features.

9.2 Feature-Driven Development

Features are independent pieces of functionality that provide an end-to-end service to an external actor. We can now start to populate our skeleton architecture with features from our functional requirements. Features provide value to users and customers and offer end-to-end fulfilment of a user need. Each feature can be designed, implemented and tested independently [3]. Incremental development consists of implementing features one after another.

In a layered architecture, we talk of features as a *thin-slice* through the system. Each layer contributes some functionality to a feature, corresponding to the responsibilities of that layer. Similarly, we can think of a data fragment making its way through a pipes and filters pipeline. The *thin-slice* in this context is an information fragment being processed and transformed by the stages of the pipeline.

© Springer Nature Switzerland AG 2022
J. M. Bass, *Agile Software Engineering Skills*,
https://doi.org/10.1007/978-3-031-05469-3_9

A feature is not a prototype. A feature comprises working code, whereas a prototype might be a low-fidelity mock-up. A prototype might have some values. But, in agile, we prefer to focus on working code.

We can create acceptance tests for features. Finally, we can demonstrate features at the end of each iteration and gain meaningful feedback from stakeholders.

We can't demonstrate a sub-system. We can't demonstrate a database with no user interface, for example, just as we can't demonstrate a user interface that has no data storage or business logic behind it. That's why in feature-driven development, we always focus on end-to-end functionality. Collect some specific piece of data from a user, manipulate that data, store it, manage it, transform it and let's see the result. A client or user should be able to understand the goal of a feature and, when that working code is demonstrated, give us feedback.

9.3   System Modelling

System modelling is where you develop visual representations of the context or of system you are creating. Each model provides a different view or perspective of the system. Models usually use some kind of graphical notation, which is often based on one of the Unified Modelling Languages (UML).

Models are most useful for their ability to stimulate discussion, and ultimately consensus, on what something does or how something works. Models can record decisions about design choices, for example. But it is the role of models in the process of discussion that is most important.

We tend to think of two main types of model: static and dynamic. Static models depict unchanging aspects of the system such as its internal structure, whereas dynamic models help us understand the runtime behaviour as the system is executed.

We can construct models of the world as it exists before our system is implemented, known as 'As Is' or *domain* models. These models are used at early stages of the development process, perhaps during the requirements phase, to clarify what happens in the real-world domain. *As Is* models allow us to consider strengths and weaknesses of current arrangements and develop requirements for the proposed new system.

More importantly for our concern now is the construction of 'To Be' models, models that describe static or dynamic aspects of the proposed new system. The *To Be* models describe things that don't yet exist. They provide conceptual visualisations of the system that is yet to be constructed. As such, they are used to develop ideas, consider design trade-offs and communicate within the team.

We can identify four views of the system, which we might want to model:

- Interaction perspective
- External perspective
- Structural perspective
- Behavioural perspective

Chapter 7 explored user stories, use cases and use case diagrams for modelling interactions between our proposed system and the outside world. Now I can talk about models from structural and behavioural perspectives.

9.4 Class Diagrams

Class diagrams are used to create structural models that visualise the organisation of a system or the current environment. We can develop our ideas about the components that make up a system and their relationships with each other. We can use our model development to discuss the design of the overall system architecture, as described in Chap. 8.

Class diagrams are used to develop object-oriented systems. The diagrams show the classes in the system and their associations. A class is a generalisation of an object instance that exists in the system. Also, an association represents a relationship between two classes.

When you develop class diagrams during early stages of the software engineering process, objects represent something that exists in the real world. In a car rental application, this might include cars, rental agreements, invoices, payments and so on.

9.4.1 Deriving Class Diagrams

Where do the class diagrams come from? Well, from requirements (use cases or user stories), of course. But how? The trick, I learned from some very clever and experienced architects, is to look for nouns and verbs. What? I know! Nouns and verbs? What are they? I'm not very good at English grammar, so perhaps I'd better explain.

9.4.1.1 Noun and Noun Phrases

Nouns are words that describe a person, place, thing, quality or idea. In software design, when we see nouns in our requirements, we are thinking of things that might appear in the system we are developing or in its application domain.

For example, if we think about banking, the noun `account` might be implemented as a bank account in our software. Similarly, in an online travel booking system, the noun `ticket` might be implemented as a passenger ticket in our software. In the English language, there are more nouns than any other kind of word.

Nouns are implemented in software as data items (attributes), data structures or classes. During the design process, we can decide which nouns become classes and which ones become attributes. We might employ decisions about cohesion, coupling and encapsulation in order to make such decisions.

9.4.1.2 Verb and Verb Phrases

In contrast, verbs describe actions. As kids, we called them *doing words*. In software engineering, verbs that appear in our requirements might end up being implemented as methods or operations.

For example, if we think about banking, the verbs `open` or `close` might be implemented as operations on a bank account in our software. Thinking of an online travel booking system, the verbs `purchase` or `cancel` might be implemented as operations on a passenger ticket in our software.

9.4.2 Domain Models

These models of the real world, as it exists before our system is implemented, are often called conceptual models [6] or are prepared for domain analysis [7].

Figure 9.1a shows two simple classes, named `car rental customer` and `hire agreement`, and a one-to-one association. This tells us that each customer can have only one (and actually must have exactly one) rental agreement. Can you hire more than one car at a time? Well, you could, I suppose. For example, if you need a hire car and then are going to need a van to move something big or heavy, that means allowing the rental car to sit unused while you use the van, which seems extravagant to me. But, it is certainly difficult to actually drive two cars at the same time, so maybe this one-to-one mapping relationship is okay.

Figure 9.1b shows a more detailed class representation with attributes (encapsulated data) and methods (operations the class can perform). This class shows the conventional representation of a class in the UML, with three boxes: the name box at the top, the attributes box in the middle and methods at the bottom.

Things get more useful in Fig. 9.2, where the class diagram shows a generalisation or inheritance relationship. A `Corporate Car Hire Agreement` inherits methods and attributes from `Car Hire Agreement`. Consequently, we think of the `Corporate Car Hire Agreement` as a specialisation of `Car Hire Agreement`.

We can use class diagrams to model other relationships, such as composition. A car might be made up of `engine, transmission, body, wheels` and `fuel tank` components, as shown in Fig. 9.3.

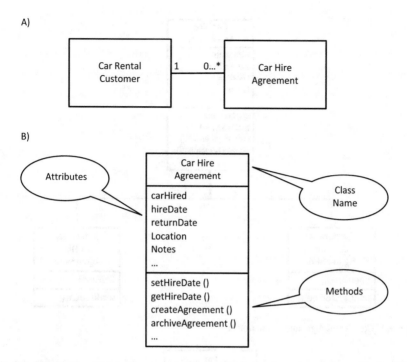

Fig. 9.1 Simple Car Rental Classes. (**a**) Simple Classes and an Association. (**b**) Car Hire Agreement Class (Incomplete)

9.4.3 High-Level Design Class Diagrams

At an early stage of the design process, class diagrams are used to model real-world entities that will be implemented into the software. This is in contrast with requirements modelling, where our focus is on the *As Is* context. Our focus, during the design is on the *To Be* structure of the system. The goal is to identify and name classes and their associations and then to find and name attributes and operations which will be implemented as methods.

9.4.4 Detailed Design Class Diagrams

Then, as the design process progresses, the class diagrams are annotated with further details, such as the attribute data types, method call and return parameter date types. So the goal is to make detailed decisions about the class diagrams such that they can be implemented in software.

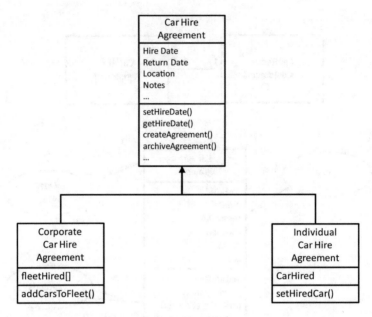

Fig. 9.2 Car Rental Agreement Inheritance

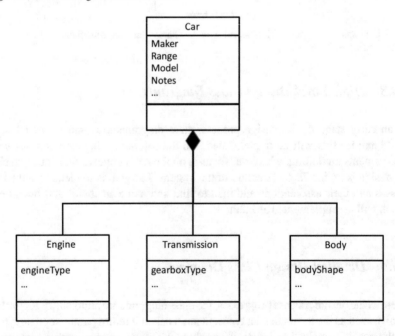

Fig. 9.3 Class Diagram Illustrating Composition Relationships

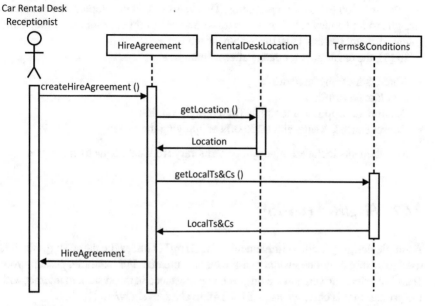

Fig. 9.4 International Car Rental Agency, Sequence Diagram

9.5 Object Sequence Diagrams

Sequence diagrams are used to model the interactions between actors and objects within the system. This is modelling dynamic behaviour. Generally, a sequence diagram corresponds to a specific use case. The actors and objects involved are listed along the top of the diagram. The interactions are shown by using annotated arrows. The diagram in Fig. 9.4 shows the interactions involved in a car rental desk receptionist creating hire agreement for a customer.

9.6 Design Patterns

Design patterns are reusable descriptions of abstract design fragments solving problems that re-occur in different application domains [5]. A pattern is the description of a problem and the essence of its solution. The patterns often include object-oriented characteristics such as inheritance or polymorphism expressed using UML class and sequence diagrams. Design patterns fulfil a really useful function on object-oriented design [6].

An objective of design patterns is to provide best practice solutions to recurring problems identified. The pattern captures experience of implementing good-quality solutions to the problem at hand. Hence, patterns are designed to provide a best practice solution to common problems. This helps so that developers do not have to struggle to find a new solution, to a well-known old problem, every time they build a new software system. Patterns enable design reuse.

In [5], the catalogue, for each pattern, contains a:

- Name, a meaningful identifier
- Problem description
- Solution description, a template for a design solution
- Consequences, results and trade-offs of applying the pattern

The elements included in design patterns vary from catalogue to catalogue.

9.6.1 Singleton Pattern

A simple design pattern to implement is the Singleton; as the name suggests, it is used to ensure only one instance of the class is created. For example, perhaps your class is a printer driver, and we only want one instance in the system to interact with the printer. In this case, we use a Singleton class, as shown in Fig. 9.5.

When using a conventional constructor, we use the new keyword to create an instance of an object. However, we made the constructor Private in the Singleton class, so using the new keyword generates a compile time error, since the Constructor method is not visible, shown in Fig. 9.6.

Singleton Class

```
public class SingletonObject {
    /* Make the instance private and static */
    private static SingletonObject instance = new SingletonObject();

    /* Make the constructor private  */
    private SingletonObject() {
    }

    /* Use this method to return the instantiated object */
    public static SingletonObject getInstance() {
        return instance;
    }

    public String showMessage() {
        return "This is from the singleton";
    }
}
```

Fig. 9.5 Implementation of Singleton Class

Instantiating the Singleton Object (Incorrect)

```
/* the following line gives a compile time error */
//SingletonObject so = new SingletonObject();
```

Fig. 9.6 ERROR: Instantiation of Singleton Object (incorrect)

Instantiating the Singleton Object (Correct)

```
SingletonObject so = SingletonObject.getInstance();
System.out.println( so.showMessage() );
```

Fig. 9.7 Correct Instantiation of Singleton Object

The correct way to instantiate the Singleton object is to use the `getInstance()` method, as shown in Fig. 9.7.

Hence, we have ensured only one instance of the `Singleton` is ever created.

9.6.2 Model View Controller

In interactive systems, such as database-driven web applications, model-view separation is a good design principle [6]. We want to be able to manage and store data separately from the display of that information. This is a good separation of concerns.

We might want to display data on different, multi-channel devices (such as tablets and mobile phones as well as conventional web browser-supported devices). We don't want to pollute our underlying data model with intricacies of these data display issues. Conversely, if we want to migrate from one underlying SQL database system to another, we would prefer not to have to re-write the whole user interface.

The model-view controller design pattern, a simplified version of which is shown in Fig. 9.8, helps us implement this model-view separation design principle. We introduce a set of controller classes that manage the interaction between the views and the model.

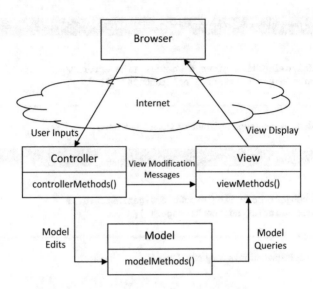

Fig. 9.8 Model View Controller Design Pattern (Adapted from [5])

9.6.3 Factory Pattern

A Factory creates and returns objects of a particular type. The Factory is an implementation of a Creator pattern mentioned in Sect. 8.5.4. For simple systems, using Constructor methods in your classes is fine. But in larger and more sophisticated systems, a Factory gives us a single point in the system for maintaining creation source code for a family of similar objects.

For example, look at Fig. 9.9; here we have a class for creating instances of the type Cars. The interface class is shown in Fig. 9.10.

An example implementation of the Car interface is in Fig. 9.11. Now, we can look at the Factory itself, as shown in Fig 9.12. Finally, how do we create instance of the Car? We simply call the getCar() method, as shown in Fig. 9.13; the full code is available from [2].

In this simple example, this does not seem much clearer than using a constructor. Imagine, if we had a large number of Car classes to create. To make changes, if needed, to all the Constructor methods would be time-consuming. In contrast, the Factory method would give us a single point of maintenance.

9.7 Technology Stack Selection

The technology stack is a range of programming languages, frameworks, libraries, development environments and deployment environments used on your project. If you are working in an academic, HackCamp or Hackathon environment, choosing the best technology stack will be an important team decision.

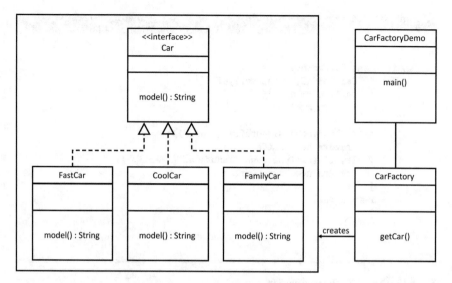

Fig. 9.9 Factory Pattern for Creating Cars (Adapted from [5])

Car Interface

```
public interface Car {
    String model();
}
```

Fig. 9.10 Car Interface Definition

FastCar Implements the Car Interface

```
public class FastCar implements Car {
    public String model() {
        return "Fast Car";
    }
}
```

Fig. 9.11 Car Interface Implementation

If you work in the commercial sector and join an existing project team, you probably won't get much say in the project technology stack. The company will probably have already selected technologies. You can focus on familiarising yourself with the chosen technology stack.

Car Factory

```java
public class CarFactory {
    public Car getCar(String carType) {
        if(carType == null){
            return null;
        }
        if(carType.equalsIgnoreCase("Fast")){
            return new FastCar();
        } else if (carType.equalsIgnoreCase("Family")){
            return new FamilyCar();
        }
        return null;
    }
}
```

Fig. 9.12 Car Factory Implementation

Creating an instance of the Car using the Factory

```java
Car car2 = carFactory.getCar("Family");
System.out.println(car2.model());
```

Fig. 9.13 Using the Car Object Factory

However, if you do need to select the technology stack for a Hackathon, HackCamp or project, there are two main steps:

1. Identify the current *skill set* within the team. You can do Exercise 2.2 to produce a skills inventory from Chap. 2.
2. Collect evidence and assess the *Pros/Cons of the technologies* your team members currently know.

In addition, when choosing your technology stack, there are four main technology issues to think about:

- Consider how candidate technologies impact your chosen *delivery model* (installable desktop application, web app, cloud-hosted service and so on).
- Consider how candidate technologies impact your *functional and non-functional requirements*.
- Consider how candidate technologies contribute to achieving your *architectural goals*.
- Consider how candidate technologies impact your *product/project goals*.

In a HackCamp or Hackathon setting, where you need to deliver a project solution in a short time, then sticking with technologies you know is a good idea. The technology stack has to meet project requirements. But, a somewhat inappropriate technology stack that your team already knows and allows you to make progress is better than spending the time sitting around learning new skills when time is limited.

If the candidate technology stack that team members know does not meet project requirements, then you will have to select and learn something new. This is best accomplished before a project starts. But if that is not possible, then you will have no alternative and will have to learn new technologies, as you go.

9.8 Model-Driven Engineering

Model-driven engineering is where we can automatically generate a complete or partial system from our system models. These days, good software development tools (such as integrated development environments: Eclipse [4], NetBeans [1], etc.) allow the automatic generation of skeleton classes and certain methods, such as accessor (`getter()`) and mutator (`setter()`) methods.

In certain domains, for example database design, commercially available tools allow you to draw diagrams representing storage structures which are then automatically implemented as database tables at the press of a button. Such graphical software tools for creating databases are domain-specific examples of the more general, model-driven engineering, concept.

9.9 Exercises

Now for some exercises on software design from Chap. 9. You should work through these exercises to sharpen your design skills. Once you are done, have a look at the hints, tips and solutions in Sect. 9.10.

Exercise 9.1 (Learning Journal)

9.1 Make some notes about what you learned from Chap. 9, in your learning journal.

Exercise 9.2 (Class Diagram, Student Record Information System)

9.2 A student record information system is used to manage student progression. Students register for option modules and programmes. Modules have lecturers. Students can transfer from one option module to another within the first 4 weeks of the semester. Modules are assigned to a year with a programme by administrators. Lecturers upload marks for mandatory and option modules which are then ratified by administrators on behalf of exam boards.

Exercise Tasks I used this scenario, in Chap. 7, to create use cases and a use case diagram. We can use the same scenario to create a class diagram. Consequently, your objective is to analyse the scenario above and build class model by doing the following tasks:

1. Identify nouns in the scenario.
2. Identify the verbs in the scenario.
3. For each noun, decide which should be classes and which should be attributes of classes.
4. For each verb, identify method names and which class should comprise each operation.

Be careful about which class you put the methods into. Do you put methods into the calling class? Or, should methods be operations on data encapsulated by a class? It is better when classes have responsibility for operations on the data they encapsulate.

Exercise 9.3 (Class Diagram, Library Information System)

9.3 A library information system is used to manage holdings (comprising books, multi-media recordings, magazines and journals) in both hard copy and online form. Holdings registered in the information system can be searched using titles, keywords and holding type. Senior librarians are responsible for archiving old, damaged and unused holdings as well as purchasing new holdings. Librarians register purchased holdings on the library information systems. Borrowers can borrow and return holdings.

Exercise Tasks Again, you saw this scenario, in Chap. 7. We can use this scenario to create a class diagram. Consequently, your objective is to analyse the scenario above and build class model by doing the following tasks:

1. Identify nouns in the scenario.
2. Identify the verbs in the scenario.

(continued)

Exercise 9.3 (continued)

3. For each noun, decide which should be classes and which should be attributes of classes.
4. For each verb, identify method names and which class should comprise each operation.

As in Exercise 9.2, be careful about which class you put the methods into. Do you put methods into the calling class? Or, should methods be operations on data encapsulated by a class? It is better when classes have responsibility for operations on the data they encapsulate.

Exercise 9.4 (Class Diagram, Flight Booking System)

9.4 The Flight Booking System (FBS) provides online services to travellers for flight and hotel reservations using a reservations transaction handling system such as Amadeus or Sabre. Travelers can search, reserve, book and cancel flights. Traveller cancelations can be performed up to 24 hours before departure. Frequent fliers can cancel reservations with no penalty within 6 hours of departure.

Exercise Tasks Now, let's use this scenario to create a class diagram. Consequently, your objective is to analyse the scenario above and build class model by doing the following tasks:

1. Identify nouns in the scenario.
2. Identify the verbs in the scenario.
3. For each noun, decide which should be classes and which should be attributes of classes.
4. For each verb, identify method names and which class should comprise each operation.

As in Exercises 9.2 and 9.3, be careful about which class you put the methods into. Make sure you create classes that have responsibility for operations on the data they encapsulate.

Exercise 9.5 (Class Diagram, Flight Broker System Exercise)

9.5 A travel agent wishes to expand its business by investing in an online flight reservation system. The agency works as a broker for booking and selling flight tickets using a number of airline companies around the world.

(continued)

Exercise 9.5 (continued)

In order to locate the requested flight, the agency communicates with air companies to retrieve their flight schedules and seat availability.

The agency has two types of clients, individual and corporate clients. Individual clients often request to search for an appropriate flight and compare prices. When searching for a flight, the user may want to sort the results by price, airlines or number of connections.

After choosing the desired flight from the results, they could make initial booking or progress to purchase and payments. Alternatively, they could cancel the search. The system should maintain a database of client accounts through which clients could retrieve all their current bookings and/or past journeys. They may also use the system to cancel or amend a journey; this is dependent on the type of ticket they have purchased. The system should support the following ticket types:

- Full fare ticket, a 1-year open fully refundable and changeable ticket
- Open ticket, a 3-month open ticket which may be changed or refunded subject to 20
- Saver ticket, valid for one trip and may not be changed

Corporate clients enjoy the services of individual clients plus additional ones. They benefit from a 30-day credit facility; the credit amount varies for different clients. A corporate client may purchase tickets using credit or direct payment. If using credit payments, corporate clients may only purchase new tickets if they have not exceeded their credit limit and they do not have any outstanding payments exceeding the 1-month period. They may also use the system to request credit increase. Such request is rejected if the client has outstanding payments exceeding the 1-month period; otherwise, it is forwarded to the agency's staff for processing.

The system may also be used by the agency's staff (agents) to query the system for outstanding bookings pending confirmation or payment. The agents use the information for following up the bookings with clients. The agents may also use the system to retrieve outstanding corporate accounts for following up the settlement of such accounts.

Exercise Tasks Now, let's use this scenario to create a class diagram by performing the following tasks:

1. Identify nouns in the scenario.
2. Identify the verbs in the scenario.
3. For each noun, decide which should be classes and which should be attributes of classes.
4. For each verb, identify method names and which class should comprise each operation.

Student	Lecturer	Teaching Assistant
Name String DateofBirth int MonthofBirth String YearofBirth int StudentId int	Name String DateofBirth int MonthofBirth String YearofBirth int StaffId String	Name String DateofBirth int MonthofBirth String YearofBirth int ContractNumber int
getName() : String setName(String) getDateofBirth() : int setDateofBirth(int) getMonthofBirth() : String setMonthofBirth(String) getYearofBirth() : int setYearofBirth(int) getStudentId() : int setStudentId(int)	getName() : String setName(String) getDateofBirth() : int setDateofBirth(int) getMonthofBirth() : String setMonthofBirth(String) getYearofBirth() : int setYearofBirth(int) getStaffId() : String setStaffId(String)	getName() : String setName(String) getDateofBirth() : int setDateofBirth(int) getMonthofBirth() : String setMonthofBirth(String) getYearofBirth() : int setYearofBirth(int) getStaffId() : String setStaffId(String) getContractNumber() : int setContractNumber(int)

Fig. 9.14 Factory Pattern Implementation Exercise, Data Transfer Objects

Exercise 9.6 (Factory Pattern Implementation)

9.6 Data transfer objects are simple objects that encapsulate a collection of data items and provide accessor and mutator methods. Let's create three fictional data transfer object classes, as shown in Fig. 9.14.

A calling class should be able to request any one of the three data transfer objects from the factory that you implement. You will notice that many of the attributes of the data transfer objects are the same but that each also has a unique attribute.

Exercise Tasks Practice using and interpreting design patterns by implementing a factory pattern to implement the set of data transfer objects shown in Fig. 9.14.

Exercise 9.7 (Learning Journal)

9.7 What happened during the exercises from Chap. 9? What went well? What could have gone better? Reflect on the exercises you have completed, and make some notes in your learning journal.

9.10   Hints, Tips and Advice on Exercises

9.1 *Learning Journal Exercise*

In Chap. 9, we have discussed feature-driven development, system modelling, class diagrams, object sequence diagrams, design patterns and model-driven engineering. Think about what you have learned about each topic. Take a few minutes to write some notes.

9.2 *Class Diagram Exercise 1 Example Solution*

See example solutions in Figs. 9.15 and 9.16.

9.3 *Class Diagram Exercise 2 Example Solution*

See solution in Fig. 9.17

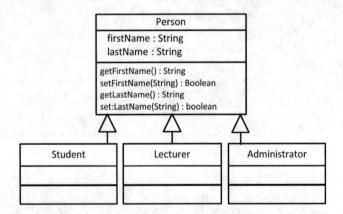

Fig. 9.15 Class Diagram Exercise 1 Person Class

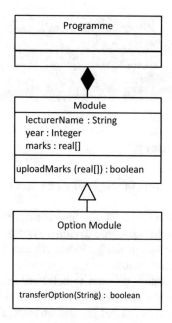

Fig. 9.16 Class Diagram Exercise 1 Programme Class

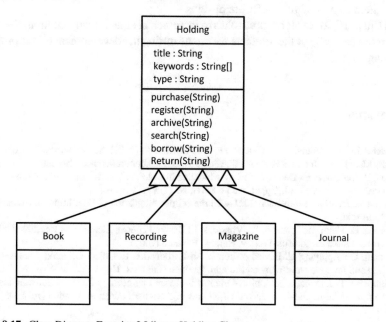

Fig. 9.17 Class Diagram Exercise 2 Library Holding Class

9.6 *Factory Pattern Exercise*

After you implement your factory pattern, have a look at the source code available in [2].

9.11   Chapter Summary

In Chap. 8, the idea of creating or employing an overall architectural style for the system was discussed.

Once an architecture is in place, we can focus on developing designs for specific software features. We can use static and dynamic system models, created using the UML, to explore and discuss our design ideas. We can then use models to record and disseminate our design decisions.

We also use reusable design patterns to solve recurring problems that appear during object-oriented design and implementation. Well-known patterns, such as `Singleton`, `Model`, `view`, `controller` and `Object factory`, need to become part of your regular software development toolkit. I encourage you to think about using them as part of your software designs.

In Chap. 10, we explore approaches to incremental agile implementation. We will look more carefully at the artefacts we create during the development of our project working code.

References

1. Apache Software Foundation: Welcome to apache netbeans (2020). https://netbeans.apache.org/
2. Bass, J.M.: CarFactory. GitHub (Jan 2022). https://github.com/julianbass/CarFactory
3. Coad, P., LeFebvre, E., De Luca, J.: Java Modeling in Color with UML: Enterprise Components and Process. Prentice Hall, Upper Saddle River, NJ (1999)
4. Eclipse Foundation: Eclipse ide 2021–12 | the eclipse foundation (2021). https://www.eclipse.org/eclipseide/
5. Gamma, E., Helm, R., Johnson, R., Vlissides, J.: Design Patterns: Elements of Reusable Object-Oriented Software. Addison-Wesley, Harlow, England (2005)
6. Larman, C.: Applying UML and Patterns: An Introduction to Object-Oriented Analysis and Design and Iterative Development, 3rd edn. Prentice Hall PTR, Upper Saddle River, NJ (2004)
7. Lethbridge, T., Laganiere, R.: Object-Oriented Software Engineering: Practical Software Development using UML and Java, 2nd edn. McGraw-Hill Higher Education, London (Jul 2005)

Chapter 10
Development

Abstract During software development iterations, we create computer programs. Programs, or more precisely software source code files, are examples of development artefacts. We also create other artefacts when we make commercial-strength software. We need to learn how to create and manage backlogs. We introduce the concepts of good-quality source code and how to create software that is consistent and readable for other members of our team. Finally, we need to test our code. So we will explore unit testing the code we write.

10.1 Introduction

Development artefacts are the things produced by self-organising teams during the software development process. Obviously, producing working code is the whole point of software development. Hence, software source code and release artefacts spring to mind. But a large number of other artefacts are also produced [2]. Software source code is discussed further in Sect. 10.4.2.

Some artefacts are produced to enable communication between different stakeholders in the development process. Some people call these *boundary objects*. *Boundary objects* enable a dialogue between people with different outlooks, perspectives of backgrounds. *Boundary objects* might include reference architectures and models such as class diagrams which can stimulate a dialogue with knowledgeable (or influential) people.

10.2 Planning Artefacts

Planning artefacts are produced before the design phase of an increment begins. That means during the preceding increment. Hang on! 'Where do planning artefacts come from for the first increment?' I hear you say. Well, some people use a device. Call it *increment 0*, or Sprint 0 as I mentioned in Sect. 6.4. *Increment 0* is a setup phase for the project. An advantage of calling the project setup phase *increment 0* is that it is time-bound.

In the Rational Unified Process, the setup stage is called the *inception phase*. But the focus of the *inception phase* is to create a detailed and fully costed requirements specification. We don't do that in agile. But we do need a place to work and computers to work on, and we need some other artefacts before we can get started.

10.2.1   Kanban Boards

Physical or virtual Kanban boards, in software development, provide a visual summary of the project status. There are lots of variations in the use of Kanban boards, but at their simplest, they comprise three columns *To Do*, *In Progress* and *Done*. Work items start in the *To Do* column. Then, at each stand-up coordination meeting, work items are moved from one column to the next. In simple terms, work items move from left to right through columns, as the project progresses.

Variations to the simple three column model might involve splitting the *To Do* column into a product backlog and an iteration backlog. Some teams introduce an *In Test* column. The main point, however, is that everyone in the team can see the overall status of the project and for development team members how their own effort contributes. We discuss Kanban boards further in Sect. 13.3.2.

10.2.2   Product Backlog

In the scrum method, the product owner elicits and prioritises requirements in the form of a product backlog. The product backlog is a prioritised list of user stories, highest priority at the top. As the development project unfolds, the product owner re-prioritises requirements, keeping the most important user stories at the top of the list.

10.2.3   Test Plan

A test plan is a strategy or policy that defines how everyone in the development project is going to handle testing to achieve required levels of code quality. You can present the test plan how you like, such as a report, wiki or presentation. But the test plan must be available online and followed by everyone.

The test plan describes the testing to be performed at each stage of development. Usually, planning considers the desired level of test coverage (the number of code pathways tested). Unit testing is often performed by developers themselves and must be completed before code is integrated with code produced by others. Some people advocate manual testing, which is certainly better than no testing at all. But automated testing is really the way to go.

Once your tested code has been integrated with the code produced in previous increments, you need to test if the old code still works properly. This is regression testing. Regression testing is used to test if the old code still works when new code is added. Usually you need automated test tools to do regression testing.

Are unit and regression tests the only tests you need? I hope not. What about load testing? Integration testing? User acceptance testing? Your test plan should describe your overall test policy. There is more about test automation in Chap. 16.

10.3   Iteration Artefacts

Iteration artefacts are produced, well, during each iteration, as the name suggests.

10.3.1   Iteration Backlog

An iteration backlog comprises a subset of requirements from the product backlog. At the start of each iteration, the highest-priority user stories are extracted from the product backlog. We populate the iteration backlog with enough user stories to fully occupy the team for a single iteration. Too much work is unsustainable and demoralising. Insufficient work is inefficient. Choosing an appropriate number of user stories for the iteration backlog requires good work estimates.

10.3.2   User Story Estimates

Iteration planning, which will be discussed further in Sect. 13.2, includes the estimation of work items. User stories can be estimated. But, more precise estimates can be derived from breaking user stories down into technical tasks and estimating each of those. A *T-shirt sizing*, or planning poker, approach can be used.

10.3.3   Burn Down Chart

A burn down chart illustrates project progress during an iteration. The y-axis represents story points and the x-axis the number of days in the iteration. The example, shown in Fig. 10.1, shows a 14-day iteration. Stories are only shown on the burn down chart when they are actually completed. That means the burn down

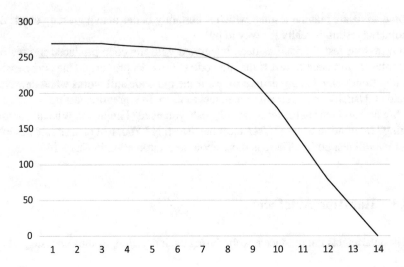

Fig. 10.1 Idealised illustrative burn down chart

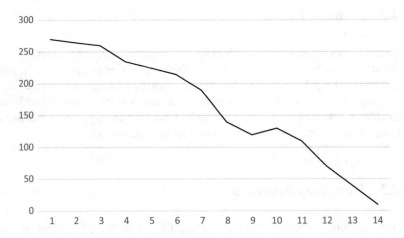

Fig. 10.2 Sample burn down chart

process does not really get started during the first few days of the iteration shown in Fig. 10.1.

The example, shown in Fig. 10.2, also shows a 14-day iteration. But, notice how in this example the graph curve actually goes up on Day 9. This suggests that something happened to increase the number of story points during the iteration. Perhaps a new user story was introduced, which is not normally encouraged. Or perhaps a spike occurred some problem or challenge emerged and something was re-estimated. Notice also that the curve does not actually get to zero at the end of the iteration. This suggests the team were unable to successfully implement and test some stories.

10.4 Feature Artefacts

Feature artefacts are produced for each feature. Not every feature needs every artefact. Consequently, you choose the ones you need.

10.4.1 Prototypes

Some people seem to think you don't need prototypes or mock-ups in incremental development. The need for a prototype, they say, is made redundant by a minimum viable product that is delivered early and enables feedback from customers or users. That view is probably true if, by prototype, you mean some elaborately coded simulation of your system.

But, I think it is prudent under some circumstances to think of producing mock-ups, particularly user interface mock-ups, to get approval before coding really begins. The idea is that you create a low-fidelity, low-cost visualisation of something. This might be because you are working on a new type of application and have little experience to draw on. Or, it might be because you are working with a new customer and you are uncertain of their expectations.

A prototype is a good example of a boundary object. You are creating a low-fidelity interpretation and saying to stakeholders, 'what do you think of this?' or 'how does this look? Is this want you want?' This process enables you to gather feedback on a single aspect of the system you are developing. But, it also has the benefit that you are, sort of, winning commitment for your work from the customer. It is hard for them to say later that they don't like the look of something, when they have approved a prototype.

10.4.2 Source Code

Working code is what software development is all about. Working code is derived from source code. All the other stuff is about enabling source code development to take place.

Many developers feel under pressure from deadlines and hence rushed into creating messy code. However, messy code actually slows you down, and what you need is elegant code. Elegant code is easily readable by people and machines. What makes elegant code? Robert Martin has created a compelling list [6], including:

- Meaningful names.
- Functions (methods) should only do one thing, and do it well.
- Good and elegant code does not need comments.
- Good formatting improves communication.
- Use objects to hide data and expose operations.

- Use exceptions to handle errors.
- Clarity, simplicity and density of expression in unit tests.
- Small classes.

Use meaningful names in your code. Method names, variable names, parameter names, filenames—names are everywhere. Elegant code uses names that reveal intent. Carefully chosen names expose the purpose of the artefact. Avoid redundant information, and make names that are pronounceable and searchable. Class names are often nouns or noun phrases, while method names contain verbs or verb phrases.

Functions (methods) are the first unit of organisation in software. Good functions are small, understandable within a few minutes, focused on only one tasks and perform that task well. Functions have few arguments or use objects as arguments that encapsulate complexity.

Comments in source code are a source of clutter. Good-quality code with meaningful names and small functions does not need comments. Comments are sometimes used to explain code that is complex or opaque. It is better to improve the underlying code, rather than write comments.

Formatting is important for code readability. Well-formatted code conveys good structure. Good formatting suggests logical organisation of source code content and ensuring openness between different concepts and density of related concepts. Good formatting is consistent within a team.

We want to use objects to conceal data structures. It is more correct to say objects *encapsulate* data structures, of course. In contrast, we want to create objects that expose functions to operate on data. This is important. Hide data. Expose operations. This approach makes it easy to add new objects without changing existing behaviour. The downside is it makes it harder to add new behaviour to existing classes.

Modern languages support exceptions. Use exceptions for handling errors. Avoid using return parameters for handling errors.

Don't release code without unit tests. Good unit tests are clear and simple and have a density of expression that makes them readable. Create one assertion and one concept per test.

High cohesion implies small classes. We want classes that focus on particular things. Good classes are responsible for one thing. Avoid using the words *'if'*, *'and'*, *'or'* or *'but'* to describe classes. You might be concerned that making classes responsible for only one thing will result in system that is difficult to understand. But in fact, there will be the same number of moving parts, and a system with a larger number of small classes will be easier to maintain.

10.4.3   Unit Tests

Unit tests are used to verify specific components of our software system. Usually we test classes (such as the constructors that instantiate objects) and methods (checking calling and return parameters) as well as attributes of classes (have variables been initialised and so on). As with regression testing, you could in theory do unit testing manually. But seriously, it is just so much more efficient to automate this stuff. I'll talk more about test automation in Chap. 16.

10.4.4   Issues

We use the word *issues* as a collective term for defects, feature requests, feature enhancements and so on. Generally, teams supporting live systems carefully keep track of *issues*. The defects and change requests are *triaged* to decide which give the most benefit for the lowest cost or least effort. Most software organisations don't have the resources to fix *issues* that are expensive but only bring small value. In safety critical software, a zero defect policy is desirable, but expensive to achieve.

Some vendors give clients a chance to vote on issues to help decide which are the most important. Teams might provide customers with a list of known issues for each release. That makes it look like you have a handle on things, even if you don't have the resources to fix everything. Obviously, defects that have a big impact and are inexpensive to fix need dealing with urgently. Otherwise, you will get a bad reputation for shipping poor quality software.

When development teams are supporting a live product, choosing between putting effort into new features, feature enhancements or defects requires careful balancing. To resolve issues, some teams set aside effort during each increment. Other teams choose to periodically dedicate an entire iteration to feature enhancements and defects (perhaps every second or third iteration).

Defects are deviations from expected behaviour. Defects in common parlance are bugs. Strictly speaking, a defect is not a software development artefact. No one manufactures defects (unless you are working on software implemented fault injection, but that is a bit of a niche application area). The artefact is the defect record we create, keep and manage. We use tracking tools (such as Bugzilla [3] or Jira [1]) to implement an *issue* database.

Feature enhancements are not defects; they are requested improvements to our software. Feature enhancements have to be prioritised, usually by a product owner or someone else with a good understanding of user needs. We decompose feature enhancements into technical tasks and estimate them, at the start of an increment. These enhancements can then be included in the development iteration just like new features.

10.5   Release Artefacts

Once source code is written and thoroughly tested, it can be released. In scrum, product owners decide when code is suitable for release to customers. Then, source code has to be packaged, ready for release. There are benefits to automating the packaging and release process, as discussed in Chap. 21.

In web applications, a `.war` file must be created comprising all the Java Server Pages, Java Servlets, XML, Java classes and so on that comprise a release. The `.war` file becomes executable when placed in a folder accessible by a web server.

Some places use a containerisation approach to releases. Containers, such as Docker [4], offer a standardised deployment platform which can then be deployed or replicated onto different server instances. Docker uses operating-system-level virtualisation to isolate and bundle software applications, libraries and configuration files. Multiple containers can run on an operating system instance and hence are lighter weight than virtual machines. On larger-scale systems, orchestration software, such as Kubernetes [5], are used to manage containerised deployments. We discuss cloud deployment further in Chap. 19.

10.5.1 Release Code Binaries

The code binaries are what gets deployed into a production environment to provide a service for users. Novices and learners often experiment by running binaries on a local machine. Mobile or embedded application binaries must be executed in a simulator or downloaded onto the device. Similarly, web application binaries must be uploaded to a web server.

10.5.2 Regression Tests

When new features are integrated into the main software trunk, we need to check if the existing features have not been adversely affected. During regression testing, we re-run tests to re-evaluate previously tested software features.

Regression testing is where automation pays off. Re-running automated test suites takes little effort, just machine time. It gives you (and others) more confidence in your software when you re-run a full test suite and everything passes okay. There is more about test automation in Chap. 16.

10.6 Exercises

Now it is time to tackle some exercises on software design from Chap. 10. You can have a go at these exercises to sharpen your development skills. When you are finished, review the hints, tips and solutions in Sect. 10.7.

Exercise 10.1 (Learning Journal)

10.1 In this exercise, write in your learning journal about what you have learned from Chap. 10.

Exercise 10.2 (Kanban Board Exercise)

10.2 This exercise is simple. Create and maintain a Kanban board for your next iteration. That's it. As a team, decide on the columns for your Kanban board. A good choice might be 'To Do', 'Doing' and 'Done'.

Exercise Tasks Once the Kanban board is set up, the process is as follows:

- At each coordination meeting, listen carefully to the status reports from team members.
- For any work items that meet the agreed definition of done, move the sticky notes from the 'Doing' or 'In Progress' column to the 'Done' column.
- For any work items that a team member picks up from the 'To Do' column, move the associated sticky note to the 'Doing' column.

At the end of the iteration, you should see all the work items in the 'Done' column. You can celebrate your success!

Exercise 10.3 (Test Plan Exercise)

10.3 In this exercise, you will conduct some research, prepare a test plan and write a report published on your team Slack channel. Conduct some research to find out about your options when considering a test strategy.

Exercise Tasks The test plan preparation process is as follows:

- Conduct online research.
- Make a proposal to your team members about test strategies (keep it simple, at first).
- Gain consensus, as much as you can, on tests everyone in the team should conduct.
- Write a document, shared with the team, describing the agreed strategy.

At the end of the iteration, all work items should have been evaluated in accordance with your plan.

Exercise 10.4 (User Story Estimation Exercise)

10.4 In this exercise, you will estimate some user stories.

Exercise Tasks The user story estimation process is as follows, and work as a team:

- Take the higher-priority user story from the product backlog.
- Break the user into technical tasks.
- Gain consensus, as much as you can, on the T-shirt size for each task (small, medium, large, extra large).

Repeat the estimation process until you have enough work item to fill a complete iteration.

Exercise 10.5 (Burn Down Chart Exercise)

10.5 This exercise is simple. Plot a burn down chart for your next iteration. Remember work items only go on the burn down chart when they are done.

Make sure that your burn down chart is truthful representation of your iteration. The point is to learn from whatever the iteration might throw at you. There might be spikes that cause you to re-estimate work items. If so, the burn down chart curve might actually go up, not down. So be it. Hopefully, the team will be able to recover from this slight setback.

Exercise Tasks The process should be something like this:

- Make a set of burn down chart axes reflecting the duration of your iteration.
- On the first day of the iteration, make a point of the axes reflecting the total expected number of story points for the iteration.
- Each time a work item is completed, tested and successfully integrated into some test trunk, deduct the corresponding number of story points from the previous point plotted on the burn down chart.
- Keep plotting completed work items each day until the iteration is complete.
- Look at the completed burn down chart in your iteration retrospective. Reflect on what you see. What can you learn from this?

Keep preparing burn down charts for each iteration. Reflect on the burn down charts from the three previous iterations. If you keep seeing evidence of inefficiencies in your development process evidences in your burn down charts, then perhaps you should discuss this in a retrospective.

Exercise 10.6 (Learning Journal)

10.6 Thinking about the exercises from Chap. 10 you have completed. Make some notes in your learning journal about what you have learned.

10.7 Hints, Tips and Advice on Exercises

10.1 *Learning Journal*

Chapter 10 has covered planning artefacts, iteration artefacts, feature artefacts and release artefacts. Write some notes about what you have learned on each of these topics.

10.2 *Kanban Board Exercise*

Let's assume, to start with, you are using a physical board. Attach sticky notes to the board. Each sticky note should present one work task in the current iteration. At the start of the iteration, all the sticky notes will be in the 'To Do' column. After work items are assigned to team members, and work begins on that task, the sticky notes should move into the 'Doing' column. Finally, once a work item is completed (designs produced, code written and the feature has been tested), it should be moved to the 'Done' column.

Remember in agile, work items are either 'Done' or not done. There is no concept of a work item that is 20% or 80% done. The team must decide on a definition of 'Done'.

See the sample Kanban board in Fig. 10.3. Notice that in this example, there is a 'To Do' column and a 'Done' column. But notice that 'Doing' column has been split into two: 'Draft' and 'Edit'. This sample Kanban is for visualising an academic writing process. A software development project might choose to split the 'Doing' column into 'Develop' and 'Test'. Notice also that the Kanban board in Fig. 10.3 has so-called swim lanes, which separate out different activities. In this case, the Kanban board shows 'journal' writing separately from writing 'teaching' materials.

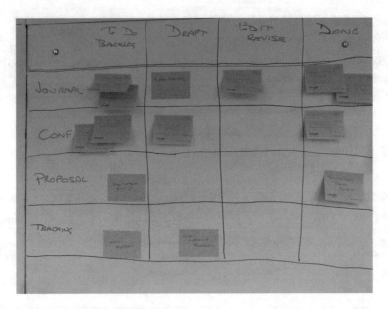

Fig. 10.3 Sample physical Kanban board

10.3 *Test Plan Exercise*

Testing and test automation is discussed in more detail in Chap. 16. Further, for your research, you can try some simple and accessible sources like [8] or something more authoritative, like [7].

In a HackCamp or Hackathon setting, the bare minimum you should aim for is unit testing and acceptance testing. If you are using incremental development (which of course you should), then regression testing is also a good idea.

A more mature team will also focus on integration and performance testing. The plan itself should be incremental. Make sure your team follows a basic test plan, before attempting to adopt a more sophisticated test plan.

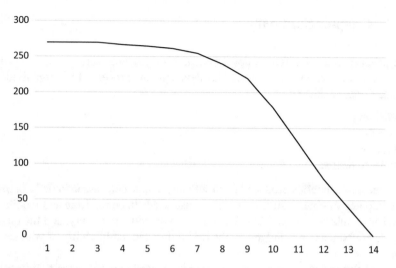

Fig. 10.4 Sample burn down chart for a 14-day sprint

10.4 *Burn Down Chart Exercise*

See the simple sample burn down chart in Fig. 10.4.

Think about your definition of done when maintaining your burn down chart. Some teams only record work items when they are done, done. For others, work items are recorded only if they are done, done, done! So, what is the difference between done, done, done and done, done, done? Well, it depends on the policies your team apply. For some teams, done means built, unit-, integration- and regression-tested. For other teams, done, done might mean build and unit tested. While for others, phrases like done, done, done reflect some process like that.

The important points are:

- The policy is clear to everyone.
- The policy is consistently applied.
- Only remove story points associated with work items that are done from the burn down.

Remember: you can still use a burn down chart with T-shirt sizing by consistently assigning a number story points to a given short size.

10.8   Chapter Summary

The primary goal of software development is to produce working code. Further, other artefacts are created during the development process. I've organised the artefacts created during:

- Planning
- Iteration
- Feature
- Release phases

The executable binaries produced from software source code are intended to control the computer, of course. But, source code also needs to be readable and modifiable by other members of your team. The code is a shared commodity, and the quality of code craftsmanship is judged by the readability and modifiability of your source code.

In addition to source code, you and your team need to produce tests. Tests allow you to monitor the quality of the code you are producing. The number of defects is a proxy measure for code quality.

In Chap. 11, we'll explore some techniques to help create secure software systems. Security is needed to keep client data safe and avoid your system being exploited by bad actors.

References

1. Atlassian: Jira | Issue & Project Tracking Software (2019). https://www.atlassian.com/software/jira
2. Bass, J.M.: Artefacts and agile method tailoring in large-scale offshore software development programmes. Inf. Softw. Technol. **75**, 1–16 (Jul 2016). https://doi.org/10.1016/j.infsof.2016.03.001
3. Bugzilla.org: About :: Bugzilla :: bugzilla.org (2019). https://www.bugzilla.org/about/
4. Docker Inc.: Enterprise Container Platform (2019). https://www.docker.com/
5. Kubernetes: Production-grade container orchestration (2021). https://kubernetes.io/
6. Martin, R.: Clean Code: A Handbook of Agile Software Craftsmanship, 1st edn. Prentice Hall, Upper Saddle River, NJ (Aug 2008)
7. Sommerville, I.: Software Engineering, 10th edn. Pearson Education, Harlow (2015)
8. wikiHow: How to Write a Test Plan (2019). https://www.wikihow.com/Write-a-Test-Plan

Chapter 11
Security

Abstract This chapter will introduce some basic techniques around cyber-security. A life cycle approach will be adopted, starting with security analysis, requirements and design and then moving on to security implementation and evaluation. Finally, we'll explore an agile secure-by-design process. The chapter will include checklists around security good practice, and some testing tools will be introduced.

11.1 Introduction

Software engineers increasingly recognise the critical importance of cyber-security. Customers, government and regulators are less tolerant of attacks leading to data loss and breaches of privacy. Simultaneously, attackers have become more persistent and sophisticated in their approaches. Further, state actors are suspected of sponsoring critical infrastructure attacks. In this chapter, we will advocate actionable agile approaches to cyber-security.

An incremental approach to software development has been advocated in Chap. 10. We advocate tailoring the incremental process to include careful consideration of security issues. Consequently, cycles of security analysis, design, implementation, testing and operations are integrated into a secure product development life cycle [1]. We establish an iterative continuous improvement process comprising prevention and detection of security problems [9]:

- Prevention

  - Use technologies/frameworks/components that take care of security,
  - Shared responsibility for security by the whole team including product owner,
  - Minimise errors by ensuring maintainable code,

- Detection

  - Automated security checking,
  - Manual, risk-based, checks focusing on changes made during a specific increment.

© Springer Nature Switzerland AG 2022
J. M. Bass, *Agile Software Engineering Skills*,
https://doi.org/10.1007/978-3-031-05469-3_11

Since software is being incrementally deployed, security and quality assurance must be tackled iteratively. Product security is maximised through cycles of planning, implementation and evaluation. The agile OWASP SAMM model identifies six key themes, as follows [9]:

- Governance,
  - Strategy and Metrics,
  - Education and Guidance,
- Design,
  - Threat Assessment,
  - Security Requirements,
- Verification,
  - Requirements-Driven Testing,
  - Security Testing.

Strategy and metrics define the overall direction and measures used to assess compliance with security needs. Education and guidance aim to enhance knowledge and skills for personnel involved in software development projects. Threat assessment is used to identify and characterise potential attacks. Security requirements promote the inclusion of functionality or countermeasures to address security concerns. Requirements-driven testing uses abuse stories which describe, from the perspective of an attacker, how a system is misused. Security testing uses tools to discover vulnerabilities in the runtime environment. We can address these themes, by taking a life cycle perspective.

11.2   Security Analysis

Security analysis comprises definition of objectives and threat model creation.

11.2.1   Security Objectives

The expected behaviour of the system under development and its operating context are called the *security environment*. This environment determines the likely threats our application will face. Internet connections offer access to many, potentially malicious, actors. Consequently, our web applications and software services must be designed to defend themselves appropriately.

11.2.2 Threat Model

After considering our product's *security environment*, a model of potential threats must be developed. The acronym *Stride* can help us to consider a good range of potential threats:

- Spoofing,
- Tampering,
- Repudiation,
- Information disclosure,
- Denial of service,
- Elevation of privilege.

For each threat, an attack tree can be developed. The tree root represents the attack goal. The tree leafs represent ways that goal can be achieved.

11.3 Security Requirements

There are two main types of security requirements: those designed to help create countermeasures and abuse, or attacker, stories. We can also use attack personas to help understand potential attackers.

11.3.1 Security Mitigation Requirements

The threat model is used to develop a set of requirements which can be prioritised and managed. The requirements are used to identify design tasks intended to mitigate security threats, for example, the authentication user story shown in Fig. 11.1.

Authentication User Story

```
As a <registered user>
I want to <log on to the system>
so that <I can see and do only the things that I am authorised to see and do>
```

Fig. 11.1 Authentication user story

This user story can then be used to create a set of test criteria [2], such as:

- User logs on successfully,
- User fails log on because of invalid credentials,
- User forgets credentials,
- User is not registered.

11.3.2   Abuse Stories

Abuse (or *attacker*) stories are used like conventional user stories during the development process. Abuse stories are developed and prioritised prior to each iteration. Then the abuse story is used to define work tasks and acceptance criteria, which in turn help to influence the evaluation process for potentially shippable code at the end of the iteration.

11.3.3   Security Personas and Anti-personas

Personas are synthetic biographies of fictitious users of a future product used during requirements gathering, as mentioned in Sect. 7.7. A set of security personas (or anti-personas) can be developed to help team members get inside the mindset of potential attackers.

Consider the fictitious personas of *Mary*, *Paul* and *Joan*.

- *Mary* is a semi-professional fraudster,

  - She targets large (>$10k) attacks,
  - She is not a coder,

- *Paul* is member of a hacker club,

  - He has little financial acumen,
  - He wants to deface sites or leave some other calling card,

- *Joan* is on a low-income,

  - She has little technical competence,
  - She wants to maximise social security claims.

These personas can help team members understand specific types of attack and justify appropriate countermeasures.

11.3.4   Risk and Risk Management

Risk management is about identifying, ranking and mitigating risks. The objective here is to prioritise the important risks and requirements in terms of severity and likelihood, hence:

$$Risk = Criticality * Likelihood$$

We can adopt a qualitative approach to working out the likelihood, such as having a scale of five criteria:

- *Frequent* Occurs often or in quick succession (once per month),
- *Likely* Occurs on multiple occasions,
- *Occasional* Occurs from time to time (twice a year),
- *Remote* Can occur but not likely,
- *Rare* Is not frequently experienced (once in 3 years),

We can then create a matrix showing the relationship between criticality and likelihood, as shown in Fig. 11.2.

A risk register is a document listing risks and their potential severity and estimated likelihood. The risk register is mainly used to describe mitigations for each identified risk. The risk register is created and then regularly reviewed.

For example, large and long-running projects require multiple cooperating self-organising development teams, as described in Chap. 18. In these multi-team projects, a risk register review during each sprint is desirable, to assess any potential adverse impact of inter-team dependencies during each iteration.

	Rare (1)	Remote (2)	Probably Occasional (3)	Probable (4)	Frequent (5)
Maximum (5)	Medium (3)	Medium (3)	High (4)	Maximal (5)	Maximal (5)
High (4)	Low (2)	Low (2)	Medium (3)	High (4)	Maximal (5)
Medium (3)	Minimal (1)	Low (2)	Low (2)	Medium (3)	High (4)
Low (2)	Minimal (1)	Minimal (1)	Minimal (1)	Low (2)	Medium (3)
Minimal (1)	Minimal (1)	Minimal (1)	Minimal (1)	Minimal (1)	Low (2)

Fig. 11.2 Risk exposure matrix (Adapted from [5])

11.4   Security Design

Secure system design is based on several underlying assumptions. We assume all user input is compromised and that malicious attackers have access to all user output. It is also wise to assume that attackers know everything a about our system and how it works.

We tend to avoid complex centralised and monolithic designs in modern software development. This is good because systems are composed of several simpler, single-purpose, subsystems. However, from a security standpoint, this can make our systems seem fragmented, with each fragment contributing its own attack surface.

In larger software systems, the number of subsystems and components itself becomes large. Consequently, each subsystem or module needs to be defended by technical security controls that help deter, resist, detect or protect against attacks. These security controls will need to be threaded through your architecture and code design.

To enhance security, it is safest to assume other components are compromised and not rely on perimeter defences, specifically, view public-facing services with suspicion. For example, in a layered architecture, we must assume the layer above is compromised. This attitude encourages us to question the identity of the calling party. We also carefully check the input we receive and what we return back up. We also keep an audit trail of what information we got, when we got it and what we did with it.

In agile software development, we want to keep our designs and code as simple as possible. In fact, we even periodically refactor our code to help drive simplicity. But, the technical security controls we introduce inevitably increase complexity. The point is that *unnecessary complexity* is the enemy of good, secure, design.

11.4.1   Security Patterns

Security patterns, like design patterns in general, seek to capture good practice in architecture design. Patterns provide a route for non-expert users to benefit from specialist expertise. There are several readily available security pattern catalogues, such as [3, 10] or [15]. To illustrate the concept, I'll briefly describe just three patterns, the *demilitarised zone*, *authorisation enforcer* and *controlled object factory*.

The *demilitarised zone* (DMZ) is a security pattern that advocates a gateway network layer between a private intranet and the public internet. Hosts in the DMZ are permitted only limited access to hosts on the internal network. Firewalls are used to prevent unauthorised access from the internet to the DMZ and also from the DMZ to the intranet. Consequently, the DMZ provides an additional layer of internal network protection from external attack.

Authorisation implements a permission system to ensure that users are entitled to perform the operations they request. While there is a runtime overhead of performing authorisation checks, this approach limits the ability of attackers to execute functionality. A *secure service façade* delegates requests to an *authorisation enforcer*, which then retrieves the appropriate information and performs authorisation at a method level. The *authorisation enforcer* likely uses an *authentication enforcer* to authenticate users before an authorisation decision is made.

A *controlled object monitor* restricts access to an object by intercepting requests from processes. The *controlled object monitor* checks whether the requester is authorised to use the object. A *controlled object factory*, drawing upon the concepts of a conventional object factory pattern (mentioned in Sect. 9.6.3), instantiates instances of controlled objects. Controlled objects may encapsulate sensitive data (such as credit card details, for instance).

11.5 Security Implementation

Security implementation is where countermeasures and security features are created.

11.5.1 Abuse Story Implementation

The first stage of developing abuse stories is to identify a catalogue of potential attacks which can then serve several purposes in each iteration, that is, to:

- Enable prioritisation of stories, based on business risk and budget,
- Derive security requirements and add them to the iteration's user story backlog and create acceptance criteria,
- Allow the project team to define countermeasures,
- Estimate the countermeasure implementation overheads.

There are two main approaches to developing abuse stories. An informal first approach might be to review each user story, creating one or two negative cases against each scenario. A simple approach is to insert 'no' or 'not' into each user story.

The second, more formal approach is to convene a workshop to review business features in the increment and create a prioritised list of attacks. The workshop includes a business analyst (domain specialist), risk analyst, penetration tester, technical lead and quality assurance analyst (or functional tester). The responsibilities of the workshop participants are shown in Fig. 11.3. This group creates potential business and technical abuse cases and takes place after sprint kick-off, so that the user stories for the iteration are known.

These abuse stories then become security requirements following the usual process of estimation and countermeasure implementation. Abuse stories appear

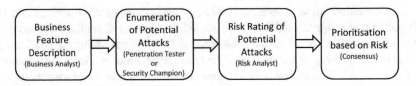

Fig. 11.3 OWASP abuse case workshop (Adapted from [6])

on Kanban boards and are the subject of discussion in stand-up meetings and retrospectives.

11.5.2   OWASP Top Ten

For web applications, the Open Web Application Security Project (OWASP) Top Ten lists and describes the most common and serious software security risks [8]. For each risk listed, OWASP identifies:

- *Threat agents*, types of entity that carry out attacks,
- *Attack scenarios*, pathway used to perform attack,
- *Impacts*, potential consequences of attack,
- *Prevention*, advice on thwarting mode of attack,
- *Resources*, references to useful information about attack resilience.

The OWASP list and resources are very comprehensive, and web application developers need to familiarise themselves with this material [8].

11.5.3   Authentication

Thinking about the authentication use case in Fig. 11.1, there is an OWASP cheat sheet that discusses the design and implementation of this user story [7].

For example, in one poor-quality pseudo-code implementation, it seems like a good idea to check if the user exists in the database before checking their password, as shown in Fig. 11.4.

But, using this approach, the execution time varies slightly between valid and invalid usernames. A malicious attacker can use this information to determine if a username exists in the data store. A better approach is to simultaneously check both username and password, as shown in Fig. 11.5.

The correct response, when authentication fails, is 'Login failed; Invalid user ID or password'. The intention here is to give no clue as to the failure cause. Following a similar pattern, for password recovery, the correct response is 'If that email address is in our database, we will send you an email to reset your password'. Again, the

Authentication - AVOID!! [7]

```
IF USER_EXISTS(username) THEN
    password_hash=HASH(password)
    IS_VALID=LOOKUP_CREDENTIALS(username, password_hash)
    IF NOT IS_VALID THEN
        RETURN Error("Invalid Username or Password!")
    ENDIF
ELSE
    RETURN Error("Invalid Username or Password!")
ENDIF
```

Fig. 11.4 Poorly implemented authentication user story

Authentication - Improved [7]

```
    password_hash=HASH(password)
    IS_VALID=LOOKUP_CREDENTIALS(username, password_hash)
    IF NOT IS_VALID THEN
        RETURN Error("Invalid Username or Password!")
    ENDIF
```

Fig. 11.5 Improved authentication user story implementation

purpose is to avoid giving away information about the existence or, otherwise, of valid user email addresses. Further, it is argued that multi-factor authentication reduces the chances of account compromise by 99.9% [14].

11.6   Security Evaluation

There are two main approaches to evaluating security, using reviews or testing.

11.6.1   Manual Security Inspections and Reviews

Security inspections are best conducted during each iteration. The reviews can check people, processes and policies, as well as technology decisions and architectural designs (and not just source code implementations). This means reviews are flexible, don't require any support technology and can be applied early in the increment development process. However, reviews are time-consuming and require considerable skill to be effective. Inspections and reviews are most effective, if performed constructively and collaboratively.

11.6.2 Automated Security Testing

Source code quality and security testing tools can help give assurance about our application. SonarQube can be used to analyse code in several languages and can identify numerous code quality and potential security weaknesses [13]. SonarQube can access software directly from your online source code repository. A small and simple configuration file must be added to your repository so that SonarQube can understand your environment.

Another useful tool is BDD-Security [4], a security testing framework that uses behaviour-driven development concepts. BDD-Security integrates with Selenium (WebDriver) [11] to perform runtime tests on web applications and APIs.

11.7 Agile Security Processes

From a security perspective, it is helpful to revisit an agile process comprising roles, artefacts and ceremonies.

11.7.1 Roles

In many organisations, security teams tend to work rather independently from the software development teams. This is not an ideal situation. It is better for a security specialist to work within a development team, while also working with other security specialists on a shared agenda. The security specialist takes the role of a security champion in daily stand-up and retrospective meetings, providing advice and support. The security champion also helps exchange good practice between other teams.

11.7.2 Artefacts

Abuse stories, as I've mentioned, describe how to compromise a system from an attacker's perspective: 'As an attacker, I want to…'. Abuse stories help developers understand security risks, can help to define specific security tests and are particularly useful at early stages of development. Abuse stories do not usually get placed on the product backlog, since they do not result in specific development work items.

11.7.3 Ceremonies

Ceremonies specifically designed to create security artefacts in agile are comparatively under-developed. This can be mitigated by including security issues in conventional iteration planning and sprint review ceremonies. Including security user stories among tasks in the Kanban board can help maintain awareness and commitment.

11.8 Exercises

Here are some exercise you can try to learn more about the topics covered in Chap. 11. Have a go at each exercise and then look at the hints and tips in Sect. 11.9.

Exercise 11.1 (Learning Journal)

11.1 Use your learning journal to make some notes about the material in Chap. 11. This could be just a few bullet points or a longer essay.

Exercise 11.2 (Source Code Review Exercise)

11.2 Choose or create a project with a public GitHub repository. Execute a security review against your source code. For example, configure your public repository for use by SonarCloud [12]. Commit some code and watch the security review tool execute.

Exercise 11.3 (OWASP Top Ten Review Exercise)

11.3 Choose or create a simple database-driven web application. For your web application, carefully review the Open Web Application Security Project (OWASP) Top Ten list [8]. Make sure you have a mitigation strategy in place for each item in the Top Ten list.

Exercise 11.4 (Learning Journal)

11.4 Reflect on the exercises from Chap. 11. Write in your learning journal about what happened during each exercise.

Exercise 11.5 (Learning Journal)

11.5 Reflect on the chapters in Part II. Reflect on what you have learned about:

- Requirements,
- Architecture,
- Design,
- Development,
- Security.

Make some notes in your learning journal about each of these topics.

11.9 Hints, Tips and Advice on Exercises

11.1 *Learning Journal*

Chapter 11 has covered security aspects of analysis, requirements, design, implementation, evaluation and agile processes. Review the chapter and write about what you have learned on each topic.

11.2 *Source Code Review Exercise*

When you execute the security review tool against your source code, if all goes well, you will be provided with a report. The report, depending upon the complexity of your source code, should give you advice on potential problems and fixes.

11.3 *OWASP Top Ten Review Exercise*

There is detailed advice available from Open Web Application Security Project (OWASP) on mitigation of all the problems identified in the Top Ten list [8]. Make sure you spend some time reviewing that material.

11.10   Chapter Summary

Security has become an increasingly important concern for product developers. In this chapter, we have explored security analysis and how to create a threat model. Then, following a life cycle model, we discussed security requirements, design and implementation. Finally, techniques for evaluating security were suggested. Security breaches undermine reputations and can be career-ending in extreme cases. There are useful and actionable resources freely available, such as from the OWASP foundation, which developers need to become familiar with.

We are now ready to apply the skills described in Part II to our *Tabby Cat* case study. We can then move onto Part III, on *Process*. In this next part, you will have a chance to learn more about agile ceremonies, lean development methods, version control and automated testing.

References

1. Apvrille, A., Pourzandi, M.: Secure software development by example. IEEE Secur. Priv. **3**(4), 10–17 (Jul 2005). https://doi.org/10.1109/MSP.2005.103
2. Bell, L., Brunton–spall, M., Smith, R., Bird, J.: Agile Application Security: Enabling Security in a Continuous Delivery Pipeline. O'Reilly (Sep 2017)
3. Fernandez-Buglioni, E.: Security Patterns in Practice: Designing Secure Architectures Using Software Patterns, 1st edn. Wiley (Jun 2013)
4. IriusRisk: BDD-Security. IriusRisk (Mar 2021). https://github.com/iriusrisk/bdd-security
5. Nancy R. Mead, C.C.W.: Cyber Security Engineering: A Practical Approach for Systems and Software Assurance, 1st edn. Addison-Wesley Professional (Oct 2016)
6. OWASP Foundation: Abuse case cheat sheet (2021). https://cheatsheetseries.owasp.org/cheatsheets/Abuse_Case_Cheat_Sheet.html
7. OWASP Foundation: Authentication cheat sheet (2021). https://cheatsheetseries.owasp.org/cheatsheets/Authentication_Cheat_Sheet.html
8. OWASP Foundation: Owasp top ten web application security risks (2021). https://owasp.org/www-project-top-ten/
9. OWASP Project: Samm agile guidance (2021). https://owaspsamm.org/guidance/agile/#General
10. Schumacher, M., Fernandez-Buglioni, E., Hybertson, D., Buschmann, F., Sommerlad, P.: Security Patterns: Integrating Security and Systems Engineering, 1st edn. Wiley (Jul 2013)
11. Software Freedom Conservancy: Seleniumhq browser automation (2021). https://www.selenium.dev/
12. SonarCloud: Automatic code review, testing, inspection & auditing (2021). https://sonarcloud.io/
13. SonarSource: Sonarqube (2021). https://www.sonarqube.org/
14. Weinert, A.: Your Pa$$word doesn't matter (Jul 2019). https://techcommunity.microsoft.com/t5/azure-active-directory-identity/your-pa-word-doesn-t-matter/ba-p/731984
15. Yskout, K., Heyman, T., Scandariato, R., Joosen, W.: A System of Security Patterns. No. CW-469 in Department of Computer Science, Katholieke Universiteit Leuven (December 2006). https://www.researchgate.net/publication/242679421_A_system_of_security_patterns

Chapter 12
Tabby Cat Project: Getting Building

Abstract In this chapter, we start building the *Tabby Cat* project. We will use this project to apply the ideas from the chapters in Part II of the book. We describe requirements in the form of user stories, as we did in Chap. 7. We select an architectural style from those described in Chap. 8. Finally, we employ object-oriented design patterns, like those in Chap. 9. As we said in Chap. 6, *Tabby Cat* is software for displaying source code repository developer activity. We want to obtain activity data from a public repository, extract important information using searching and filtering and display the results.

12.1 Introduction

In this chapter, we want to explore the technical aspects of the *Tabby Cat* software. We start by creating *Requirements* using techniques from Chap. 7. Next we move on to selecting an architectural style *Architecture* from Chap. 8. We then employ design patterns and practices from Chap.9. Finally, our implementation uses software source code *Development* techniques from Chap. 10 and *Security* from Chap. 11. The *Tabby Cat* project, as I've mentioned elsewhere, has been provided by Red Ocelot Ltd., our software start-up company [9].

12.2 Requirements

First, we can establish some high-level epic user stories for the *Tabby Cat* project.

- As a developer, I want to download public (GitHub) repository activity information, in order to learn about development events
- As a developer, I want to display information about commits, issues and metrics in order to understand the repository activity history

© Springer Nature Switzerland AG 2022

J. M. Bass, *Agile Software Engineering Skills*,

https://doi.org/10.1007/978-3-031-05469-3_12

Notice we have chosen to obtain information from GitHub repositories. Other repository platforms are available. You might choose to fork and extend the *Tabby Cat* software [2] to work with other platforms such as Apache Subversion or GitLab. Make sure you have read Chap. 7. Complete Exercises 7.2 to 7.14. It is a good time to review your learning journal.

12.2.1 Functional Requirements

Now, we can decompose our epics into more specific user stories for the *Tabby Cat* software.

- As a developer, I want to select a public repository, in order to learn about the activity history,
- As a developer, I want to download the activity history, in order to learn about the activity history,
- As a developer, I want to sort the activity history, in order to identify specific activities in the repository
- As a developer, I want to search the activity history, in order to identify specific activities in the repository
- As a developer, I want to display repository metrics, in order to identify specific properties of the repository

The *Tabby Cat* software should implement these user stories while supporting possible future functional extensions later.

Review Your Learning Journal
I have recommended that you create and update a learning journal when you do the exercises in each chapter; see Exercise 7.1. Now is a good time to reflect on your journal notes for the chapters from Part II.

- Re-read your learning journal from the chapters and exercises in Part II of the book,
- Think about what went well when you did the exercises,
- Think about what didn't go so well,
- Make some notes, in your learning journal, about the strengths and weaknesses of your work in these areas,
- Create some actions or set some targets for your future learning.

12.2.2 Non-functional Requirements

For the *Tabby Cat* project, at this stage, we do not need to concern ourselves too much with non-functional requirements. Our purpose is to build confidence and gain experience of building a functional solution. This is not a safety-critical application. Data privacy is not a big issue, since we have chosen to use public source code repositories. Consequently, anything in the repository is already public domain. The application doesn't need to support many users (to quantify what we mean by 'many', let's say a few tens of users, not hundreds).

However, we might want to add new functionality to the *Tabby Cat* project later. Consequently, future enhancement is a priority for this project. We plan to employ good practices to ensure extensibility. We will also use organisational structures and design patterns that enable future enhancement.

Finally, if you fork or clone this software, check limitations on the application programming interface (API) used to collect repository data. Quite often, open-access (free) APIs impose limits on the number of requests you can make. They don't want people running large numbers of requests against their servers. Check the *terms of use*, and avoid accidentally running too many requests during development and testing.

12.3 Architecture

We can summarise our functional requirements as:

- Select a remote repository,
- Download activity data from the chosen repository,
- Display the commit history,
- Add search terms or filters to see a targeted subset of the activity history.

We want to achieve a separation of concerns between our business functions and our UI. Both can be developed independently, perhaps by different team members or teams. From a front-end perspective, we need to consider how we're going to display dynamic data. For this illustrative case study, the user interface need not be very sophisticated. For the back-end, we need to consider obtaining the repository activity data. While initially, we will only be doing relatively simple data processing, we anticipate that future functionality might become more complex.

The user stories in Sect. 12.2 suggest a flow of processing. There are four steps illustrated in Fig. 12.1: from (1), selecting the repository to investigate; then (2), making a request on the GitHub API of the selected repository; next (3), reading in the activity history from that repository; and finally, (4), producing the activity history display. Remember to read Chap. 8 and complete Exercises 8.2 and 8.3.

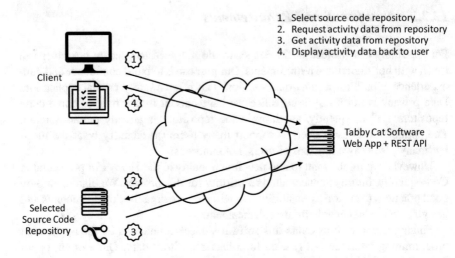

Fig. 12.1 *Tabby Cat* project outline architecture

12.3.1 Architectural Style

We have selected the clean architectural style popularised by Bob Martin [5]. This style comprises four main elements, entities, use cases, interface adapters and frameworks and drivers, as described in Sect. 8.3.5.

Entities provide the system with enterprise business logic. The entities comprise relatively slow-changing functionality. These are plane objects that represent the business domain of your system.

Use cases are where you provide the business rules of your application. The use cases are pure business logic and don't know how results will be presented.

Interface adapters retrieve and store data. A novel feature of this architectural style is an attempt to provide consistent management of network interfaces and databases. The interface adapters translate between use cases and specific drivers and frameworks for presenting data.

Frameworks and drivers comprise the database drivers and graphical user interface libraries we select for our application.

An important idea in this architectural style is that entities and use cases are independent of frameworks user interfaces and databases. In simple terms, entities and use cases comprise business logic. And, interface adapters and frameworks and drivers comprise implementation detail. Consequently, a simplified architecture of our system is shown in Fig. 12.2.

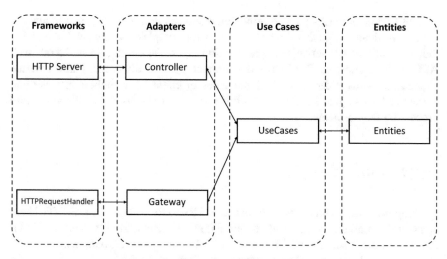

Fig. 12.2 *Tabby Cat* clean architecture outline design

The next question we need to ask ourselves is: how will the overall architectural style we've adopted influence our technology choices. We know we're making a software-as-a-service style web application; some approaches might include:

- Monolithic web application that serves html,
- Monolithic web services that expose a REST API with a stand-alone client (i.e. client-server)
- Micro-services, where many small web services are aggregated to create a single coherent API which is consumed by a stand-alone client(s).

The monolithic web application is superficially simple, but quickly becomes difficult to maintain. There are risks of code for the user interfaced being mixed with code for application functionality and the lack of clarity that can result.

In contrast, the second option of monolithic web services exposing an interface to a stand-alone client is a little more complicated to implement, but neatly separates the user interface and application logic. In principle, we can separately deploy the server-side presentation layer from the REST services, if we want to.

Decomposing the services into micro-services would allow each micro-service to be deployed independently. Independent deployment of services is useful if you are supporting very large user populations or where services vary considerably in their processing complexity (and hence hardware requirements). But micro-services add complexity to achieve these benefits.

Although our requirements are quite simple, we have chosen the client-server architectural style to illustrate this commonly used approach. The RESTful services will be designed around the specific types of repository information we want to collect. Consequently, looking at the user stories, in Sect. 12.2, we can see we want to collect information about commits, issues and metrics.

This approach means we can provision resources in a more targeted manner—we can vertically scale the server to account for complex and high-volume traffic independently of the server-side presentation layer. We could also make our web API public to allow for third-party development, potentially creating new revenue streams, or perhaps develop additional types of client i.e. a mobile app. We can select the Java language ecosystem to fulfil our current needs and tackle any future processing requirements.

12.3.2   Client-Server

We propose a stand-alone web API that serves RESTful requests over HTTP. There is no user interface component to our RESTful API; it simply accepts HTTP requests in the form of a HTTP verb and URI which then responds with a HTTP status code and accompanying payload (in the form of JSON).

We need some way of serving out client code (HTML/JS/CSS) to the user's web browser, though. To this end, we employ a popular (open-source) web server, nginx [6]. Our nginx web server has two purposes. Firstly, it is processing incoming requests to our domain and sends the relevant static files back. Secondly, it acts as a reverse proxy, forwarding requests to the back-end RESTful API server. Using a reverse proxy allows the client code to remain unaware of the back-end server location, it can simply send requests to itself, and the nginx web server will proxy them to wherever they need to go.

12.4   Design

Now, make sure you have read Chap. 9 and completed Exercises 9.2 to 9.6.

12.4.1   Back-End Design

Looking more carefully at Fig. 12.1, we can decompose this into the following *challenges* our system needs to resolve:

- Step 1

  - Accepting and processing incoming HTTP requests,
  - Converting incoming HTTP requests into an internal format for use,
  - Mapping the external URI to internal business logic,
  - Processing the request,

- Step 2

  – Querying an external HTTP API,

- Step 3

  – Mapping the response from the external HTTP API into an internal format,

- Step 4

  – Returning a response to the requester.

We then identify the components we will need in our system. We are following the clean architecture style we mentioned in Sect. 12.3.1. The main components we identify are:

- A HTTP server component, which accepts HTTP requests and sends HTTP responses,
- A controller component, which converts HTTP requests into an internal format and maps to internal business logic,
- Use case components which represent our core business logic,
- Some entities which provide a more meaningful internal representation,
- An internal HTTP request handler, for querying the GitHub API,
- A gateway component, for converting between external data (database, GitHub API) and internal data (entities).

From our requirements, we identify four entities that we will need to model: *Commit, Issue, Metrics* and *Source Repository*. The Commit entity might aggregate other entities like author, etc. The Issue entity, at the name suggests, is for issues recorded in the repository we are investigating. The Metrics entity is for repository metrics. Finally, there will be a Source Repository entity for managing a handle on the external repository.

In the first instance, we envisage that these entities will be simple objects that just contain data. Our use cases, for this initial iteration, are also simple retrieval operations i.e. GetSomething. So we identify the following:

- GetCommits, get a list of commits for a given repository,
- GetIssues, get a list of issues for a given repository,
- GetSourceRepository, get a source repository from the system database,
- GetSourceRepositoryMetrics, get the metrics for a given repository.

Hence, we can flesh out our simple design into something a bit more complete, as shown in Fig. 12.3.

After creating our initial design, now is a good time to consider if there are any problems that can be solved using common object-oriented design patterns [4]. Looking at the diagram in Fig. 12.3, we need to make external HTTP requests from within our software. We could embed HTTP requests into our source code. But, these calls could end up going in several gateways. Also making HTTP requests is quite a common thing to have to do. Hence, there are a couple of third-party libraries

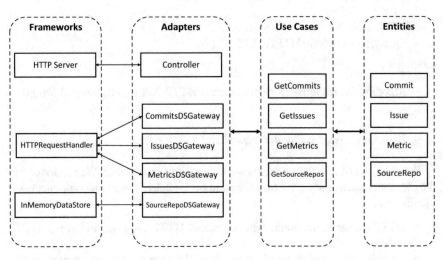

Fig. 12.3 *Tabby Cat* clean architecture design

that can help us with this, such as [1] and [3]. We have selected the OKHttp library [3]. To avoid coupling our code to this external code (that we don't control) and to simplify the overall interaction, we employ the façade pattern. We'll discuss this in more detail when we consider the implementation, Fig. 12.6.

12.4.2 Front-End Design

A popular way to structure GUIs is to use the MVC architectural style, as mentioned in Sect. 9.6.2 and shown in Fig. 12.4a. Our initial design follows this pattern; hence, we have some models, some views and some controllers. We also need to make external API calls to our back-end service, it would be tiresome to have to do this every time, so we will need a wrapper to encapsulate the http request logic. This way, if our API changes for some reason, there's only one place we need to change it.

Our front-end models can loosely map to the back-end models. However, we might make some minor changes. For instance, we want our view to update from a list of commits; therefore, we might create a Commits (plural) model, instead of just a Commit (singular) model. Similarly, we want to list all repositories (Repos), but we also want to select a specific repository (Repo). Consequently, we identify four models, Commits, Repo, Repos and Issues, as shown in Fig. 12.4. Based on how we may want to display the data to the user, the repository metrics have been incorporated into the Repo model.

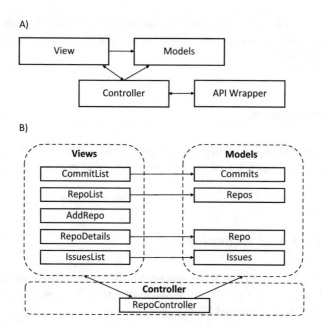

Fig. 12.4 *Tabby Cat* model-view-controller design. (**a**) Simple MVC. (**b**) Tabby Cat MVC design

Now we have our models, we need to think about what views we want to display, and from our requirements, we will need:

- A view to list available repositories,
- A view for adding a new repository,
- A view for showing the repository details (with a child view which lists commits and issues).

We therefore identify five views, as shown in Fig. 12.4:

- `RepoList`, lists available repositories,
- `AddRepo`, a form for adding repositories to the system,
- `RepoDetails`, the entry point into a repository, listing the name, owner and metrics as well as providing functionality to select developer activity,
- `CommitList`, a list of commits for a given repository,
- `IssueList`, a list of issues for a given repository.

Given the relative simplicity of this application, we don't imagine we'll need more than a single controller to handle our model/view interaction.

Looking at our MVC design, shown in Fig 12.4, we would like to maintain a unidirectional data flow. First, the user interacts with view. Then, the controller updates the relevant model. Finally, the model updates the view. However, we'd like to keep this as loosely coupled as possible. Therefore, we use the observer pattern [4] where our models are the *Subject* and our views are the *Observer*. Our controller will bind each view to the relevant model that it needs to observe. That way, whenever our model updates, it will iterate through all its observers updating them with its new state.

12.5   Development

Make sure you have read Chap. 10 and completed Exercises 10.2 to 10.5. We can now see a representation of our overall architectural implementation shown in Fig. 12.5.

12.5.1   Back-End Technologies

In the *Tabby Cat* project, we have decided to build a web-based service, serving a RESTful API over HTTP. We are familiar with both Java and JavaScript. Let's consider some further Java and Node.js design issues:

- Node.js is single threaded, but, due to the runtime environment and 'event loop' model it uses, can offer significant performance per resource cost for high I/O-based applications (think of a web server dealing with lots of small requests) [7].
- Java on the other hand is multi-threaded, spawning a new thread (with accompanying memory) for each new request that comes in. This means individual

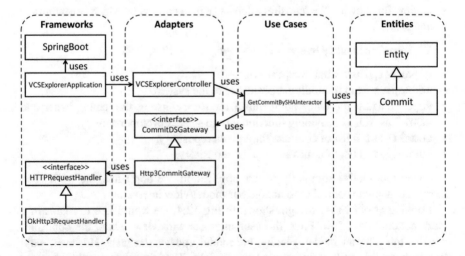

Fig. 12.5 *Tabby Cat* clean architecture implementation

requests can be complex, but the total number of I/O requests is limited (based on available resources in the runtime environment).

- Node.js has no types out of the box but can be added via Typescript; however, this introduces another layer of complexity.
- Java is strictly typed without any additional overhead.

This list is my no means exhaustive. These are simply examples of the issues you might consider. I encourage you to look at empirical research resources that experimentally compare different languages. Be wary of online discussions that are based on opinion, instead of fact.

We have only considered Java and Node.js in this discussion; it could be worth looking at languages such as C# or Python and see how they compare. As with most things, it's about trade-offs—Java might be 'good enough' and we already know the language, but it might be that Python is just perfect for the job and might therefore be worth the initial investment in learning. On the other hand, maybe a HackCamp or Hackathon setting is not ideal for learning a new language. Using our experience and an evaluation of the available technologies and our skill sets, we have decided to choose a Java-based server-side application for implementing a REST API over http.

One other issue we should consider is how we integrate *Tabby Cat* source code with third-party libraries. We want to use an external library to simplify accessing the GitHub API and making activity history requests. As mentioned earlier, we have chosen to use the OKHttp3 library for this [3]. We could just embed calls to this library within our own code, but this can add complexity when it comes to future source code maintenance. Consequently, it is good practice to use a *façade* pattern [4] to hide the complexity of the OKHttp3 library, as shown in Fig. 12.6. We have provided a generic request handler HttpRequestHandler and a specific

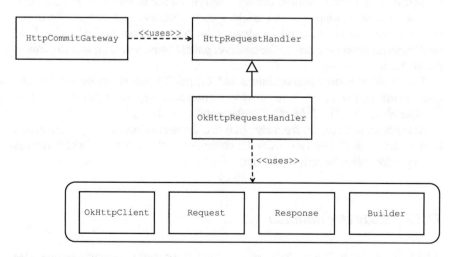

Fig. 12.6 *Tabby Cat* façade pattern

instantiation of that handler, the `OkHttpRequestHandler`, that wraps calls to the external library.

12.5.2   Front-End Technologies

We need to complete a design exercise for front-end technologies, as well. In our case, we are familiar with vanilla JavaScript, HTML, jQuery and React.

- vanilla JavaScript and HTML are simple, no compilation or complex build tool needed out of the gate, play well with conventional UX/UI design tools that produce HTML/CSS and can be hard to maintain beyond a certain size/complexity
- jQuery + HTML, similar to vanilla JavaScript, have lots of rich libraries and tools that simplify using vanilla JavaScript but still suffer the same issues in terms of complexity and size
- React excels at making modular, reusable components which can be plugged together to build sophisticated applications and strong support community and rich sets of UI libraries and excels at creating single-page applications (SPAs)

As with the back-end technologies, it might be worthwhile to investigate other technologies, for instance, Vue or AngularJS. Our user interface for the purpose of this case study does not have to be very sophisticated. Hence, a simple vanilla JavaScript and HTML front-end is fine.

One risk with implementing the model-view-controller is the complexity associated with the controller. The model encapsulates functionality for managing and manipulating data. Simple. The view is responsible for the user interface and user experience. That's clear. But the controller... What goes in there? A simple suggestion is that the controller contains everything not in the view or the model. This is, of course, simplistic and crude. But, it illustrates that complexity in the controller can get out of hand. A clever solution, employed in *Tabby Cat*, is to implement an observer pattern. The observer pattern provides a neat way to connect the model and view [4].

The observer pattern implements, a sort of, publish and subscribe model. The idea, shown in Fig. 12.7a, is to provide a consistent way to update the state of multiple observers. The *Tabby Cat* implementation is shown in Fig. 12.7b.

At runtime, you can see from Fig. 12.8 that the user selects activity information from within a view. The view calls the controller to select a model which returns activity information directly to the view.

12.5.3   Code Organisation

An important issue facing developers is how to organise the source code files for the project. This is particularly true when a team of developers is involved.

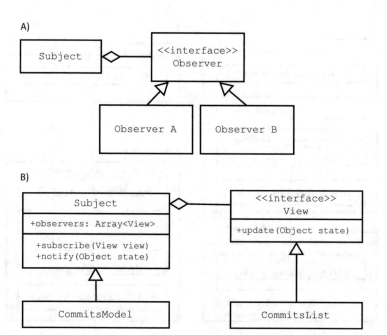

Fig. 12.7 *Tabby Cat* observer pattern. (**a**) Observer pattern. (**b**) Observer pattern, Tabby Cat implementation

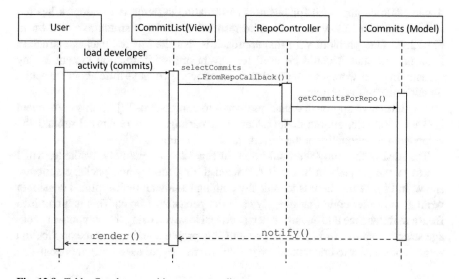

Fig. 12.8 *Tabby Cat* observer object sequence diagram

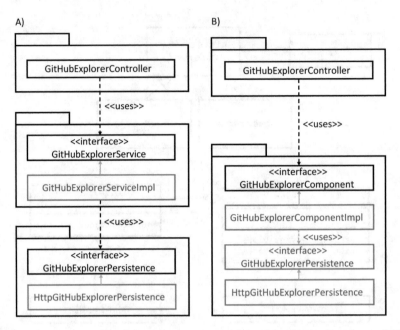

Fig. 12.9 *Tabby Cat* source code organisation (Adapted from [5]). (**a**) Layered code organisation. (**b**) Component code organisation

A conventional approach for business information systems is to adopt a layered architecture and follow that with a corresponding package structure as shown in Fig. 12.9a. One problem with this approach is that the layered package structure is so generic that it could be used for any business information system in any domain. In other words, the layered package structure conveys little about the actual functionality of the system.

An alternative approach organises code into components [5]. In this component package structure, source code folders and packages are organised around the component functionality in the system, as shown in Fig. 12.9b.

The idea is that only the bold boxes in Fig. 12.9 are publicly available, while access to the greyed-out boxes is restricted. Using the layered package structure shown in Fig. 12.9a, there is technically nothing to stop an undisciplined developer writing controller code that directly calls the persistence layer. This is a bad idea from a maintenance and evolution perspective. However, using the component package structure shown in Fig. 12.9b prevents this problem and makes the application source code easier to understand when intuitive names are used for components.

12.6 Security

Our focus here has been to build a functional system. We've already observed, in Sect. 12.2, that non-functional requirements are not at the forefront of our minds, right now. Consequently, security issues are not exceptionally stringent beyond the concerns of any internet connected application or software service.

Take this opportunity to read Chap. 11 and complete Exercises 11.2 and 11.3. Now is a good time to review the Open Web Application Security Project (OWASP) Top Ten list that describes the most common and serious web application software security risks [8].

12.7 Illustrative Implementation

An example implementation of the *Tabby Cat* project is available on GitHub [2]. The *Tabby Cat* project source code shows how we chose to implement an illustrative example based on ideas in the book. We've tried to keep things simple while also adopting good development practices. In particular, we have tried to make the software simple to enhance and extend.

References

1. Apache Software Foundation: Apache httpcomponents – httpclient overview (Feb 2022), https://hc.apache.org/httpcomponents-client-5.1.x/
2. Bass, J., Monaghan, B.: Tabby Cat GitHub Explorer. Red Ocelot Ltd (Jan 2022). https://github.com/julianbass/github-explorer
3. Block, Inc: Overview - okhttp (2022). https://square.github.io/okhttp/
4. Gamma, E., Helm, R., Johnson, R., Vlissides, J.: Design Patterns : Elements of Reusable Object-Oriented Software. Addison-Wesley, Harlow, England (2005)
5. Martin, R.C.: Clean Architecture: A Craftsman's Guide to Software Structure and Design, 1st edn. Addison-Wesley (Sep 2017)
6. Nginx, Inc.: nginx (January 2022). https://nginx.org/en/
7. OpenJS Foundation: Node.js (Jan 2022), https://nodejs.org/en/
8. OWASP Foundation: Owasp top ten web application security risks (2021). https://owasp.org/www-project-top-ten/
9. Red Ocelot Ltd: Enhancing digital agility (2022). https://www.redocelot.com

Part III
Process, Tools and Automation

Part III of the book focuses on *process*. We want to learn how to create a systematic and repeatable software development *process*, for creating worthwhile products. Each of the chapters in Part III has exercises.

First, in Chap. 13, the coordination activities and meetings in a typical business information system development *process* are described. You can learn about coordination meetings and some engineering practices like pair programming and test-driven development.

In contrast, Chap. 14 investigates the benefits of lean software development. I'll explore key ideas around *value*, *waste* and *speed* in a software development *process*.

Version control helps you create a revision history of your software and provides a means for sharing code with others in your team. Version control is discussed in Chap. 15.

Testing helps identify defects in your code and is considered in Chap. 16. From a *process* perspective, we are most interested in test automation.

In Chap. 17, the ideas from all the chapters in Part III are applied to the *Tabby Cat* case study. I explore the process and automation skills needed to read information from a selected GitHub repository using an API and display the activity data.

Other Book Parts

As I've said, the overall design of this book is around Part I on *people*, Part II on *product* and Part III on *process*. These parts of the book are stand-alone, more or less. So, if your main interest is in the *people* aspects of software development, for instance, then you might want to skip back to Part I. However, if your main interest is in technicalities of developing a *product*, you could skip back to II. To further support you in learning the skills you need, there are some more advanced topics, in Part IV.

Chapter 13
Agile Ceremonies

Abstract This chapter explains how iterations work in software development. There are planning ceremonies at the start of each iteration and a review at the end. One aspect of the iteration review is to get customer feedback on the software that has been produced. Another aspect of the review is to enhance learning and improvement within the software team. We will talk about other potentially useful techniques like pair programming, test-driven development and swarm programming.

13.1 Introduction

Ceremonies are the group collaboration activities performed as part of an agile development process; see Fig. 13.1. Ceremonies are usually meetings, of one sort or another, conducted during each iteration.

13.2 Iteration Planning

Planning is essentially about deciding what to work on (and consequently what not to work on) in the coming (hopefully short) time window. We want to plan for a short iteration, as a way of mitigating the risk of change (in the environment, in customer needs or wishes, in the teams and so on). Planning involves mapping customer priorities to estimates of our production capacity.

Iteration planning is conducted at the start of each iteration, as shown in Fig. 13.1, and comprises four tasks:

- prioritisation of requirements,
- breaking up of requirements into technical tasks,
- estimation of technical tasks and consequently requirements,
- work item assignment within the team.

© Springer Nature Switzerland AG 2022
J. M. Bass, *Agile Software Engineering Skills*,
https://doi.org/10.1007/978-3-031-05469-3_13

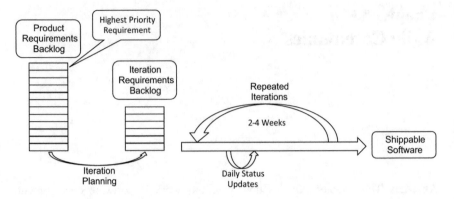

Fig. 13.1 Agile process

On large-scale projects, more extensive planning is required. Release plans are used to coordinate cooperating teams and periodic risk assessments performed to prepare mitigations; see Chap. 18. But for now, let's focus on merely planning for the iteration ahead.

13.2.1   Prioritisation

The product owner, not the development team, prioritises requirements for implementation. There is one exception, which is where team members notice some technical dependency between tasks. That is, some high-priority requirement, selected by the product owner, depends on some lower-priority requirement being implemented first. In this situation, the team can advise the product owner that the higher-priority requirement can be implemented but will not work. The product owner can then decide if they want to increase the priority of the lower-priority requirement.

13.2.2   Features and Technical Tasks

Our first task during iteration planning, with a prioritised requirements backlog, is to get consensus on what a user story comprises. So, we break each feature up into a set of technical tasks. Does this user story require any front-end interface screens? Does this feature need to use data storage? What business logic operations are part of this feature? We need to divide the user story into all its constituent technical tasks. By creating a list of smaller work items, we can more confidently estimate the effort required to implement each and hence the overall feature.

We can summarise the process as follows:

- Select highest-priority user story from the backlog,
- Discuss the purpose and scope of the user story,

- The product owner answers questions about the user story,
- The discussion is complete, once all questions have been answered,
- The user story is broken up into constituent technical tasks, depending upon the application domain; think about user interface tasks, application logic and data storage tasks as separate items.
- Repeat the process for the next high-priority user story in the product backlog.

We do not need to perform this process on every user story in the backlog, for every iteration. We only need to split stories which are going to be implemented during the coming iteration. After we have split a user story into technical tasks, we can estimate the effort required for implementation.

13.2.3 Estimation

We need to know how many features we can fit into an iteration. That is a difficult question to answer. Not least because team members may have different perceptions of what is required to implement a feature. The two techniques worth mentioning are story points and T-shirt sizing. Both approaches tend to use the planning poker technique.

13.2.3.1 Story Point Estimation

Story points are a relative measure of the size or complexity of user stories. The integers used to approximate size are taken from a Fibonacci number sequence: 1, 2, 3, 5, 8 and 13. Using this number sequence, the estimates for larger sizes are less precise; consequently, there is no need to differentiate between sizes 9 and 10. Instead, it is sufficient to distinguish between 8 and 13.

Larger, story point sizes, depending upon the business domain of the application under development, could indicate that the user story is in fact an epic that needs to be further decomposed into user stories. If large user stories cannot logically be decomposed, then story point sizes like 20, 40 or 100 might be considered. However, we do need each user story to fit into an iteration; consequently, epics do have an upper size limit (or iteration durations lengthened).

Planning poker is commonly used to allocate story points to technical tasks. To perform planning poker, the team members collectively:

- Take each technical task; in turn, the first round of voting starts,
- Discuss each technical task, if necessary,
- Write down (secretly) their estimates for the work item,
- When everyone has finished writing, team members reveal their votes for the tasks,
- Look at the story points assigned and see if there is close consensus (in novice teams or a new application domain, close consensus is unlikely),

- If there is consensus, on the story point allocation, move on to the next technical task,
- If there is no consensus, constructively discuss the highest and lowest story point estimates and try to understand why someone thought it was a larger or smaller task,
- Following this discussion, move into a second round of voting
- Continue rounds of voting and discussion until consensus emerges around the story point value for a task,
- Then, move on to the next technical task or user story.

The planning poker approach to estimation is consensus-based and draws upon all the team expertise available. This approach fosters discussion, which is a valuable source of learning for novice or less experienced members. Teams tend to improve estimation accuracy over time.

13.2.3.2   T-Shirt Sizing

A simple and easy way to estimate tasks is to agree a small set of categories and fit the features into the agreed groups. So, we can think of tasks or features as being *small, medium, large* and *extra large*. We think of this estimation process as fitting tasks in a (small) group of size categories. How many size categories are reasonable for your context? Three, four or five? How accurate (or precise) do you expect your estimation to be? More than five size categories require considerable effort for a novice team.

If a task is bigger than the usual range of categories, we take further action, as we did with story point estimation. For example, if a task is *extra, extra large* (which is an epic user story), it requires further analysis to break it down into a more manageable size.

We can use a similar planning poker process as we used with story point estimation. Everyone secretly writes their size estimate for a technical task on a sticky note. The sticky notes are all revealed simultaneously (so no one can change their score, when they see other people's estimates). Team members can then see the variation in size estimates within the group. Teams usually discuss the thinking behind the largest and smallest estimates. After the discussion, team members are invited to offer a revised size estimate. Everyone writes a second estimate on a sticky note, which is then shared again. After a few rounds of discussion and voting, consensus is achieved on the size of that specific technical task.

T-Shirt Sizing, Burndown Charts and Velocity

Some people describe agile methods, like Scrum, as *empirical* methods. The idea is we can keep track of the number of story points completed in an iteration. This figure, the number of story points completed in an iteration, is called the team *velocity*. We can also plot burndown charts, during the iteration, showing story points as they are completed, as discussed in Sect. 10.3.3.

A perceived disadvantage of T-shirt sizing is the lack of integer values for each size. A simple way to combine velocity, burndown chart and T-shirt sizing is to consistently assign an integer value for each size. For example, large might equate to 13 points. Medium equals 8 points and so on. Now we can use T-shirt sizing as an empirical method.

13.2.4 Task Assignment

After requirements have been estimated, we now have an idea how many tasks can fit into an iteration. We can now decide who, in the team, is going to tackle each task. A defining characteristic of a self-organising team is that people volunteer for tasks. Sometimes, people pick up a task because it is similar to others they have successfully completed in the past. On the other hand, sometimes people pick up tasks to learn something new. The aspiration for the team, achieved in experienced groups, is that anyone be capable of doing any tasks.

You might imagine relying on volunteers to pick up tasks means that there are tasks no one wants that don't get taken up. But practitioners say this is unusual. More commonly, self-organising teams develop a sense of shared commitment to group outcomes. So, unpopular tasks do tend to get shared around the group over successive iterations.

13.3 Coordination Meetings

The daily *stand-up*, a coordination meeting involving everyone in the team, is an important activity in agile methods. It is where everyone finds out what is going on in the team.

Everyone in the team answers the following three questions:

1. What have I been doing, since the last stand-up?
2. What will I be doing, between now and the next stand-up?
3. Are there any impediments preventing me from making progress?

Some groups like to add a fourth question: *Am I going to create any blockers that might impede others?* This fourth question is typically useful in larger projects where there are dependencies between the codes produced by different team members.

Example: Why Might Anyone Create an Impediment?
The fourth question *am I going to create any blockers that might impede others?* is sometimes useful where one or more team members are creating a class or API which is relied upon by other members of the team. When changes are made to that API, this could potentially cause code already written by others to fail. In such cases, it is polite to warn people that the interface or API they use is changing.

13.3.1 Virtual Stand-Up Meetings

Where groups are working remotely or geographically distributed, a stand-up meeting can be conducted online. Obviously, given the choice, we'd all rather be in the same room at the same time. However, there are often lots of reasons why someone isn't able to physically be with the rest of the team. The ubiquity of video or audio conferencing facilities makes virtual team meetings more attractive than not having a meeting at all.

Partly online coordination meetings are common, that is, where one or two members of the team participate online, while the rest of the group gather around a Kanban board. If you are technical team member, you just need to answer your three questions when your turn comes, so that can work. In offshore development contexts, the team might be offshore, and the product owner is in a remote location (from the team's perspective) that is considered onshore. But if you are the product owner, you are a kind of observer anyway, so that does not matter so much.

However, being the only online participant in a meeting where everyone else is co-located is not fabulous. The solitary remote worker tends to feel left out of the discussion and often can't interject to make a comment. It is difficult to achieve a sense of team cohesion in this arrangement, trust is weak, and the risk of conflicts emerging is high.

13.3.2   *Kanban Boards*

Coordination meetings are usually held in front of a visual (often physical) display of project status. The idea is to make visual the team's efforts towards project goals. Kanban boards were mentioned in Sect. 10.2.1.

The Kanban board originates in the world of advanced manufacturing and just-in-time production emanating from the Japanese car industry. In its simplest form, it consists of three columns: *To Do*, *Doing* and *Done*. The requirements, features or, more likely, technical tasks identified in iteration planning are added to the board using sticky notes. Each sticky note represents a technical task. All the tasks start off in the *To Do* column. As the project progresses, the sticky notes all work their way over to the *Done* column. The sticky notes are usually moved during coordination meetings, as the status of an item changes. This gives a visually appealing sense of project progress. Each team member can see their effort as part of the wider range of team activities.

Online tools, such as Trello [1], can be used to support virtual teams using Kanban boards. This retains the visual illustration of project progress while enabling remote working. Tasks or user stories modelled using online Kanban boards can be embellished with acceptance test criteria and links to definitions of done.

13.4   Customer Demonstrations

A customer demonstration is where you demonstrate working code to your customer or client at the end of an iteration. Preparation for the customer demonstration requires the following steps:

- Scrum master arranges a convenient date and time with the product owner or client,
- Scrum master arranges a venue, which might be online of course,
- Scrum master makes sure that all the team members are available and aware of the time and venue,
- Scrum master makes sure you have the right technology to demonstrate the software (install and check the demonstration environment),
- Identify a team member to make notes during the customer demonstration,
- As a team, rehearse the demonstration, and make sure the demonstration runs smoothly and that any hand-off from one presenter to another is seemless,
- As a team, make sure you wear appropriate (usually smart casual or business) dress.

During the customer demonstration, the meeting agenda is as follows:

1. Introduce the purpose of the meeting,
2. Review the requirements you were supposed to implement,
3. Demonstrate each new feature of the software,

4. Review any requirements that you were unable to implement for any reason,
5. Collect and carefully record any feedback from the product owner or client.

An important benefit of the incremental development approach is the idea of getting feedback at intermediate stage of the project development process. Customers, clients or users (whichever most appropriately describes your situation) need to be able to see progress towards project completion and influence the direction of travel. If you are serious about software development, you genuinely want reassurance that the code you are writing is fit for purpose and meets the needs that have been identified.

It is the customer demonstration that offers both sides the opportunity for this feedback. You get reassurance from the customers that you are on the right track. And customers see evidence of progress towards the completed system. You do this by demonstrating each of the features, in turn, that have been implemented during the last iteration.

Demonstrate how each feature works and the defensive programming measures you have implemented. So, for example, where your software requires user input, you will show how the programme responds if the wrong type of information is provided. You may also demonstrate how the working software has benefited from testing and other quality assurance measures.

13.4.1 Retrospectives

Another important benefit of the incremental development approach is the idea of learning from each iteration. Committed software developers genuinely want to improve their team effectiveness. The retrospective is an opportunity to do that. Retrospectives are better than infrequent and ineffective end-of-project reviews.

In research interviews I've conducted with practitioners, one or two have said 'ohh, we don't bother with retros any more, we didn't find them useful. We kept going over the same ground'. That is a sign of a team with deep-rooted unresolved problems; a sign of a dysfunctional development process.

A healthy team uses retrospectives to experiment and learn. Try new ideas. Keep the ones that work. Discard ideas that don't work. And repeat. A simple way you can conduct a retrospective is for everyone in the team to think of:

- Three things that *worked well*, in the previous iteration,
- Three things that, as a team, you *could be doing better*,
- Three *improvement actions* for the next sprint.

The things that worked well are the good practices you want to keep doing. Then, the things you could be doing better are the areas for potential improvement. As a team, you look for consensus areas. Often you find several team members will point out similar areas where things could improve. Once you have identified three potential areas of improvement, from among the suggestions from team members, you can develop a set of actions. Actions are practical steps you can take to address improvement areas.

> **Example Action from a Retrospective**
>
> A common problem, for novice teams, is that stand-up meetings drift off-topic and consequently take too long. This can happen gradually, but becomes a problem for busy teams. For example, when someone raises an impediment in a stand-up meeting, a discussion starts on the causes or solution to that impediment.
>
> If long stand-up meetings are identified as an area for improvement by several people in the retrospective meeting, then the team might agree to be more disciplined about sticking to answering the three questions. The scrum master, who usually facilitates the stand-up meetings, should gently remind people to stay on-topic. Further, the scrum master convenes separate meetings, for those interested, to discuss the issues raised in the stand-up. At the next retrospective, we expect to see fewer concerns about long stand-up meetings.
>
> If the same issue were to remain a problem raised at the next retrospective, then some firmer stand-up facilitator is needed. Perhaps someone else should run the meeting with a stricter mandate to keep the meeting on-topic. The idea of the retrospective is that the team take collective responsibility for quality improvement over time.

13.5 Pair Programming

Pair programming is where two developers work together in a pilot-co-pilot configuration [4]. This is not a case of one person programming while the other rests or watches. Rather, it is that both developers are occupied on different activities during the development process.

In pair programming, one developer is more focused on low-level syntax and language mechanics. Usually, this developer has the keyboard and is actually typing source code.

While one developer is typing and thinking about syntax, the other is considering higher-level structure and readability. This second developer is focused on source code quality and acceptance testing.

Another common use of pair programming is for developing new talent. There is some evidence that novice team members operate at the level of the more experienced team member when working in pairs [2] and that pairs significantly outperform individuals [5]. Pair programming can be used to support new developers acquiring software skills for the first time. Or, pair programming support the induction of experienced software developers joining a team and learning to find their way around an existing code base. In either situation, the learner controls the keyboard. You don't learn much by merely watching an experienced hand. Obviously, the mentor adopts a warm, constructive and supportive demeanour.

13.6 Test-Driven Development

Test-driven development takes a counter-intuitive approach to software development in which automated tests are written before the code itself [3]. Developers extract the test criteria recorded against each requirement. These test criteria are then written into unit tests. The tests fail at first, when executed, because no code has been written. Then code is written to meet the requirements. One by one, the automated tests will pass. At the end of the process, code will have been written to pass all the tests.

So the general test-driven development cycle goes as follows [3]:

1. Write a test,
2. Make it run
3. Make it right.

Make it run means quickly filling in functionality to get tests to pass. *Make it right* means refactor the code into an elegant form, by removing duplication and simplifying, while still passing all the tests, of course.

The approach has been shown experimentally (albeit with student, rather than practitioner, subjects) to be less effective, in terms of defect reduction, than code inspections [6]. But, it is suggested test-driven development improves developer morale, since the conclusion of the development process is signified by passed tests.

13.7 Specialist Agile Ceremonies

There are some specialist ceremonies that development teams use, usually when things are not going well. Sometimes our initial estimates of a user story turn out to be wrong. Perhaps, as a development team, we misunderstood the requirement. Or, maybe implementation of the story turns out to be much more complicated than expected. Often, pair programming is enough to get us out of such a fix. However occasionally, a more dramatic solution is called for.

13.7.1 Spikes

A spike is where the estimate, for a requirement or technical task under development, proves to be inaccurate. This usually means some new, previously hidden, complexity associated with a requirement has emerged. We can mark the task on our Kanban board, re-estimate the effort required and re-prioritise. The advantage of treating the story as a spike is that we can remain committed to other stories in the sprint and do not get distracted with the troublesome one.

We might choose to park the story for a future sprint. But, this is undesirable, because we have failed to meet our commitment to the product owner or client. In consultation with our product owner, we might decide that the spike is too important to just park for a future sprint.

Having identified a story as a spike, we might also consider adding resources to that story. In this situation, quite a lot of teams use pair programming to resolve the issue. While, in the Extreme Programming method, it is recommended that developers use pair programming all the time [4], some practitioners prefer to use pair programming only under specific circumstances. A common, special case, use of pair programming is to address spikes.

Alternatively, we might reduce the priority of some other activity, so that we can resolve the spike. There are some other approaches to resolving spikes, such as swarm programming or even pulling in additional specialist support from outside the team.

13.7.2 Swarm Programming

In swarm programming, more than two developers work together. This can be useful if team members want to work together to tackle some new task or technology that no one has used before or where progress for the whole team is blocked by one particular problem that needs to be solved. The idea is that the swarm makes development quicker, and comes up with higher-quality solutions, than an individual or pair.

Usually swarm programming is used to tackle specific issues. For example, some teams use swarm programming to address a high-priority spike. Alternatively, a swarm might be used to achieve consensus on an architectural style.

13.7.3 Mob Programming

Mob programming takes the ideas of pair and swarm programming to the extreme. In mob programming, the whole team works together all the time. The team is co-located, working together at one computer performing all requirements, design and development activities. So, in mob programming, the team has workshops for defining stories, working with customers and designing, testing and deploying software.

13.8   Exercises

Now create a learning journal for Part III *Process*. You can use the learning journal to make notes on the things you learn from this part of the book. The journal should include a section for each book chapter. You can also use the learning journal for planning your future skills development.

Don't look at the hints, tips and solutions chapter, at this stage. First, complete an exercise (but still, do not look at the hints or tips). Next, reflect on the exercise. Then look at the hints, tips and advice in Sect. 13.9.

Exercise 13.1 (Learning Journal)

13.1 Write in your personal learning journal about what you have learned from Chap. 13. Briefly review the chapter now.

Exercise 13.2 (Sprint Planning Exercise)

13.2 As a group, practise conducting a sprint planning exercise. You will need to create technical tasks for each high-priority requirement. Estimate each requirement. Decide how many (and which) requirements you can accommodate in the next iteration. Make sure someone in the team has chosen tasks to work on. There is more detailed advice on how to conduct sprint planning in Sect. 13.9.

Exercise 13.3 (Stand-Up Meeting Exercise)

13.3 As a group, practise conducting a stand-up meeting. Make sure the meeting stays focused on project status. During the meeting, did you learn who is working on what? Make sure the meeting lasts no more than 15 minutes.

Exercise 13.4 (Customer Demonstration Exercise)

13.4 As a group, rehearse conducting a customer demonstration. Perhaps a colleague or friend can stand in for your client. You want to have done a previous, private, rehearsal of the demonstration, so you can advertise the new features of your software in a positive light. In your practice customer demonstration, record any constructive feedback you are given. Review all the feedback later, and action any comments you have been given.

Exercise 13.5 (Retrospective Exercise)

13.5 As a group, rehearse conducting a retrospective, at the end of an iteration. Each team member should:

- Write down three areas of good practice that the team should continue in future iterations,
- Write three potential areas for improvement.

Everyone shares their notes with the team, on a whiteboard, or virtual whiteboard perhaps. The scrum master then groups together the areas of good practice and improvement. Then, the scrum master groups together similar topics within the areas of good practice or improvement. Look for areas of consensus.

Now, having identified a shared set of (no more than three) areas for improvement, create a set of actions. These actions should be practical steps that the team can take to improve their work in the improvement areas.

Exercise 13.6 (Learning Journal)

13.6 Use your learning journal to reflect on the exercises you have completed. Think about what you have learned and make some notes.

13.9   Hints, Tips and Advice on Exercises

13.1 *Learning Journal*

In Chap. 13, we have discussed aspects of iteration planning, coordination meetings, customer demonstrations, pair programming, test-driven development and specialist ceremonies. Review the material in the chapter and write some notes about what you have learned.

13.2 *Sprint Planning Exercise*

The sprint planning process comprises four main activities:

- Expand requirements into technical tasks,
- Estimate requirements to see how many can be accommodated in the new iteration,
- Select requirements for inclusion in the new iteration,
- Ensure that all the requirements have been accepted by someone on the team.

Look at the high-priority requirements on your backlog. The prioritisation will have been done by the product owner. For each requirement, create the full set of technical tasks needed for implementation.

Now that you have a list of technical tasks for each requirement, you can more accurately estimate the effort needed to implement the requirement. Think about which method you want to use for estimation. Practise and rehearse using your chosen method on a toy example before you use it on a project. The purpose of estimating is to create an equitable allocation of work to team members and to ensure your team will not be over- (or under)-utilised during the next iteration.

Once estimation is complete, you can choose a specific set of requirements for the next iteration. This might be straightforward. Or, there may be some tasks forced upon by dependencies. So, you need to implement something that is only needed right now in order to finish something else. Or, you may need to pull up some smaller tasks because you do not have team capacity to undertake another large task. So, as you can see, there are some trade-offs here.

Finally, team members have to choose work tasks. Remember scrum master don't assign work. But they do need to ensure all tasks are assigned to someone. So some encouragement or cajoling might be needed to get all the tasks taken up by someone.

13.3 *Stand-Up Meeting Exercise*

Remember the stand-up meeting ground rules. Everyone should answer the following three (or four) questions: (1) what have I been doing since the last stand-up? (2) What will I be doing between now and the next stand-up? (3) Are there any impediments preventing me from making progress? And, maybe, (4) am I going to create any blockers that might impede others?

Listen carefully to the discussion. If anyone diverts onto other topics, make sure you make a note of the issue and set up a separate meeting for that discussion. Steer people (firmly, but politely) in the stand-up back onto the three questions.

13.4 *Customer Demonstration Exercise*

Make sure you have arranged a venue. Make sure that all the team members and product owner are available and aware of the time and venue. Introduce the purpose of the meeting and review the requirements you were supposed to implement. Demonstrate the features of the software. Review any requirements that you were unable to implement for any reason.

13.5 *Retrospective Exercise*

There are several ways of conducting retrospectives, but you might consider using the following steps:

- Everyone in the team writes three sticky notes: 'things we should continue to do'
- Collect all the sticky notes together on a blank whiteboard
- Everyone writes three sticky notes: 'potential areas for learning or improvement'
- Collect all the sticky notes together on a blank white board
- Spend a few minutes, as a group, reviewing all the sticky notes
- Try to collect the 'potential areas for learning or improvement' into groups or categories. Look for themes.
- Choose the top three 'potential areas for learning or improvement'. The top three are likely to be areas of consensus or at least mentioned on more than one sticky note.
- Create one action point for each of the top three 'potential areas for learning or improvement'. You should encourage implementation of the action point during the coming iteration.

13.10 Chapter Summary

In agile methods, the specific meetings teams use to develop software are often called ceremonies. I have described ceremonies used to start and finish iterations. This includes estimation and work allocation during iteration planning and kick-off. Demonstrations of working code provide opportunities for feedback and retrospectives and an important forum for team learning. I've also discussed ceremonies used during the iterations themselves, such as coordination meetings, pair programming and test-driven development. Kanban boards, whether physical or online, provide visibility to team members of project progress. Next, in Chap. 14, we'll explore the principles and ideas behind *lean* software development.

References

1. Atlassian: Trello (2019), https://trello.com
2. Balijepally, V., Mahapatra, R., Nerur, S., Price, K.H.: Are two heads better than one for software development? The productivity paradox of pair programming. MIS Quarterly 33(1), 91–118 (2009)
3. Beck, K.: Test Driven Development, 1st edn. Addison Wesley, Boston (Nov 2002)
4. Beck, K., Andres, C.: Extreme Programming Explained, 2nd edn. Addison Wesley, Boston, USA (Nov 2004)
5. Lui, K.M., Chan, K.C.C., Nosek, J.: The effect of pairs in program design tasks. IEEE Trans. Softw. Eng. 34(2), 197–211 (2008). https://doi.ieeecomputersociety.org/10.1109/TSE.2007.70755
6. Wilkerson, J.W., Nunamaker, J.F., Mercer, R.: Comparing the defect reduction benefits of code inspection and test-driven development. IEEE Trans. Softw. Eng. 38(3), 547–560 (2012). https://doi.ieeecomputersociety.org/10.1109/TSE.2011.46

Chapter 14
Lean

Abstract This chapter will introduce the concept of *lean* software development. The lean approach treats each user story or work item as an artefact flowing through a development process. Lean focuses on concepts such as value, waste, speed, people, knowledge and quality. We take a holistic view of the development life cycle, concentrating on maximising the efficient flow of work items. We also touch on the influential lean start-up model, an approach to starting a technology company using revenue (rather than investment) to support growth. There are many useful ideas in lean which we can apply alongside agile methods. Some teams view adopting lean as a natural progression once they have become proficient at agile.

14.1 Introduction

Lean concepts emerged in the just-in-time (or smart) manufacturing movement from Japan in the 1980s. In smart manufacturing, the ideas are about responsive production, low inventories and high quality. These ideas have proved very useful, when applied to software development.

Let's consider seven principles:

- Eliminate waste,
- Build quality in,
- Create knowledge,
- Defer commitment,
- Deliver fast,
- Optimise the whole,
- Respect people.

Eliminate waste, waste is anything that does not add value. We need a deep understanding of value, so we can remove anything superfluous. Waste is anything that does not add customer value or any form of delay. We'll come back to topic of waste in Sec. 14.3

© Springer Nature Switzerland AG 2022
J. M. Bass, *Agile Software Engineering Skills*,
https://doi.org/10.1007/978-3-031-05469-3_14

Build quality in, to achieve quality in software development, we take steps to avoid creating defects, rather than focus on issue tracking. It is still necessary to fix defects, but avoidance is better than cure.

Create knowledge, software development is a knowledge-creation activity. Requirements and designs can only really be validated when they are implemented as working code. We need to deeply learn about customer needs in order to fulfil them.

Defer commitment, it is tempting to make irreversible decisions early. But it is better to carefully consider options, experiment with alternatives and only make irreversible decisions when necessary.

Deliver fast, consider competing on time. Organisations that compete on time are often very efficient, because delays are often expensive.

Optimise the whole, we want to think of developing, testing and deploying features to clients as a holistic, end-to-end process. Any bottlenecks or impediments negatively affect the flow of requirements and features into products clients want to use.

Respect people, our goal is to help our team members build their expertise. We then want to support people using their skills and knowledge to make decisions.

These lean principles underpin our thinking when we adopt a continuous improvement approach.

14.1.1   Respecting People

I devoted the whole of Part I to the topic of people, their roles, membership of self-organising teams and managing other stakeholders in the process. In short, software development is a team sport. We need technical expertise, and we need an environment in which we can work together.

Management's objective is to coach and mentor staff members so that they acquire the skills and behaviours we need. Managers help people to develop. The model of management is a servant-leader approach. Managers provide the resources team members need to complete work items and offer support with learning new skills. Managers remove impediments that create inefficiencies in the development process.

Many lean organisations provide time for professional development. Perhaps half or 1 day per week is set aside for personal projects that can help team members acquire new skills and knowledge that can, in turn, help the organisation grow and improve. These projects can be used to learn entirely new techniques or to study exciting new technologies.

Just like in agile methods, the lean approach is dependent on the self-organising team. The self-organising team takes responsibility for delivering good-quality software. Team members assign themselves work items and commit to continuous improvement of quality. Over time, the team develops a collective responsibility for delivering good-quality code, on time.

Sometimes a team member may be keen to take on a stretch task, a work item that creates an opportunity to learn new skills. At other times, team members may be happy to exercise the skills they currently have. The point is that selecting work items empowers team members to have more control over their activities during the work day.

14.1.2 Create Knowledge

Lean proponents advocate a scientific approach to knowledge gathering. In lean, systematic data collection is used to inform empirical decision-making. Like many agile and lean approaches, knowledge gathering is cyclic.

A systematic knowledge gathering process involves [4]: problem definition, situation analysis, hypothesis creation, experimentation, result verification and standardisation.

Problem definition. When undertaking a cycle of knowledge gathering, it is important to make sure you focus on the real problem and not a symptom. Keep asking yourselves, as a team, what is the underlying cause of the issue you are trying to deal with. In other words, make sure you focus on a real and significant problem. Carefully define the problem, in terms of scope, parameters and time scales.

Situation analysis. Collect data, ideally based on measurements of your process, to provide evidence about the problem. We analyse aspects of our development process to understand the causes of the problem we have identified.

Hypothesis creation. A hypothesis is an untested explanation based on evidence. We want to create a testable hypothesis for the problem we have identified and using the evidence we have collected. The hypothesis aims to explain the problem. At this stage, we do not know, for sure, if the explanation is correct.

Experimentation. Experiments can now be conducted to test the hypothesis. We make changes to our working practices intended to address our chosen problem. We don't just changes things at random. The changes we make must be carefully calibrated so we can assess the consequences. Can evidence be gathered to confirm our hypothesis is correct? Or, is further work needed to create a new and better hypothesis?

Result verification. We perform analysis of our experiments. We want to confirm that our changes are creating the intended outcomes. We also need to check if there are any harmful unintended side effects. We can now be confident that our hypothesis has correctly explained our problem and that our changes and experiments have made an improvement to our process.

Standardisation. The follow-up to this knowledge gathering cycle is to make sure the new approach becomes routine and that the best practice is disseminated to others.

14.1.3   Build Quality In

A common goal, for advocates of lean, is to *strive for perfection*. We can think of quality assurance in two senses: prevention and detection of errors. Pair programming (see Sect. 13.5) and code reviews can help with prevention. Test-driven development (see Sect. 13.6) and test automation can help with detection. We'll talk more about automated testing in Chap. 16.

Our goal must be to use sensible coding standards and best practices [3], as discussed in Sect. 10.4.2, and to be alert for code smells [2] that might indicate future maintainability problems. We use appropriate folder and package structures to logically organise our source code. Source code is split into subsystems (perhaps layers or other moving parts) depending upon the architecture style we have selected; see Chap. 8. Further, in larger systems, some sensible organisation of functionality into groups might also be required.

Using good naming conventions helps with readability. We carefully choose meaningful names that convey the purpose of the source code element. Use naming styles that are consistent with language conventions and used uniformly. Removing dead code helps achieve simplicity. We avoid unused imports, variables, methods and classes. Any redundant code must be refactored.

We try to automate as much as possible. We like automated testing: unit, regression and acceptance testing. We also like version control as explained in Chap. 15. Frequent merging of branches helps to minimise and resolve inconsistencies. We will discuss continuous integration and DevOps in Chap. 21. Perhaps DevOps is too much for a student or novice project, but it's a good idea for mature commercial teams to consider. Automation helps us to apply policies consistently and repeatably. Manual processes are error prone and tend to get forgotten when teams are under pressure from tight deadlines.

Software tools to review code quality, such as SonarCloud [6], help us to identify potential problems early. We can run a quality test each time code is pushed to our main trunk in version control. A dashboard in SonarCloud then helps us identify issues and even gives advice on mitigation.

14.2   Value

Value is mainly considered in terms of monetary quantities. We want to focus our resources (often developer time) on the highest value activities. The highest value activities will change over time depending upon on state of the project and development life cycle and evolving client needs. Simply put, we want to maximise value.

The lean focus on value is about identifying where value is created in our development process. Some of our activities will create more value than others. We need to estimate the value generated by our activities in order to understand the value in our processes. We would certainly like to eliminate any of our activities that do not produce value at all.

14.2.1   Non-monetary Value

I like to think of value more broadly than money and identify other sources of value. For example, disaster recovery software is used to manage the logistics delivering emergency aid and relief. We might consider disaster recovery software value in terms of the number of lives saved. Environment mitigation software might be valued in terms of the number of habitats saved or restored. What better examples of value can there be? Consequently, it is legitimate to think beyond monetary value, if you are developing software in a commercial context or for a third-sector or non-governmental organisation.

14.2.2   Value Stream Mapping

Value stream mapping is a technique for identifying blockages and inefficiencies in your software development process. We need to list the stakeholders in our processes, the activities they perform and the dependencies between each activity. We can then estimate the value of each activity, to search sources of inefficiency. There is some advice and guidance on performing value stream mapping in Exercise 14.2.

14.2.3   Definition of Done

We need a set of (value) criteria for work items to move from one part of our value stream to the next. This might take the form of a checklist or some other set of criteria. For example, code ready for merging into the main trunk must have passed all unit tests and locally integrate with the code in the trunk without creating errors. Code ready for review must have passed unit tests and integration as well as static quality assurance tests and regression tests. Finally, in this example scenario, code might be ready for deployment only if:

- *Unit tests* have all been passed,
- *Code reviews* have been completed and any actions addressed,
- *Security tests* the full suite of security tests performed,
- *Code quality tests* have passed.

Some people use informal names to distinguish these stages of completion. Code ready for deployment is *done, done, done*. Code ready for review is *done, done*. Code ready for merging into a branch is simply *done*.

14.3 Waste

Imagine starting a stopwatch the moment an idea for a new software feature is identified. Then imagine stopping the stopwatch, the moment you get paid for that feature. Our goal is to minimise that time interval. What can you do to remove any activity that does not add value in that time interval? In manufacturing, seven sources of waste have been identified. These seven wastes have been translated into the software development context [4]; see Table 14.1.

Let's briefly consider each of these forms of waste.

14.3.1 Partially Done Work

Our overall objective is to get worthwhile features, deployed and used by paying clients as efficiently as possible. Any incomplete work *in the system* or under development is a source of waste from that perspective. We can explore some examples of partially done work.

Documentation that is missing code. Design documents and requirements specifications that have yet to be implemented represent a source of waste. These documents need to be prepared when they are needed not any earlier.

Code not checked into trunk. Code sitting in personal repositories that has yet to be *checked in* to the main repository is not adding value to the development process. We check in code frequently.

Untested code. Code can be tested at development time. Acceptance testing and code reviews should be conducted promptly. Untested code is not adding value to our product.

Table 14.1 Seven wastes in manufacturing and software development (Adapted from [4])

Manufacturing	Software development
In-process inventory	Partially done work
Over-production	Superfluous features
Extra processing	Rework
Transportation	Hand-offs
Motion	Task switching
Waiting	Delays
Defects	Defects

Undocumented code. Where external stakeholders require documentation, this needs to be produced promptly, ideally more or less concurrently with code development.

Undeployed code. Code that is checked in to the trunk and that has been reviewed, tested and approved can be deployed to clients promptly. Approved code needs to be deployed, to bring value to clients.

14.3.2   Superfluous Features

Historically, in software development, adding unnecessary features has been a major source of inefficiency. As a community, software developers have been too enthusiastic to anticipate customer needs by adding features that are *obviously* going to be useful, when, in fact, those features are not needed, after all. We have sometimes been wrong in our attempts to guess requirements resulting in unnecessary complexity and bloated products. A better posture is to not add features, if there is any doubt about their utility. We must only develop features when the need is current and obvious.

14.3.3   Rework

Rework is where we have to recreate something because we didn't do it correctly the first time. Rework (bad) is not the same as refactoring or feature enhancement (often good). Rework means doing something again, which is obviously a form of waste.

14.3.4   Hand-Offs

Hand-offs, where an incomplete work item is passed onto someone else, result in lost tacit knowledge about the task. This lost tacit knowledge must either be re-learned by the work item recipient or, perhaps worse still, they proceed without the benefit of the tacit knowledge potentially resulting in defects. It is healthy to minimise hand-offs, which is an important justification for self-organising teams comprising people with the full range of required skills.

14.3.5   Task Switching

Knowledge work, such as software development, requires deep concentration. Switching from one task to another is distracting and causes waste. Having multiple activities on-the-go simultaneously means that you spend more time resetting your mind than actually productively working. Multi-tasking three different 1-week tasks will take longer than working on the three 1-week tasks sequentially.

14.3.6   Delays

Delays and waiting time are obviously undesirable in an agile development process. Some of the most significant waiting times occur before we even start development, such as:

1. Waiting for project approval,
2. Waiting for people to be assigned to the project,
3. Waiting for assigned people to become available.

A common problem faced by developers is waiting for sufficient information to be able to develop code. This can be because insufficient effort went into user story elaboration or because clients assume it is enough to describe desirable features only in broad terms. Scrum masters are supposed to remove impediments, such as waiting for information, but disengaged clients can undermine agile processes.

14.3.7   Defects

We try to minimise defects in our code. The longer a defect exists in our code, the more expensive it is to fix. Further, if a defect reaches customers, it damages our reputation for quality as well. We use frequent automated unit and acceptance testing as well as code reviews to try to catch defects early, ideally during the development cycle.

14.4   Speed

In lean, speed in delivering value to clients is a consequence of assiduously removing waste. Speed is the absence of waste [4]. By combining efficient development processes, with automated testing (see Chap. 16) and deployment (see Chap. 21), we can ensure each iteration rapidly creates production code.

Short delivery cycles increase learning. You are forced to find ways to simplify installation and product upgrades, because you plan to do those activities frequently. Your quality assurance processes are designed to be performed within iterations, not after iterations have finished.

Analysis of queueing theory suggests that to reduce average cycle times, we should 'even out the arrival of work', 'minimise number of things in process', 'minimise size of things in process', 'establish a regular cadence', 'limit work to capacity' and 'use pull scheduling'.

Even out the arrival of work. It is difficult to control project approval processes or sales of bespoke software. However, it is undesirable if requests are queued for months at a time. We strive to maintain a steady flow of work. Allowing big product backlogs to build up is not ideal.

Minimise number of things in process. I've already suggested that task switching is inefficient. Work-in-progress (WIP) limits are used to make process bottlenecks more visible. This enables more precise matching of resources to demand.

Minimise size of things in process. It is a difficult discipline, but reducing the size of work items is a good tactic for reducing average cycle times. Try to split work items up so that as many as possible are small.

Establish a regular cadence. Iterations provide a valuable insight into the productivity of teams. You learn how much can be accomplished and build confidence in estimation. This means it is easier to make promises to clients and then honour them.

Limit work to capacity. Working over capacity means people work long hours and consequently get tired and careless. Short-term over-capacity working can be useful, even desirable. But as a long-term strategy, it is not wise.

Use pull scheduling. Work items can be pulled from a backlog into development and production, as a consequence of some external demand. This is usually established through prioritisation of the product backlog. We pull high-priority items first. The point is to pull according to customer need.

In summary, problems in our development process slow down our cycle times. Tackling these inefficiencies one by one, using a continuous improvement process, helps us to streamline our software production processes.

14.4.1 Work-in-Progress Limits

As mentioned, WIP limits provide a mechanism for controlling the number of work items being processed. Establishing WIP limits is a policy decision that can help us manage the flow of items through our work processes.

The WIP limit is derived from the capacity of the team to perform a particular task. When looked at from this perspective, what is the point of giving a team more work than they have the capacity to perform? The WIP limit provides a mechanism for making the team's capacity more visible.

As part of creating a WIP limit, it might be desirable to create a buffer (the buffer might be shown on a Kanban board, for example) for items blocked by the WIP limit. The buffer can be useful for accommodating small fluctuations in arrival rate of work items. The buffer also has an important role in making visual an unhealthy build-up of work items in a buffer. Having identified a work item build-up in our buffer, we can add resources to clear the backlog or analyse our processes to better understand our work item flow. For example, we might use a developer swarm, as a temporary fix, to empty the buffer; see Sect. 13.7.2.

14.4.2   *Work Item Variability*

A major challenge for teams seeking to reduce cycle times is variability in the size and complexity of work items. Building new features is fun and attractive; enhancing the source code in existing features is less so. New features tend to be large work items. Feature enhancements vary in size.

Refactoring to simplify our code base is important. Refactoring, as we've said, is making changes without affecting programme outputs. Refactoring is to help with maintainability and readability of source code, but is difficult to estimate. Often refactoring is overlooked by product owners when they prioritise work.

The effort, required for defect fixing, is difficult to estimate; by the time you've figured out the problem (the time-consuming and difficult part), implementing the solution is often relatively straightforward. Consequently, some teams don't perform estimation on maintenance tasks; they view it as waste [1].

Teams estimate the effort needed to create new features, but don't waste their time estimating defect fixes and minor feature enhancements. Each iteration comprises a blend of new features and maintenance tasks. Team members and product owners collaborate to achieve the right blend over time.

In larger-scale projects (see Chap 18), some teams are solely dedicated to maintenance tasks: bug fixing and minor feature enhancements. But it seems rather uninspiring to be limited to maintenance tasks, if another team gets to build all the new features.

An approach I like, which is dependent upon the number and size of work items arriving, is for teams to perform a maintenance iteration from time to time. Perhaps every third iteration is focused on defect fixing and minor feature enhancements. The other iterations are (largely) focused on new feature development. This way, everyone gets to share the full range of work items.

14.5   Lean Start-Up

Lean thinking has also been influential among technology entrepreneurs, notably through the work of Eric Ries [5]. This approach advocates a fierce focus on experimenting and monitoring customer reaction. The idea is to get early feedback from developing products and business models with minimum investment, by using prototypes or mock-ups to assess market reaction. The goal is to generate revenues and continue experimenting to maximise income. Consequently, this model focuses on attracting paying customers, rather than obtaining investment in an untested idea. Three important concepts of lean start-up ethos are bootstrapping, minimum viable product and pivot.

14.5.1   Bootstrapping

The lean start-up model focuses on generating revenue, early in the business development process. The approach advocates testing ideas, through revenue generation, before making substantial investments. Some people call this *bootstrapping*, because it is an attempt to pull the business up by its own bootstraps. The *bootstrap* approach is a reaction to the focus on raising investment that was popular during the *.com* (pronounced 'Dot Com') bubble earlier in the century.

14.5.2   Minimum Viable Product

The idea of a minimum viable product is to make tangible the essence of a solution, with the least possible investment of time and resources. Then, the minimum viable product can be used to test concept viability with potential customers. The minimum viable product's purpose is to support short cycles of evaluation with each new feature.

The definition of *essence*, in the minimum viable product, is the central challenge. What set of features are needed to make the solution work? And, by implication, what features are not necessary? We need to identify only the essential features, because we don't want to invest time and resources on superfluous features.

The minimum viable product typically includes end-to-end information flows and hence requires simple interfaces to cooperating subsystems. Sometimes it is helpful to think of the minimum viable product as a skeleton of the system or core solution.

14.5.3   Pivot

If our minimum viable product is not energising potential customers, we may decide our solution idea is not as promising as we hoped. This may cause us to pivot, or change direction, towards a variation of our solution idea. In a sense, the minimum viable product failure has worked perfectly. We have not invested heavily, or 'bet the house', on an idea that is not going to work.

The pivot may be a rather dramatic change of direction. The solution may serve a different market or perform a different function, than our original idea. A new minimum viable product needs to be constructed and further experiments performed. Many technology start-ups have gone through the experience of a pivot towards a different idea to their original concept.

14.6   Exercises

Now for some exercise, you can try to learn more about the topics covered in Chap. 14. Complete an exercise and then you can look at the hints and tips in Sect. 14.7.

Exercise 14.1 (Learning Journal)

14.1 For this first exercise, make a few notes in your learning journal on lean process from Chap. 14.

Exercise 14.2 (Value Stream Mapping Exercise)

14.2 As a group, practise conducting a value stream mapping exercise. You will need to have an existing development process that you can analyse.

- Identify stakeholders, or actors, involved in the development process,
- List the activities performed by each actor or stakeholder,
- Determine the dependencies between activities performed.

Now you need to move into a research phase. You need to gather data on each activity. You are seeking to estimate, on average, how long each activity takes to perform. By measuring effort expended on each activity, you can start to identify inefficiencies in your development process. There is more advice on how to conduct value stream mapping in Sect. 14.7.

Exercise 14.3 (Seven Wastes Exercise)

14.3 Think about the seven sources of waste: partially done work, superfluous features, rework, hand-offs, task switching, delays and defects. Which is creating the worst problems in your team? What single thing can you do to substantially reduce that source of waste?

Exercise 14.4 (Handling Requests Exercise)

14.4 How many items are in your overall product backlog? At what rate do items arrive and get completed? How long will it take to complete the current backlog? Do you have items in the backlog that will never get completed?

Exercise 14.5 (Knowledge Gathering Exercise)

14.5 What is the biggest problem that your team faces? Use the knowledge gathering cycle: problem definition, situation analysis, hypothesis creation, experimentation, result verification and standardisation. Experiment with solutions.

Exercise 14.6 (Cycle Time Exercise)

14.6 Think about the ways to reduce cycle time: even out work arrival rates, minimise the number of in-progress items, minimise the size of work items, establish a regular cadence, introduce work-in-progress limits (according to capacity), and use pull scheduling. Conduct experiments to reduce cycle time, by tackling the most promising approach.

Exercise 14.7 (Story Test-Driven Development Exercise)

14.7 Facilitate a discussion in your team. What is the difference between story test-driven development and unit test-driven development? Discuss the advantages and disadvantages of each. Should you be using story test-driven development? Why?

Exercise 14.8 (Learning Journal)

14.8 Reflect on the exercises you have completed from Chap. 14. Think about what you have learned and make some notes in your learning journal.

14.7 Hints, Tips and Advice on Exercises

14.1 *Learning Journal*

In Chap. 14, we have described lean value, waste, speed and start-up. Review these topics and write some notes about what you have learned.

14.2 *Value Stream Mapping Exercise*

Create cost estimates for the different activities in your development process.

You might put together a rough and ready swimlane diagram of your development process, like the one in Fig. 14.1. You can then estimate costs of the ceremonies and artefacts in your process. Some items will be estimated per product or iteration and some per feature. This approach might reveal potential areas of process refinement.

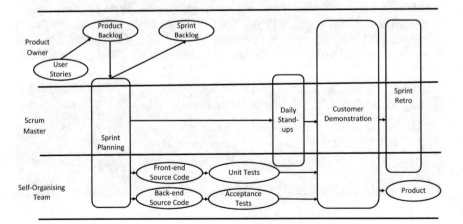

Fig. 14.1 Simple process swimlane

14.3 *Seven Wastes Exercise*

I suggest you use a swimlane diagram, such as the one in Fig. 14.1, as a starting point. Create an inventory of the sources of waste in your process. Choose the most egregious source of waste and experiment with steps towards elimination.

14.4 *Handling Requests Exercise*

What does your inventory of current requests look like? If you are over-whelmed, maybe it is time to build a business case for funding an additional team.

Do you suffer from a constant stream of emergency work items? What is the cause of these requests? What proportion are caused by defects in your team's code? What proportion are feature enhancements? Do they emanate from specific clients or user communities?

14.6 *Cycle Time Exercise*

How long does it *really* take you to deliver a feature? From 'concept to cash' as the Poppendiecks put it [4]. The true duration will likely shock you, if you have not thought about it before. You should be conducting experiments to reduce this duration.

14.8 Chapter Summary

In this chapter, we have explored a set of eight lean principles: *eliminate waste, build quality in, create knowledge, defer commitment, deliver fast, respect people, optimise the whole* and *eliminate waste*. We have investigated in more detail the lean concepts of *value, waste, speed, people, knowledge* and *quality*. Value and value stream mapping invite us to understand inefficiencies in our processes. Waste is anything that does not add value to our product, including delays and superfluous activities. When you tirelessly work to eliminate waste, you will likely achieve much faster delivery of value. When we say speed, we really mean the need to minimise development cycle times. This is a perspective on maximising work flow though our process. Lean proponents advocate a systematic and scientific approach to knowledge gathering. Experiments are conducted to test hypotheses aimed at improving the efficiency of development processes. When using a lean approach, we focus on quality. We aim to prevent, as well as detect errors in our products.

The lean start-up ethos is used to create new technology businesses, particularly in the software sector. The lean start-up approach focuses on (1) bootstrapping, to attract revenue rather than investment; (2) minimum viable product, as a vehicle for cheaply testing new ideas; and (3) pivot, a recognition that changes in direction might be needed along the way. Next, in Chap. 15, the focus is on using version control to establish a revision history for your software source code.

References

1. Anderson, D.J.: Kanban. Blue Hole Press (2010)
2. Fowler, M., Beck, K., Brant, J., Opdyke, W., Roberts, D.: Refactoring: Improving the Design of Existing Code, 1st edn. Addison Wesley, Reading, MA (Jun 1999)
3. Martin, R.: Clean Code: A Handbook of Agile Software Craftsmanship, 1st edn. Prentice Hall, Upper Saddle River, NJ (Aug 2008)
4. Poppendieck, M., Poppendieck, T.: Implementing Lean Software Development: From Concept to Cash. Addison Wesley (Sep 2006)
5. Reis, E.: The Lean Startup: How Constant Innovation Creates Radically Successful Businesses. Portfolio Penguin (2011)
6. SonarCloud: Automatic code review, testing, inspection & auditing (2021). https://sonarcloud. io/

Chapter 15
Version Control

Abstract Version control software tools provide content management services for source code. They offer a searchable change history and allow us to archive and restore code fragments, as we add new features to our software. Version control gives us a historic database of our system as we develop. We can use version control locally, when we are working alone. Moreover, version control really comes into its own when we work with others in a group. For team working, we can use shared source code repositories. In this chapter, we will explore simple version control use cases, such as staging and committing files. Then we will explore shared repository techniques like cloning, checkout, merging and so on. These techniques will enable you to share the new features you create with others. In turn, you will be able to learn how to incorporate their features into your code.

15.1 Introduction

Version control is about solving three main problems: creating change records, storing the changes we make to our evolving software as well as sharing and integrating code with others. I suggest you start by learning how to manage changes in your own code first. You can then learn how to share your own software and download code written by others.

15.2 Content Management

A version control system is used to record a copy of files as you make changes over time. We most often think of version control being used to record the evolution of computer software source code. But version control can actually be used for any computer files. Indeed, I used a version control system to keep a record of changes and create a backup file archive during the development of this book.

As the software you create becomes more complex, using a version control system is a very wise thing to do. Version control can help you to protect yourself

© Springer Nature Switzerland AG 2022
J. M. Bass, *Agile Software Engineering Skills*,
https://doi.org/10.1007/978-3-031-05469-3_15

Fig. 15.1 Local version
control

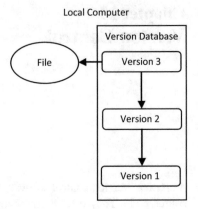

against lost files or revert to an earlier version when new ideas or features that
you add to software don't work out. Version control allows you to revert files to
a previous state. You can also use version control to easily revert an entire project
to a previous state. You can use version control on your local computer, as shown
in Fig. 15.1. You can store a snapshot of your system, as it evolves, keeping track of
changes as you go.

You have to initialise the version control database, and you have to remember to
store and document the snapshots as you go. But in return for this discipline, you
get much more control and access to a range of features you don't get if you simply
archive files to a backup storage device or a cloud server.

15.2.1   Create a Local Git Repository

Let's try this out for ourselves. I've chosen to use a version control system called git
[1]. Others are available. First make sure git is installed on your computer. Open a
command window and type this:

Check Git Installed Version

```
C:\folder>git --version
```

If git is installed, you will see a version number. If not, you will need to download
and install git in a manner appropriate for your operating system [5]. I have chosen
to use a command window for these exercises. I prefer to see exactly what is
happening, which can sometimes be obscured by graphical environments. Assuming

git is installed and running, create a folder and initialise a git repository on that folder, like this:

Initialise Git in Folder

```
C:\folder>mkdir git-test
C:\folder>cd git-test
C:\folder\git-test>git init
```

Depending on your host operating system, if you do a standard directory listing, like this...

MS Windows Command Window Directory Listing

```
C:\folder\git-test>dir
```

...nothing seems to have changed. That is because git has created a hidden folder in the current directory. You can see this, in MS Windows 10, for example, by typing this:

MS Windows Command Window Full Directory Listing

```
C:\folder\git-test>dir /a
```

You will see a hidden folder, as shown in Fig. 15.2. Git uses that hidden folder to keep copies of your files as you make changes. We don't need to worry ourselves about the internals of how git does this.

Fig. 15.2 File listing showing git hidden folder

```
Directory of C:\folder\git-test

09/03/2022  06:57    <DIR>          .
09/03/2022  06:57    <DIR>          ..
09/03/2022  06:57    <DIR>          .git
              0 File(s)              0 bytes
```

15.3   Source Code History

Now, let's work through an exercise of creating a change history for some of our own code. We can create some example files to be archived using our version control system. Use a text editor to create three files:

- MyFirstFile.txt,
- MySecondFile.txt,
- AFileIDoNotCareAbout.txt

You can put a sentence text into each file, as follows:

- MyFirstFile.txt, 'here is some text',
- MySecondFile.txt, 'this is some other text',
- AFileIDoNotCareAbout.txt, 'some unimportant text'.

Before we do anything else, what does the git version control system think is happening? We can run the `git status` command, like this:

Folder Git Status

```
C:\folder\git-test>git status
```

The output of the `git status` command is shown in Fig. 15.3. Notice that the files we created are listed in red. Git even tells us what we need to do, if we want to include the files in our version control repository.

```
C:\folder\git-test>git status
On branch master

No commits yet

Untracked files:
  (use "git add <file>..." to include in what will be committed)

        AFileIDoNotCareAbout.txt
        MyFirstFile.txt
        MySecondFile.txt

nothing added to commit but untracked files present (use "git add" to track)
```

Fig. 15.3 Using the *git status* command

```
C:\folder\git-test>git status
On branch master

No commits yet

Changes to be committed:
  (use "git rm --cached <file>..." to unstage)

        new file:   MyFirstFile.txt
        new file:   MySecondFile.txt

Untracked files:
  (use "git add <file>..." to include in what will be committed)

        AFileIDoNotCareAbout.txt
```

Fig. 15.4 Using the 'git status' command to show two staged files

15.3.1 Stage Files for Inclusion in the Version Control Repository

We need to run the git add command for each file.

Staging Files

```
C:\folder\git-test>git add MyFirstFile.txt
C:\folder\git-test>git add MySecondFile.txt
C:\folder\git-test>git status
```

The output of the git status command is a bit different this time, as shown in Fig. 15.4. We can now see the two files we *added* are shown in green. Technically, these files are *staged*, which means they are ready to be put in the version control repository. The staged files are not in the version control repository, yet. They are only ready to be put into the repository.

Staging allows us to prepare some files to go into version control and ignore some others. This way we can separately track changes we make for different purposes. We are not forced to put everything in version control at the same time.

15.3.2 Commit Files into the Version Control Repository

To put the staged files into the version control repository, we must perform a git commit operation. The git commit is followed, in this example, by the -m

```
C:\folder\git-test>git commit -m"files created with initial text"
[master (root-commit) 5ee0031] files created with initial text
 2 files changed, 2 insertions(+)
 create mode 100644 MyFirstFile.txt
 create mode 100644 MySecondFile.txt
```

Fig. 15.5 Initial 'git commit' command output

```
C:\folder\git-test>git status
On branch master
Untracked files:
  (use "git add <file>..." to include in what will be committed)

        AFileIDoNotCareAbout.txt

nothing added to commit but untracked files present (use "git add" to track)
```

Fig. 15.6 Status output after initial 'git commit' command

option to accept a message parameter. The -m option is followed by the text string "files created with initial text" of the message.

Git Commit Example; part 1

```
C:\...>git commit -m "files created with initial text"
```

The output can be seen in Fig. 15.5. Notice that the two files have been created (in the version control repository) and that the message from the git commit command is reproduced.

We can run the git status command again and see what git 'thinks' is happening. The git status is shown in Fig. 15.6.

Notice that git is not *tracking* the file AFileIDoNotCareAbout.txt because we didn't use the git add command on that file. That file is being ignored by git. Files that are not staged are not added to the version control repository.

Now you can use the text editor to add some new text to the *first file* and do a new git commit. Let's also delete the *unimportant* file, like this:

Fig. 15.7 Status output after
the second commit

```
C:\folder\git-test>git status
On branch master
nothing to commit, working tree clean
```

Git Commit Example; part 2

```
C:\folder\git-test>git add MyFirstFile.txt
C:\folder\git-test>git commit -m "first file changed"
C:\folder\git-test>del AFileIDoNotCareAbout.txt
C:\folder\git-test>git status
```

After running the final `git status` command, you will see something like the output in Fig. 15.7.

15.3.3   Making and Removing a Change

Let's illustrate how version control can help you recover from mistakes [6]. We'll deliberately add some erroneous text to our second text file, using a text editor, to illustrate the idea. In our moment of madness, we figure the text in the second file is fine, so let's commit that, like this:

Git Commit Example; part 3

```
C:\folder\git-test>git add MySecondFile.txt
C:\folder\git-test>git commit -m "error in second file"
C:\folder\git-test>git status
```

Oh no! Now, let's imagine we realise we have committed a file with errors. No matter. We can just, in this example scenario, revert to out earlier commit.

Now, we can use the `git log` command to view the commit history of our work so far. Have a look at Fig. 15.8. You can see the three commit messages and that each commit has a unique reference number. A simple, and perhaps rather crude, way to remove the text we just added to the second text file is to use the `git revert` command. The `git revert` offers several options, but in this example, we will simply throw away the last commit, like this:

```
C:\folder\git-test>git log
commit f4e490718ae52ca31719f6aa131aa097e95c4633 (HEAD -> master)
Author: Julian Bass <j.bass@salford.ac.uk>
Date:   Wed Mar 9 09:19:42 2022 +0000

    error in second file

commit d696510c4657f9947224ca2990ce7d6cd40173bc
Author: Julian Bass <j.bass@salford.ac.uk>
Date:   Wed Mar 9 09:16:47 2022 +0000

    first file changed

commit 5ee0031b855c8ca0988d69f78df712d288b5effe
Author: Julian Bass <j.bass@salford.ac.uk>
Date:   Wed Mar 9 07:30:51 2022 +0000

    files created with initial text
```

Fig. 15.8 Git log output after the third commit

Remove Last Git Commit

```
C:\folder\git-test>git revert HEAD
C:\folder\git-test>git log
```

Now when we look at the output from the git log command, we can see that a new commit has been added that reverses our previous commit, as shown in Fig. 15.9, and removes the erroneous text we had added to our second file.

15.4   Source Code Remote Archiving

Having learned some skills about using git to create a change history for some of our own code, we can now learn the skills we need to share code with others.

15.4.1   Version Control Remote Server Archiving

While using a local version control system to manage your content makes sense, adding a remote server offers a higher level of reliability. In the previous section, we created a local git repository, so we don't need to do that again. What we need to do though is:

```
C:\folder\git-test>git log
commit e8531ea44a5a1913a2fb856f7baba04fed95a26b (HEAD -> master)
Author: Julian Bass <j.bass@salford.ac.uk>
Date:   Wed Mar 9 09:26:45 2022 +0000

    Revert "error in second file"

    This reverts commit f4e490718ae52ca31719f6aa131aa097e95c4633.

commit f4e490718ae52ca31719f6aa131aa097e95c4633
Author: Julian Bass <j.bass@salford.ac.uk>
Date:   Wed Mar 9 09:19:42 2022 +0000

    error in second file

commit d696510c4657f9947224ca2990ce7d6cd40173bc
Author: Julian Bass <j.bass@salford.ac.uk>
Date:   Wed Mar 9 09:16:47 2022 +0000

    first file changed
```

Fig. 15.9 Git log output (partial) after reverting the third commit

- create an account on github [2],
- create a repository on GitHub, using your GitHub account.

I called my remote GitHub repository git-test to match the local folder name I chose. Then, you can link your local repository to your remote repository, as follows:

Setup Remote GitHub Repository

```
C:\...>git remote add origin...
    ...https://github.com/<your username>/git-test.git
C:\...>git push -u origin master
C:\...>git status
```

If everything worked, the final git status command should show you that the local repository is up to date and that is linked to origin, which is the name we gave to the remote repository on GitHub. The GitHub approach to authentication has changed over time. At the time of writing, access tokens are needed. You create an access token, copy it and then use it, in place of a password, through your command line. Don't worry; there are instructions about how to set this up, online [4].

Now each time you make changes, you have to remember to stage any files you have changed, commit the changes and push the changes to your remote server, like this:

Commit and Push (Archive) Code to Remote Repository

```
C:\folder\git-test>git add -A
C:\folder\git-test>git commit -m "describe changes"
C:\folder\git-test>git push
```

15.5   Source Code Sharing

As we have seen, modern version control systems, like git, support integration with remote servers. By using a combination of local and remote version control systems, known as distributed version control, you can share source code within a team in an orderly manner. In this way, a team member can work on a specific feature locally, which can then be shared with other members of the team using the remote server, as shown in Fig. 15.10.

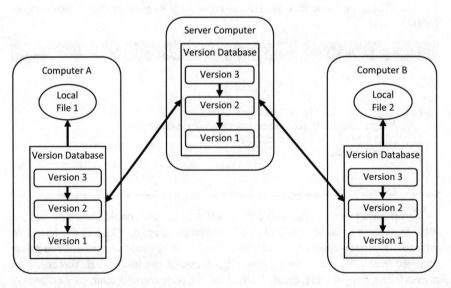

Fig. 15.10 Distributed version control

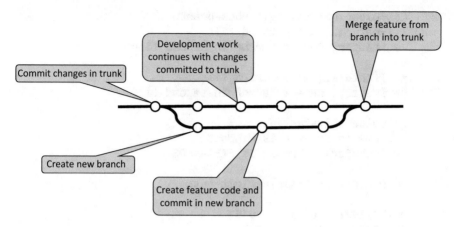

Fig. 15.11 Creating a feature branch

15.5.1 Trunk and Branches

We now have to get to grips with another new idea: branching. Branches are separate lines of development within your project. You can think of branches as development *topics*, *features* or *versions*. Branches can live for a long time, or can be rather temporary, depending on your project needs.

For example, say you release *version 1.1* of your project to some customers. But now you want to work on *version 1.2*. So you can create branches for versions 1.1 and 1.2; you can then decide to leave version 1.1 alone, in case you need to go back and investigate any bug fixes there later. You can safely work on *version 1.2* without affecting *version 1.1*. Branches to support releases (such as versions 1.1 and 1.2 for example) tend to live on for a long time.

Alternatively, maybe you want to add a new feature to your software, but you are not sure exactly how it is going to work. Then you need to create a new branch for the new feature, which you can work on separately, without disrupting the rest of the code base, as shown in Fig. 15.11. Branches for new features tend to get merged back into the main code base (often known as the trunk).

Version control systems, such as git, provide a lot of features for creating, merging and managing branches. But don't get too carried away. We don't want dozens of branches in our projects. We'll soon lose track of what on earth is going on. Here is an example of creating a branch, pushing to the remote repository and switching between branches locally:

```
C:\folder\git-test>git show-branch
* [feature1] added third file
 ! [master] Revert "error in second file"
--
*   [feature1] added third file
*+ [master] Revert "error in second file"
```

```
C:\folder\git-test>dir
 Volume in drive C is Windows
 Volume Serial Number is FA85-AE0B
```

```
 Directory of C:\folder\git-test
```

```
09/03/2022  10:11    <DIR>          .
09/03/2022  10:11    <DIR>          ..
09/03/2022  09:14             43 MyFirstFile.txt
09/03/2022  09:26             23 MySecondFile.txt
09/03/2022  10:11             27 MyThirdFile.txt
               3 File(s)             93 bytes
```

Fig. 15.12   Directory listing of feature1 branch in git

Git Branch Example, Part 1

```
C:\folder\git-test>git branch feature1
C:\...>git checkout feature1
\* use editor to put text in third file */
C:\...>git add -A
C:\...>git commit -m "added third file"
C:\...>git push --set-upstream origin feature1
C:\...>git show-branch
C:\...>dir
C:\...>git checkout master
C:\...>dir
```

The first directory listing is shown in Fig. 15.12. You can see the third file that you added; mine has the unimaginative title of MyThirdFile.txt. Now, for this example, when you switch back the master branch, what happens to that third file? Remember that the idea of branches is to allow separate lines of development to be performed without interfering with each other.

The second directory listing is shown in Fig. 15.13. As you might have guessed, that third file has disappeared. The third file exists in the feature1 branch and not in the master branch.

```
C:\folder\git-test>git checkout master
Switched to branch 'master'

C:\folder\git-test>dir
 Volume in drive C is Windows
 Volume Serial Number is FA85-AE0B

 Directory of C:\folder\git-test

09/03/2022  10:13    <DIR>          .
09/03/2022  10:13    <DIR>          ..
09/03/2022  09:14                43 MyFirstFile.txt
09/03/2022  09:26                23 MySecondFile.txt
               2 File(s)             66 bytes
```

Fig. 15.13 Directory listing of master branch in git

As I mentioned, sometimes we want long-lived branches; branches that live forever. But sometimes the whole point of the branch is to create a new feature to be implemented into the main trunk of code. In this case, we need tools that allow us to join branches together:

Git Branch Example, Part 2

```
C:\...>git checkout master
C:\...>git merge feature1
C:\...>git commit -m "added feature1 to master"
C:\...>git push
C:\...>git show-branch
C:\...>git branch -d feature1
C:\...>git push
C:\...>git show-branch
```

In this simple example, the git merge feature1 command works without any problem. We can then remove the branch that is no longer needed with the git branch -d feature1 command.

The git merge, in this simple example, went well because we were simply adding a new file into the code trunk on the master branch. Things get a bit more complicated when the code or text we are merging goes into one file. Thankfully, git has been well-designed with many tools to support merging. For example, you can explore the changes made to files by using the git diff command.

So far, the merging we have been doing is local. It is quite useful to be able to create local branches, merge and delete them. But, what about picking up code written by someone else? What we really want to have is an orderly way to allow different team members to create features and then, once the features are working and tested, integrate them into a shared trunk. A simple way to achieve this is to use feature branches and the remote GitHub server.

One person can create a new branch; let's call it feature1. That person downloads the main trunk from the GitHub repository and works on feature1 locally. In the meantime, another person can create a new branch; let's call it feature2. That person also downloads the main trunk from the GitHub repository and works on feature2 locally to them.

After completing their work, the first person merges their feature1 code with the main trunk. That main trunk now includes feature1. Sometime later, the second person merges their feature2 branch with the new main trunk on the GitHub repository. The main trunk now includes both feature1 and feature2. However, while they are working on the branches locally, feature1 and feature2 are kept separate from each other.

While the feature branch technique is conceptually simple and elegant, it can encourage people to work independently for long periods of time. Imagine you work on feature1 or feature2 for a few hours or even a day or two, not much harm is done when you merge that feature with the main trunk. But, what happens if you work on a feature for several weeks or months? Maybe there will have been major changes to the main trunk that make merging a complicated nightmare. To avoid this, some people suggest working locally on new features, but keep them in the same main truck branch and keep merging frequently. As you add new files, they get added to the main trunk every day.

Caution!

It is potentially damaging to merge any feature to the trunk on the remote GitHub repository. We always download the trunk to a local repository. We can resolve any merge conflicts, before then pushing the merged code back to the remote repository. It is dangerous to resolve merge conflicts on the remote server. You can overwrite or lose source code that is already there.

In summary, to add new code to our repository, we:

1. use a git pull command to get the main trunk from the remote onto the local repository,
2. git merge the main trunk source code with our local new feature and resolve any merge conflicts,
3. git push the merged source code back on the remote GitHub repository.

If you fail to follow this three-step (pull, merge, push) process, you are asking for trouble. This is important!

As I've mentioned, branches are very useful where we want to keep a frozen copy of a source code release. Let's say we complete version 2.1 of our software system and we want to start work on version 2.2. We can create a new branch, dedicated to the version 2.1 release. We can then version control that branch, with defect fixes and feature enhancements, without worrying about new features being added on the main branch. When version 2.2 is released, we can create a new branch for that release as well. We can repeat this cycle for each new release, knowing that we have a separate version control history for each release.

15.6 Exercises

For learning purposes, it is good to do these exercise activities with unimportant files, because you can learn about the git commands and the use of local and remote repositories without worrying about losing or overwriting source code. Actually, merge conflicts are often easily resolved, but still best avoided if possible. Occasionally, merge conflicts within the same file can be tricky to resolve. There is some advice on the exercises in Sect. 15.7.

Exercise 15.1 (Learning Journal)

15.1 Write an essay or a few bullet points in your learning journal. Review this chapter. Then, write about the main things you have learned about version control.

Exercise 15.2 (Create a Local Git Repository Exercise)

15.2 Make sure you have git installed on your local computer. Your task is to:

- create a local folder,
- put a couple of text files in the folder,
- create a local git repository,
- stage the two files,
- commit the two files,
- make a change to one of the files,
- stage and commit the changed file,
- for the purposes of this exercise, discard the latest changes and go back to the first commit.

Use the git --help command to remind you what you need to do.

Exercise 15.3 (Create a Remote Git Repository Exercise)

15.3 Make sure you have git installed on your local computer. Make sure you have a local folder which has a git repository. Your task is to:

- create a GitHub account,
- create a remote repository using your GitHub account,
- back up your local git repository to the remote GitHub repository you just created

Use the online GitHub documentation to remind you what you need to do.

Exercise 15.4 (Create and Merge Git Branches Exercise)

15.4 Make sure you have git installed on your local computer. Make sure you have a local folder which has a git repository. Your task is to:

- create a new branch,
- switch over to the new branch,
- add a new file to the new branch,
- switch back to the original branch,
- now, merge the new branch with your original branch,
- remove the new branch from your git repository.

Use the `git --help` command to remind you what you need to do.

Exercise 15.5 (Sharing Code Within a Branch Exercise)

15.5 Work with a friend. You need a public GitHub repository linked to a local repository. The task for Person A is to:

- add a new file to the local master branch,
- push the master branch to the shared GitHub repository.
- Now, pause until the other person gets to this point, also

The task for Person B is to:

- create a new local folder and repository,
- clone the shared repository into your local folder,
- add a file to the master branch,
- push the master branch to a shared GitHub repository.
- Now, pause until Person A can pull this new file

(continued)

Exercise 15.5 (continued)

Use the online GitHub documentation to remind you what you need to do.
Now, the task for Person A is to:

- pull the content of the shared GitHub repository into the local repository,
- you should see the file added by Person B appear in your local repository.

The idea is that Person A and Person B do not need to carefully synchronise their activities if everyone uses the `git pull` command to obtain any new code added to the shared GitHub repository. You must do a `git pull` and then resolve any differences, before you do a `git push` command.

Exercise 15.6 (Sharing Code with Separate Branches Exercise)

15.6 Work with a friend. The task for Person A is to:

- create a new branch, and call it `feature1`,
- switch over to the new branch,
- add a new file to the new branch,
- push the new branch to a shared GitHub repository.
- Now, pause until the other person gets to this point, also

The task for Person B is to:

- create a new branch, and call it `feature2`,
- switch over to the new branch,
- add a new file to the new branch,
- push the new branch to a shared GitHub repository.
- Now, pause to watch what Person A does.

The idea is that Person A wants to merge the `feature1` branch into the master branch and put that onto the shared GitHub repository.
Now, the task for Person A is to:

- switch over to the master branch,
- pull the shared GitHub repository (there should not have been any changes on the master branch, so everything should be up to date),
- merge the `feature1` branch into the master branch,
- push the master branch to a shared GitHub repository.
- Now, pause and watch what Person B does.

Now, the task for Person B is to:

- switch over to the master branch,

(continued)

Exercise 15.6 (continued)

- pull the shared GitHub repository (this time, Person B should get the new merged master branch with the file added by Person A).
- Now, merge the `feature2` branch into the master branch,
- push the master branch to a shared GitHub repository.
- Now, pause and watch what Person A does.

Finally, the task for Person A is to:

- make sure you are in the master branch,
- pull the shared GitHub repository (this time Person A should get the new file from the `feature2` branch added by Person B).

Hopefully by following a process like this, you can learn how to work independently and then share your work, when the time comes. By using separate files in the different branches, we avoid the issue of resolving changes made within a shared file.

Exercise 15.7 (Sharing Code Within a Shared File Exercise)

15.7 Work with a friend. Repeat the procedure for Exercise 5; only this time, work on a shared file. Take turns to add text to a common file, which is then pushed to a shared GitHub repository. Then see what happens when you try to do pull the file including edits from the other person and do a merge. Hopefully, you should be able to work out how each person can add text to the same file and end up with both your text and the text from the other person in your local repository.

Exercise 15.8 (Learning Journal)

15.8 Reflect on the exercises you have completed from this chapter. What went well? What could have gone better? Make some notes in your learning journal.

15.7 Hints, Tips and Advice on Exercises

15.1 *Learning Journal*

Review the text of this chapter. This chapter has described content management, source code history, remote archiving and sharing. Write some notes about what you have learned, for each of these topics.

15.2 *Local Git Repository Exercise*

To make a local git repository, we must create a folder. Navigate to that folder on the command line. And then, use the `git init` command. Assuming you have already created a file, or two, then you can stage the files using the `git add` command. The flag `-A` simply stages all changed files in the working tree.

Local Git Initialise, Stage and Commit Example

```
C:\folder\git-test>git init
C:\...>git add -A
C:\...>git commit -m "Describe operations performed"
```

Next use a text editor to change one of the files.

Local Second Commit Example

```
C:\folder\git-test>git add -A
C:\...>git commit -m "Describe operations performed"
```

(continued)

Now you realise, for the purposes of this exercise, that the last commit was an error. You want to undo the change you made to that file and have just committed. No problem.

Revert to Previous Commit Example

```
C:\folder\git-test>git revert HEAD
```

The git revert command can be used to undo the last commit. Use the git revert --help command to see the other capabilities of the git revert command.

15.3 *Remote GitHub Repository Exercise*

Follow the online help tutorial to create a new empty remote GitHub repository [3]. Make sure the name of the remote repository on GitHub corresponds to your local repository. In this example, I called the repositories git-test. Do not perform any commit on your remote repository.

Now we have to back up the local repository contents, which presumably contain something you want to back up. To start off, you need to use the git remote add command.

Add Remote Example

```
C:\folder\git-test>git remote add origin
https://github.com/<your username>/git-test.git
```

You can then use git push to back up your local files to the remote server. The -u option saves you from having to type the <REMOTENAME> <BRANCHNAME> every time you do a git push.

(continued)

Push to Remote Example

```
C:\folder\git-test>git push -u origin master
C:\folder\git-test>git status
```

With luck, you should now have your local code backed up on the remote server. You can use your browser and GitHub credentials to search your online repository and see what is there.

15.4 *Branching Exercise*

Creating a new branch is straightforward. Just use the `git branch` command. Remember you can use `git branch --help` for more information.

Create Branch Example

```
C:\folder\git-test>git branch feature1
C:\folder\git-test>git checkout feature1
```

Our new branch, in this example called `feature1`, has been created and we are now 'in' the new branch. We can create and modify files without affecting the contents of any other branches. You should now add some new content within the `feature1` branch. This new content can now be committed and push to your remote repository on GitHub.

(continued)

Push Branch to Remote Example

```
C:\folder\git-test>git add -A
C:\...>git commit -m "Third file"
C:\...>git push --set-upstream origin feature1
```

You should now have a backup of the new branch of your local repository on your remote GitHub repository.

15.8   Chapter Summary

Version control systems give us a very sophisticated content management system for managing our source code. As we create and modify files, we can keep track of the changes we make and even archive them to remote backup servers. A version control system allows us to create branches so we can undertake separate lines of development without interfering with each other. I suggest learning version control skills in three stages; learn how to:

1. Stage and commit local files,
2. Archive your personal code to a remote server,
3. Merge your code with source code from others.

I suggest you learn the skills you need to create a change history and archive of your own files, before you learn how to merge code with other people's.

Branches are useful for creating a space for separate lines of source code development that can be worked on independently from each other. But branches should be used with caution because they can inadvertently cause problems when it comes to merging new code into the main truck. Now, we are ready learn the skills needed to test our software, in Chap. 16.

References

1. git: Git (2019). https://git-scm.com/
2. GitHub Inc.: Build software better, together (2019). https://github.com

3. GitHub Inc.: Create a repo – GitHub Help (2019). https://help.github.com/en/github/getting-started-with-github/create-a-repo
4. GitHub, Inc.: Creating a personal access token (2021). https://docs.github.com/en/authentication/keeping-your-account-and-data-secure/creating-a-personal-access-token
5. GitHub, Inc.: Git guides – install git (2021). https://github.com/git-guides/install-git
6. Loeliger, J., McCullough, M.: Version Control with Git: Powerful Tools and Techniques for Collaborative Software Development, 2nd edn. O'Reilly Media Inc, Sebastopol (2012)

Chapter 16
Testing and Test Automation

Abstract Testing is used to identify defects and provide reassurance about the quality of our software. We always test our code before we share it with others. In this chapter, we will learn the skills needed to create unit, regression, user experience and acceptance tests. We will also learn the skills needed to create simple test automations. We always try to automate the things we do, so that they are reliably repeatable. This saves time in the long run and reduces the chances that we will forget or cut corners later, when we are under pressure from short deadlines. We will also explore some techniques for performance and security testing.

16.1 Introduction

Testing in software development provides two main services: identifying defects and providing evidence that our software works as intended. We always aim to test method signatures, return parameters, data transformations and storage services before we share our source code with others. This is polite, to avoid sharing defects with our colleagues, but also demonstrates our collective commitment to quality.

The concept of *test coverage* helps us understand the need to test the different logical pathways through executing code. An individual if statement may be used to determine the runtime circumstances in which a particular method, doSomethingMethod(), is called. To achieve high coverage, our job is to ensure we test the pathways that includes the doSomethingMethod() method call as well as any pathways that do not.

An *error* is a mistake, perhaps made during requirements gathering or source code development. A *fault* is the defect in the code that arises from the error. A *failure* occurs if the fault in the code is executed and causes the wrong results to be produced. From this logic, we can realise that not all faults lead to failures. A fault in our code can lay dormant until a specific scenario in which that faulty code is executed and produces incorrect results.

If you think, for a moment, about testing every pathway through the software, every decision, every loop, every user input sequence and every possible variable

© Springer Nature Switzerland AG 2022
J. M. Bass, *Agile Software Engineering Skills*,
https://doi.org/10.1007/978-3-031-05469-3_16

value, you quickly realise that testing all combinations of inputs and preconditions is not possible in even quite simple systems.

However, we can and must use testing to check for defects and improve the quality of our software. We just need to be selective about what we test, making sure we test all the important pathways through our code. We touched upon testing artefacts used during the development process, in Chap. 10.

16.2   Test Planning

Test planning is about establishing the process and resources needed to test an application to an appropriate level of test coverage. The test plan defines what is to be tested and how test results will be recorded, as mentioned in Sect. 10.2. The testing schedule, and how testing is integrated into an incremental delivery model, will also need to be defined.

16.3   Testing Levels

Testing levels determine the focus of our testing: whether on the contents of small software components or classes on the one hand or on the integration of components into larger systems on the other hand. Common testing levels include unit, integration, systems and acceptance testing.

16.3.1   Unit Testing

Unit testing is a feature development artefact, as mentioned in Sect. 10.4. In unit testing, we isolate and test individual elements of our code, such as method signatures, return parameters and data transformations. Unit tests are often created and executed as we develop. Unit tests are usually written by source code developers, sometimes with the support of test specialists that are members of our self-organising teams during the development iteration.

16.3.2   Integration Testing

Integration testing is used to verify each new interface we add to our system. Interfaces to new subsystems are built incrementally and must be tested to expose any defects. Interface testing is done after unit testing and prior to offering up the code to other software components that depend on the new services provided.

Prior to integration testing, we can use *stubs* and *drivers* to simulate interfaces. A *stub* provides a dummy implementation of an interface. The *stub* complies with the interface requirements without executing any code to fulfil the call. A simple dummy response is provided instead. Conversely, a *driver* make dummy calls to an interface. We can implement all the source code to fulfil the interface and use the *driver* to simulate calls to our interface code.

During integration testing, we remove the *stubs* and *drivers* and perform tests to ensure everything works as expected. We normally perform one integration at a time, to ensure each interface is working before we move onto the next.

16.3.3   System Testing

We use system testing to evaluate the holistic functioning of our system. During system testing, we determine if components and subsystems cooperate in the way we expect and transform data appropriately across interfaces. System testing routinely involves software built by different individuals or teams. System testing may also involve evaluating newly developed software interacting with third-party software.

We can perform non-functional as well as functional system testing. Performance, load testing and security testing are best performed on the entire system prior to release. If a third-party test team is employed, they are more likely to perform system testing than unit or integration testing.

16.3.4   Acceptance Testing

Acceptance testing is used to ensure that each feature or increment meets its needs. Conventionally, in sequential or plan-based software development models, acceptance testing was performed towards the end of the development life cycle. But in incremental development, acceptance test criteria are developed earlier in the process and then applied as features or increments are completed. Acceptance testing is performed before customer demonstrations, so that the test results can inform judgements about software quality.

16.4   Testing Techniques

To achieve the objectives of evaluating our systems at the different stage of development, we can employ five main testing techniques: regression, user experience, performance (load), security and A/B testing.

16.4.1   Regression Testing

Regression testing plays an important role in incremental software development, as mentioned in Sect. 10.5. When new features are added, it is important to test that existing features are still working properly and that nothing in our earlier source code has been broken.

It is usually during regression testing that automated test tools really bring value to the development process. This is because previously developed suites of tests can be re-run to give assurance that features developed earlier are still working correctly after new feature source code has been integrated into our main trunk.

16.4.2   User Experience Testing

User experience testing, in contrast, is focused on evaluating our user interface design and end-to-end screen flow. In simple terms, we recruit a group of participants to use our software in specific pre-planned ways and observe. We can consider seven aspects of user experience testing:

- Create interaction scenarios to be tested,
- Identify and select target user demographic,
- Recruit participants for the study,
- Use questionnaires or interview techniques to collect participant expectations before using the system,
- Brief participants on the task to be performed during the interaction scenario
- Observe participants performing the scenario (this might include measuring task completion time),
- Use questionnaires or interview techniques to collect participant feedback after using the system.

The interaction scenarios are likely to be derived from use cases or user stories defined at the requirements analysis stage of application development. Typically several user stories will be joined into an end-to-end user scenario for user experience testing.

Members of the target user demographic should be recruited for the user experience study. Typically, we select a representative sample of a broad target user demographic for our user experience evaluation panel. Or, we select very specifically a more narrowly defined demographic segment that corresponds to a specific persona; see Sect. 7.7. We sometimes ask participants about their perceptions or expectations before they see the software system being evaluated.

To conduct the testing, study participants must be briefed on the software system and the activities they are supposed to perform. This briefing might be in the form of a simple set of instructions, or a more elaborate training activity, depending on the application.

The users are then observed performing the requested task using the software system under investigation. Observation might be informal, with researchers making notes and timing activities. For more detailed studies with more resources available, careful observation and video recording might be used. For a more rigorous, research-oriented, approach, specialist eye-tracking apparatus can be used to precisely characterise participant behaviour while using the software.

Once users have completed the scenarios, it is typical to ask them questions about their impression of the experience. This qualitative data can help decide if the software is going to be enthusiastically adopted by potential customers. Once the software goes live, we employ *A/B testing* to evaluate the new features we release, as discussed in Sect. 16.4.5.

16.4.3 Performance Testing

Performance testing is used to check that system response times are acceptable when subjected to an expected number of user requests. Tools like Apache JMeter [1] can be used to load-test applications, while Selenium [6] has features for testing web applications by simulating button presses and web-form filling. Performance testing gives reassurance that an application performs with adequate response times, when under anticipated load.

However, stress testing is often performed to explore the load under which the response time falls below acceptable levels. In stress testing, load (in terms of number of users or data throughput) is steadily increased to understand the limits of acceptable performance. We want to know how much additional capacity our system can withstand before response times become unacceptable.

16.4.4 Security Testing

We talked about security in more detail in Chap. 11. It is good practice to include security testing in a test pipeline. General code quality testing tools, such as SonarCloud, perform some security tests that can identify deficiencies in our code [7]. In addition, we can use more specialist security testing tools such as Gauntlt [8] and OWASP ZAP [4].

These tools are designed to be used as part of an automated test and build pipeline. This is known as *DevOps* in which source code development, the *Dev*, and deployment or operations, the *Ops*, are integrated using automation. Indeed, extending the phrase *DevOps* to *DevSecOps* derives from the need to include security testing in the continuous integration or continuous deployment pipeline. We'll come back to these ideas in Chap. 21.

16.4.5   A/B Testing

In A/B testing, we deploy two alternative versions of our functionality to live users and measure their responses. This approach is usually used in web-based or browser-based applications. Our objective is to measure user behaviour in real time on our live web-hosted products. At runtime, users are assigned to one version or the other of our experimental features. For example, a new landing page might be deployed, and we can use A/B testing to see which version attracts the higher number of site registrations.

We use metrics like number of click-throughs, lower abandonment rates, higher conversion rates and revenue per customer to evaluate different versions. Essentially, each roll-out of a new feature is treated as an experiment to measure impact on desirable customer behaviour.

An A/B testing framework is usually used to manage our experiments. The framework allows us to define metrics, deploy software features and measure usage. Such frameworks offer a dashboard for managing experiments and analysing test results.

16.5   Test Automation

Bearing in mind that we can't test everything, we nevertheless ensure that the main features and data pathways have been tested before we ship product. To achieve this goal, automation of our testing processes becomes essential.

16.5.1   Unit Test Automation

Automating unit testing is attractive because we want to re-run tests at later stages in the development process.

The term *XUnit* is used to describe a standard set of unit testing frameworks that have emerged for providing a consistent approach to automated unit testing regardless of the programming language used. So, for example, we can find *SUnit* (for Smalltalk), *JUnit* (for Java) and *RUnit* (for R) and so on.

The *XUnit* approaches comprise several common elements:

- Test runner, an executable programme for running tests,
- Test case, used to define specific test conditions,
- Test fixtures, a set of preconditions needed to run a test
- Assertions, a function that verifies the behaviour or state of the unit under test,
- Test execution, the execution of an individual test,
- Test result formatter, produces test results in a common output format,
- Test suites, a mechanism for running collection of tests in any order.

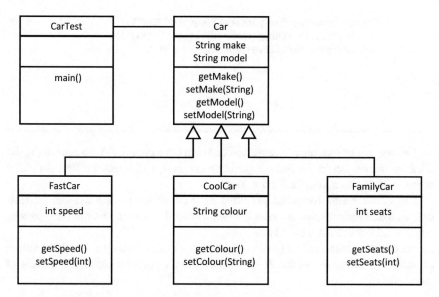

Fig. 16.1   Small application for illustrating JUnit in Eclipse [2]

To illustrate a basic use of *JUnit*, look at the small application shown in Fig. 16.1 and which is available to download from GitHub [2].

Having created the application classes and methods, we can create a test. Simply *right-click* on the project in the Eclipse package explorer, hover your cursor over the new menu item, and select a new `JUnit Test Case`. I usually collect my tests into a *JUnit* package, although on larger projects it might make more sense to have a dedicated *Test Package* for each package in the source code.

The test simply instantiates the class and then tests the values of variables using getter methods, as shown here:

Fast Car Test Method

```
package junit;

import static org.junit.Assert.*;

import org.junit.Test;

import car.FastCar;

public class FastCarTest {

    @Test
    public void test() {
        FastCar fastCar = new FastCar("BMW", "320M", 180);
```

```
        assertTrue(fastCar.getMake().equals("BMW"));
        assertTrue(fastCar.getModel().equals("320M"));
        assertTrue( fastCar.getSpeed() == 180);
    }
}
```

The test can be executed once the test case has been completed. To execute, *right-click* on the project in the Eclipse package explorer, and select the Run As\dots menu. You can then select a JUnit Test.

The *JUnit* result formatter provided by Eclipse shows the number of tests executed and their results. A green bar denotes all the tests in this run have passed, while a red bar indicates failed tests.

For this simple example, I have used the assertTrue method to check the values of attributes. However, in the *JUnit* environment, assertions come in a variety of flavours:

- assertEquals(boolean expected,boolean actual): to check if two primitives/objects are equal.
- assertTrue(boolean condition): to check if a condition is true.
- assertFalse(boolean condition): to check if a condition is false.
- assertNull(Object obj): to check if an object is null.
- assertNotNull(Object obj): to check if an object is not null.

Consequently, these test methods can be used to test different variable values as required by the application. Finally, a test suite can be created, which executes all the unit tests, as follows:

A Test Suite in JUnit

```
package junit;

import org.junit.runner.RunWith;
import org.junit.runners.Suite;
import org.junit.runners.Suite.SuiteClasses;

@RunWith(Suite.class)
@SuiteClasses({ CarTest.class, FamilyCarTest.class, FastCarTest.class })
public class AllTests {

}
```

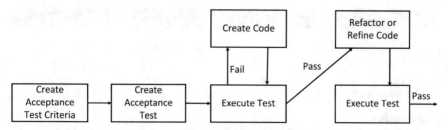

Fig. 16.2 Acceptance test-driven development

The test suite automates executing multiple tests, simplifying the processes of running every test against a specific method or class.

16.5.2   Acceptance Test-Driven Development

In test-driven development, rather counter-intuitively, the tests are written before the application code. As already mentioned in Sect. 13.6, the general test-driven development cycle goes as follows [3]:

1. Write a test,
2. Make it run,
3. Make it right.

This process can be enhanced by first establishing a set of acceptance test criteria, as shown in Fig. 16.2. The acceptance test criteria are derived from user stories defining new requirements. Using the test criteria, an automated acceptance test can be implemented. Initially this test will fail, so the code to fulfil the test is constructed until the test passes. The final stage, shown in Fig. 16.2, is to refactor the code and do a last check that the test still passes.

16.5.3   Behaviour-Driven Development

Emerging from the test-driven development community, *behaviour-driven development* employs specialist software tools, notably a domain-specific language to integrate user story-like descriptions of functionality with test criteria. The test code itself is automatically generated from the natural language descriptions. Using these non-technical, natural language, descriptions encourages collaboration between stakeholders in defining features and their acceptance criteria. In an agile context, this approach fosters collaboration.

Behaviour-driven Development User Story Structure

```
Title
  A user story title.

Narrative
  A brief feature description using the following structure:

    As a: the actor who will benefit from the feature;
    I want: the feature;
    so that: the benefit or value of the feature.

Acceptance criteria
  A set of scenarios describing the behaviours of the user
  story with the following structure:

    Given: the preconditions of the scenario, in one
      or more clauses;
    When: the event that triggers the scenario;
    Then: the expected outcome, in one or more clauses.
```

The acceptance criteria are parsed by software tools to create tests. For example, in the *Cucumber* tool set, the *Gherkin* natural language parser is used to extract test cases from such user story descriptions [5].

16.6 Exercises

These exercises can help you develop your testing skills. Have a go at an exercise and then check for hints, tips and advice in Sect. 16.7.

Exercise 16.1 (Learning Journal)

16.1 Based on this chapter, write about testing in your learning journal. You could write an essay or just a few bullet points.

Exercise 16.2 (Unit Testing Exercise)

16.2 Add a JUnit test to one of your existing projects. Once the test is working, add a second test. Now create a JUnit test suite to execute both tests in an automated sequence.

Exercise 16.3 (Integration Testing Exercise)

16.3 Add a JUnit integration test to one of your existing projects. Once the first integration test is working, add a second test. Now create a JUnit test suite to execute both integration tests in an automated sequence.

Exercise 16.4 (Learning Journal)

16.4 Writing in your learning journal can help you reflect on the exercises you have completed. Make some notes about each exercise.

Exercise 16.5 (Learning Journal)

16.5 *Learning Journal*
Reflect on the chapters in Part III. Reflect on what you have learned about:

- Ceremonies,
- Lean,
- Version control,
- Testing.

Make some notes in your learning journal about each of these topics.

16.7   Hints, Tips and Advice on Exercises

16.1 *Learning Journal*

Review the text of this chapter. This chapter has described content management, source code history, remote archiving and sharing. Write some notes
about what you have learned, for each of these topics.

16.2 *Unit Testing Exercise*

A basic use of *JUnit* is illustrated in the toy application shown in Fig. 16.1
and available to download from GitHub [2].

16.3 *Integration Testing Exercise*

Integration testing is used to evaluate the interconnection of moving parts
in the software. Such interconnections are often implemented using various
kinds of interfaces.

A common approach to interface testing is to use *stubs* and *drivers*. When
you create an interface, a stub can be used to fulfil the interface by providing
dummy and usually static data. Hence, a simplified version of the interface
is implemented which returns hard-coded test data. Consequently, we can
implement calls to the stubbed-out interface and observe that the test data
is returned as expected.

Conversely, a driver is used to call an interface that has been fully or
partially implemented. We can create driver that passes the interface some
test data and observe the response.

There are various other approaches used in integration testing, but I suggest
you start by experimenting with some stubs and drivers.

16.8   Chapter Summary

Testing plays an important role in any high-quality software development process.
On the one hand, testing is used to detect defects and identify problems. On the other
hand, testing is designed to provide reassurance that software works as intended.

This chapter has introduced four levels of testing: unit, integration, system
and acceptance testing. Unit testing gives us feedback on the function of low-
level software elements during the development process. Integration testing is used
to ensure that interfaces work as expected. In system testing, we evaluate the

interaction of the components in our system. In contrast, acceptance testing is to ensure that completed software meets its intended requirements.

We have discussed five testing techniques conducted during the development process: regression, user experience, performance, security and A/B testing. Each serves a different purpose and performs a useful service in achieving high quality in our software. Regression testing is important in incremental development to ensure that existing features continue to work correctly after new features are added. User experience testing gives us feedback on usability, while performance testing is to ensure that software is sufficiently responsive under intended load conditions. Security testing seeks to expose vulnerabilities in our code. Finally, A/B testing is used on live software systems to evaluate user reaction to new features in a runtime experiment. We can now establish process, tools and automation approaches for the *Tabby Cat* project in Chap. 17.

References

1. Apache Software Foundation: Apache jmeter (2021). https://jmeter.apache.org/
2. Bass, J.M.: Cartester (2022). https://github.com/julianbass/CarTester
3. Beck, K.: Test Driven Development, 1st edn. Addison Wesley, Boston (2002)
4. OWASP Foundation: The zap homepage (2021). https://www.zaproxy.org
5. SmartBear Software: Bdd testing & collaboration tools for teams (2021). https://cucumber.io/
6. Software Freedom Conservancy: Seleniumhq browser automation (2021). https://www.selenium.dev/
7. SonarCloud: Automatic code review, testing, inspection & auditing (2021). https://sonarcloud.io/
8. Wickett, J., Tadayon, M.: https://github.com/gauntlt/gauntlt (2021)

Chapter 17
Tabby Cat Project: Process, Tools and Automation

Abstract In this chapter, we consider the process issues and software tools required to create the *Tabby Cat* case study project. This project will create an opportunity to apply the ideas from the chapters in Part III of the book. As stated in Chaps. 6 and 12, *Tabby Cat* is software for displaying source code repository activity. We want to obtain data from a public repository and display activities using various searches and filters.

17.1 Introduction

This case study allows us to summarise and apply the most important ideas we have covered in Part III. Here, you can learn more about agile process and software tool issues. The three main sets of skills I want to focus on are ceremonies from Chap. 13, version control from Chap. 15 and test automation from Chap. 16.

The *Tabby Cat* project has been kindly provided by Red Ocelot Ltd., our software start-up company [2]. The *Tabby Cat* project source code is available on GitHub [1].

Review Your Learning Journal

I have recommended that you create and update a learning journal when you do the exercises in each chapter; see Exercise 13.1. Now is a good time to reflect on your journal notes for each exercise in the Part III chapters.

- Re-read your learning journal from the chapter exercises in Part III of the book,
- Think about what went well when you did the exercises,
- Think about what didn't go so well,

(continued)

© Springer Nature Switzerland AG 2022
J. M. Bass, *Agile Software Engineering Skills*,
https://doi.org/10.1007/978-3-031-05469-3_17

- Make some notes, in your learning journal, about the strengths and weaknesses of your work in these areas,
- Create some actions or set some targets for your future learning.

17.2   Agile Ceremonies and Lean Thinking

First, make sure you read Chap. 13 and work through Exercises 13.2 to 13.5. These ceremonies are how we collaborate in agile projects. We try to empower team members to fulfil our goal using their own creativity and skill. We think this is better than relying on a project manager who has all the creativity and tells everyone what to do.

Before we start development work, we need a prioritised list of requirements. Each sprint starts with a *sprint planning* activity, described in Sect. 13.2. Essentially, sprint planning is where we decide on the requirements to be tackled during this sprint and which team member is going to work on each. We divide each requirement (use case or user story) into technical tasks, and, in a self-organising team, members step forward to pick up each task.

Daily stand-up meetings, as described in Sect. 13.3, allow everyone in the team to keep track of progress. Remember that the daily stand-up consists of everyone taking turns to answer three questions: 'what have you done since the last meeting?', 'what are you working on now?' and 'are there any impediments stopping you from making progress?'. Separate meetings are called to deal with any challenged surfaced during the daily stand-ups.

At the end of the sprint, we have a *customer demonstration*. As mentioned in Sect. 13.4, this is where we demonstrate working code created during the sprint. The purpose of the customer demonstration is to collect feedback on our work. We prefer to find out sooner, rather than later, if we are going off on the wrong track.

We conduct a sprint *retrospective*, after the customer demonstration, as discussed in Sect. 13.4.1. During the retrospective, we can reflect on our successes during the sprint and look for opportunities to improve. Usually, we aim to have two or three action areas for improvement in each sprint.

Now read Chap. 14 and consider how you can apply lean thinking to your project. Exercises 14.2 to 14.7 should provide some ideas you can apply to your work. Perhaps most important is to focus on the *flow* of features through your development process. This mindset might help you identify *waste* to eliminate which increases the *value* of your work.

17.3 Version Control

Now, you should have read Chap. 15 and worked through Exercises 15.2 to 15.7. Version control is going to play a critical role in the *Tabby Cat* project. We want to use version control to be able to manage source code changes during the project, but also to provide a straightforward mechanism for sharing source code within the team using a shared remote repository.

There is an overhead in learning the skills required to keep your working source code in version control. First working source code must be synchronised with your local repository and then keeping your local repository synchronised with an archive in a remote repository. But, if you can get into the habit of using these software tools regularly, it will save you a lot of time in the long run.

Aim to synchronise your code locally very few minutes (by performing local commits). It is much better to commit in small increments, rather than commit the result of hours (or, worse, days) worth of effort. Frequent commits make it easier to do a roll-back, if it ever needed, and easier to track any defects introduced into the source code.

17.4 Testing and Test Automation

First, make sure you read Chap. 16 and work through Exercises 16.2 and 16.3. It is obviously good practice to unit test, as you create your source code. Depending on the language you adopt, *XUnit* style tests (*JUnit* for Java and so on) seem the way to go.

You will also need to perform regression testing on existing source code, when new features are added in each increment. This is where automated testing really comes into its own, because the automated tests are already there for the existing features and can be re-run to check nothing has broken when new features are added.

It is likely also to be a good idea to create some integration tests. Integration tests are used to check the interfaces between the *moving parts* of your system. Re-running integration tests at the end of each increment provides increased confidence that interfaces have not been accidentally broken. It is very easy to perform an enhancement on an existing interface and forget to update all the existing clients of that interface.

In Part IV, I will explore some more advanced skills that will be useful for you to acquire as your expertise in agile software development grows.

References

1. Bass, J., Monaghan, B.: Tabby Cat GitHub Explorer. Red Ocelot Ltd, London (2022). https://github.com/julianbass/github-explorer
2. Red Ocelot Ltd: Enhancing digital agility (2022). https://www.redocelot.com

Part IV
Advanced Skills

Part IV of the book deals with four more advanced topics: large-scale agile, cloud deployment, technical debt, evolution and legacy, and DevOps. The skills in these chapters become more relevant; once your agile team is functioning, you have shipped your first releases and you have a nice agile process cadence.

Chapter 18 explores large-scale agile development projects. A key feature of large-scale agile is the need to coordinate multiple self-organising teams. The trade-off here is that team sacrifice some autonomy in order to work towards a common software solution. The specialist roles, activities and ceremonies needed for big projects are discussed in Chap. 18.

Cloud-hosted application deployment, described in Chap. 19, is very attractive if you don't already have access to your own servers. Cloud-hosting can scale to the needs of a varying size customer base and can minimise capital investment costs for start-ups and new entrants. We explore some key issues, such as scaling, multi-tenancy and containerisation, for software-as-a-service deployment.

Finally, Chap. 20 explores legacy systems, technical debt and software evolution. Technical debt builds up as a natural consequence of incremental development. Periodic refactoring is desirable to reduce technical debt. Legacy systems often exhibit extremes forms of technical debt.

Continuous integration and continuous deployment, often called DevOps, are useful when using incremental development. DevOps ensures the seamless delivery of new features into your production deployed product. Automation helps to ensure consistency and quality in your deployment pipeline. Tools to help with continuous integration and continuous deployment are described in Chap. 21.

Other Book Parts

As I have emphasised elsewhere, the main focus of Part I is on *People*, in Part II is on *Product* and in Part III is on *Process*. These book parts are pretty much stand-alone and hence can be tackled in any order.

Chapter 18
Large-Scale Agile

Abstract Large-scale agile development is required where time scales are short and the scope of work is, well, large. Large-scale development focuses on cooperating teams. We have a dilemma; on the one hand, we want to empower teams to be self-organising and innovative. However, on the other hand, teams must cooperate to work together on the same product. This chapter introduces the more advanced topics around cooperating teams. We will discuss conventional approaches, such as the scrum-of-scrums approach, where dependencies between cooperating teams are resolved by scrum masters meeting and thrashing out release roadmaps and resolving impediments. We will also introduce the Spotify culture of squads, chapters, tribes and guilds. Spotify engineering culture is based on self-organising teams, known as squads. A tribe is a collection of collaborating squads organised around specific products. Within the same tribe, Chapters focus on skills development within a tribe. While guilds are communities of practice for sharing knowledge across different tribes about areas of specialism. We will explore these techniques for managing scale, distance and governance.

18.1 Introduction

When the number of requirements to be fulfilled is large, and time scales are short, then we need to use large-scale agile techniques. Rather than have one large team, we prefer to have a number of smaller cooperating teams. There are specific issues around coordinating cooperating teams. We will consider specialist artefacts and activities within roles on agile projects.

On large-scale projects, there is also a tension between consistency of approach between teams and the ability of teams to be creative and innovative. Different organisations will choose their own point on this spectrum. Some will focus on nurturing highly creative and innovative autonomous teams, while others will look

© Springer Nature Switzerland AG 2022

J. M. Bass, *Agile Software Engineering Skills*,

https://doi.org/10.1007/978-3-031-05469-3_18

to compare teams and aim for consistency. Such organisations might ask questions like:

- How can we learn from the most productive team(s) and spread best practice to others?
- Why do some teams maintain consistent velocities, while others seem to fail sprints from time to time?
- How do we achieve consistent software quality standards?

There are risks with both extremes. Highly autonomous teams might be innovative but end up having to waste time doing rework to fit in with other teams, because of uncoordinated decision-making or wrong assumptions. On the other hand, enforcing too much consistency can stifle team innovation and undermine motivation. Clearly, a balance needs to be struck. The secondary roles, in Sect.18.4 and 18.5, help cooperating teams to achieve this balance between team autonomy and team consistency.

18.2 Distance

When thinking of geographically distributed software development, so-called global software development, we can identify three aspects of distance that impact the software development process: geographical, temporal and cultural.

18.2.1 Geographical Distance

Geographical distance is, well obviously, the physical distance between team members. Engaging other team members in the same city is considered easier than if team members are in different continents. While *offshore* development refers to engaging developers from remote distances, *near-shore* development refers to team members from within the same continent. Large geographical distance means longer flights to facilitate face-to-face meetings and more time on video conferencing platforms.

18.2.2 Temporal Distance

Temporal distance refers to the issue of time zone differences between team members. Significant time zone differences impact the ability to hold online meetings during the working day. Someone is going to have to meet other team members outside normal working hours, either during the late night or early morning. Consequently, some organisations group people into teams with others that live directly north or south, rather than east or west. From this perspective, forming groups with team members from Brazil and North America, on the one hand, or from Africa and Europe, on the other hand, is more attractive, to minimise time zone differences. There are lots of out-of-hour work meetings for teams in South Asia working with clients in the USA.

18.2.3   Cultural Distance

Cultural distance, perhaps the more controversial concept here, refers to differences between community, family and social attitudes and values in different societies. Some observers identify differences in how hierarchical or deferential some organisations are, compared to others. Also, team members may be from different cultures where attitudes to issues such as gender equality, religion or sexuality vary considerably. Cultural awareness becomes a more sensitive issue in teams comprising members from distant cultures. Some large organisations offer team members training in this area.

18.3   Large-Scale Artefacts

To support the development process, in large-scale projects, several new artefacts are often developed, including risk register and architectural standards.

18.3.1   Risk Register

A risk register is a list of potential risks, an assessment of their likelihood and possible mitigations. Some regulatory authorities demand preparation of a risk register for projects. See the discussion on risk management in Sect.11.3.4. Risk registers may be qualitative, using assessments of risk severity such as *high* or *low*. Or, they maybe quantitative, using impact evaluations, such as risk of $1m loss and a probability of 50%.

A risk register, then, typically contains:

- Categories, grouping similar risk types,
- Description, a brief description of the risk,
- Impact, integer value representing potential consequences of the risk,
- Probability, the likelihood that the risk will materialise,
- Risk score, a ranking of risk, usually based on multiplying impact and probability
- Mitigation, steps to ameliorate the risk.

Amelioration steps for each risk might include approaches to identify, analyse, plan response, monitor and control.

On many large-scale projects, the risk register will be reviewed by senior executives during each iteration. The potential impact of one or other teams failing to deliver planned work will be assessed.

18.3.2   Architecture Standards

Architecture standards are used to encourage adoption of a shared architectural style and technology stack across multiple cooperating self-organising teams. Typically, the standards permit use of specific versions of language libraries, development tools, software frameworks and so on. The purpose of standards is to ensure consistency and avoid architectural conflicts between different teams working on the same product.

18.4   Large-Scale Scrum Master Activities

To support large-scale working, several new scrum master coordination activities have been identified.

18.4.1   Scrum-of-Scrums Facilitator

The scrum-of-scrums facilitator organises coordination meetings between scrum masters from different cooperating teams. The scrum of scrums is a simple way for a few cooperating teams to coordinate their work together, as shown in Fig. 18.1. The scrum masters and product owners from each team work together to divide tasks between the teams and plan to overcome dependencies between the teams.

18.4.2   Agile Coach

Many organisations will have team members dedicated to spreading best practice from team to team. These individuals aim to have an extensive repertoire of techniques that can help teams work effectively. There are several ways of conducting sprint planning or sprint retrospectives (these ceremonies are described in more detail in Chap. 13), for example. An agile coach can help teams try different approaches and see what works best for them. You might be thinking that the agile coach sounds just like a scrum master. Well, it's true. Scrum masters are supposed

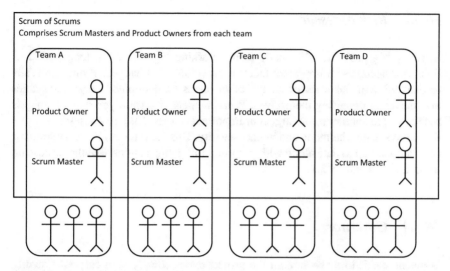

Fig. 18.1 Scrum of scrums

to help teams try new ideas and improve their effective use of agile methods. The agile coach, however, supports several (sometimes many) teams, whereas the scrum master usually only supports one team.

18.5   Large-Scale Product Owner Activities

Product owners create and prioritise user stories and decide when code is ready to be deployed and shipped. In large-scale software development programmes, the activities of identifying business needs and creating requirements are time-consuming and difficult. Product owners have been found to create several specific new activities, to cope with agile scaling [2].

18.5.1   Product Sponsor

Someone needs to develop the vision as well as create and negotiate a business case to senior executives in a large organisation. This usually requires involvement at the most senior board level. Senior executives, such as the chief executive, chief information or chief technology officer, may 'own' the project, but they are unlikely to have time to attend to all the project details. Hence, a product sponsor, who 'owns' the project, creates a product owner team which then deals with all the details associated with running the project [1].

18.5.2   Risk Assessor

In really big projects, with many teams working together for a long period of time, risk becomes an important factor to monitor. What happens if one team fails to deliver? Will the work of all the other teams be disrupted? Large companies are forever reorganising themselves. What happens if a team you depend on gets redeployed to another (more urgent or important) project? The risk assessor keeps a list of risks, their likelihood and impact severity. This list is reviewed, every sprint or two, and kept up to date along with proposed mitigating actions. See the discussion in Sect. 11.3.4 and 18.3.1.

18.5.3   Governor

Someone needs to make sure all the project teams comply with corporate quality standards and technical policies. Self-organising teams have to relinquish some autonomy when they cooperate with other teams to create a product. Usually some central architecture board or design authority determines policies and approaches, which teams then comply with.

18.5.4   Technical Architect

In large projects, cooperating project teams have to adhere to a shared architectural vision. The technical architect is tasked with creating, disseminating and encouraging adherence to this shared architectural vision. The architecture might involve a simple front-end back-end split with a web service API providing the interface between two teams, rather like the *Tabby Cat* project in Chap. 12. Once a simple architectural style is agreed, a dedicated technical architect role is hardly needed. However, in larger and more sophisticated applications with more moving parts (a euphemism for interacting subsystems of one kind or another), then an architect has an important role to play in defining approaches for achieving project goals.

The technical architect activity is provided by a specialist to enable design coordination between cooperating self-organising teams. Technical architects achieve coordination by designing, implementing and disseminating a reference architecture, a blueprint, for the overall organisation of the system (or some specific aspect of the system). The reference architecture is used to coordinate technical and high-level design policies between the scrum teams.

18.5.5   Technical Product Owner

There are, of course, variations between organisations and business sectors. Sometimes, in large projects, product owners are called product managers (particularly in consumer-facing businesses). There also seems to be a trend towards technical product owners supporting one team, within a specific business domain. The technical product owners will be used to focusing on a set of technologies or a technology stack, within their business domain. They support a more senior product owner who is more broadly product focused, supporting several teams, but who is technology agnostic.

18.5.6   Product Owner: Market Trends

The product owner prioritises the development of new features and services. This can be informed by maintaining good customer relationships in business-to-business domains or through market trend analysis. Horizon scanning market trends and competitor performance helps identify new business opportunities that can be fulfilled by new features and software services.

18.6   Spotify Culture

The music streaming service *Spotify* developed their own software innovation culture comprising teams organised into squads, tribes, chapters and guilds [3]. Spotify was launched in 2008 and had continuous growth for 10 years, at times being one of the most downloaded mobile device apps. The Spotify engineering model uses a matrix management structure, as shown in Fig. 18.2, comprising squads, chapters and tribes. In addition, guilds are communities of practice that disseminate innovations across the organisation.

18.6.1   Squads

The squad is the basic unit of software development in Spotify. A squad is similar to a scrum team, consisting of five to seven people. But Spotify squads have more autonomy over choosing a software development method, such as Scrum, XP, Kanban, lean, Scrumban and so on.

Squads have a long-term focus on an aspect of the product, such as a mobile device front-end, payment solutions or back-end services. This long-term commitment to a mission helps the squad gain deep expertise on their product area. In

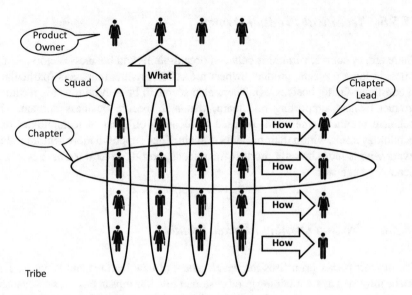

Fig. 18.2 Overview of Spotify engineering model, within a tribe

Spotify, they think of squads as mini-start-ups with a particular focus. Five key features of squads are:

- Product owner, each squad has a product owner,
- Agile coach, each squad has an agile coach to help resolve impediments and support continuous improvement,
- Self-organising team, influencing planning and work assignment,
- Squads own their own process and continuous improvement,
- Squads have a clear mission, with backlog stories focused on that mission.

The product owner assigned to each squad prioritises work considering business value and technical issues. Squads are strongly influenced by the principles of the lean start-up [4]. The minimum viable product concept means releasing early and often. While extensive use of metrics and A/B testing provides validated learning to find out what works and what doesn't, the approach of squads is summarised by the informal slogan *'Think it, build it, ship it, tweak it'*.

Squad members can spend 10% of their time on hack days, where people can try out new ideas and experiment with new technologies. Some squads choose to do one hack day every other week; other squads save up the hack days into a hack week. Hack days are a fun way to try out new tools and techniques.

18.6.2 Chapters

Chapters comprise people within a tribe, with a similar competency or skill set and focus on personal growth and development. The chapter lead is line manager for chapter members, responsible for training, performance reviews, salary setting and so on. Chapters meet regularly to disseminate best practice within a skill area, such as testing, web development or back-end services.

18.6.3 Tribes

Tribes are formed where multiple co-located squads work together on the same product. Tribes are typically limited to around 100 people. Tribes are designed to be smaller than around 100 people, to discourage formation of excessive bureaucracy, layers of management or organisational politics.

In Spotify, they think of tribes as an incubator for their squads. The squads within a tribe are assigned adjacent office space, often sharing a physical lounge space to encourage collaboration. Tribes have a leader who is responsible for creating a desirable habitat for the squads.

18.6.4 Guilds

Guilds, on the other hand, are communities of practice that operate across the whole organisation [8]. As mentioned, guilds are communities of practice for disseminating innovations. Guilds are self-managing and formed around particular set of interests. Guilds have a coordinator and organise activities for members. Anyone can join any guild, as shown in Fig. 18.3, the span squads, tribes and chapters. Successful communities of practice have a good topic, a passionate leader, a proper agenda, decision-making authority, openness, tool support, a suitable rhythm and cross-site participation.

18.6.5 Architectural Alignment

Autonomy of squads is good. Autonomy means squads have a greater sense of collective ownership of problems and solutions; they release faster and are more highly motivated. Squads have autonomy over what to build, how to build it and how to work together while building it.

However, squads also need to be aligned around a shared mission, product strategy and short-term goals. The mission is to serve a client need or solve a

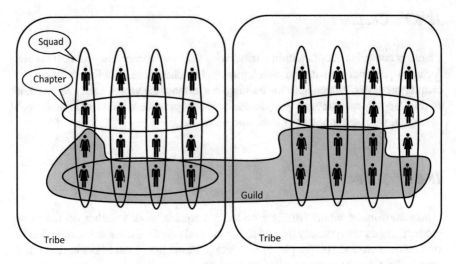

Fig. 18.3 A Spotify engineering model guild spanning two tribes

customer problem. Alignment is the extent to which organisation strategy and goals are proudly understood and undertaken by having focused squad interactions [5].

Software structure or software architecture can play an important role in fostering or impeding collaboration between teams [6]. In a simple model, each squad focuses on one layer of an architecture. Interfaces, which are published and version controlled, define the boundaries between architectural layers, but also between teams. As projects grow larger, this simple approach breaks down, because there is too much work for one squad to handle an entire layer of the architecture.

Abdallah Salameh worked with a Scandinavian FinTech company to tailor their Spotify model to foster architectural alignment [5]. Dr Salameh helped to form an *Architectural Ownership Team* comprising chapter leads and led by an enterprise architect. This change represents a decentralisation of architectural decision-making from enterprise architects to chapter leads while also freeing up time for enterprise architects to focus on over-arching enterprise aspects of architectural thinking. We found that this approach strengthened the autonomy of squads by aligning architectural decision-making and helped to share architectural knowledge among squads [5].

18.7 Other Frameworks

The scrum-of-scrums concept involves an additional coordination meeting exclusively for scrum masters, as shown in Fig. 18.1. However, the scrum-of-scrums approach has limitations. Consequently, other frameworks have been developed to support large-scale agile. There are two frameworks which we need to mention: large-scale scrum and the scaled agile framework.

18.7.1 Large-Scale Scrum

Large-scale scrum (LeSS) offers two different frameworks, one for up to eight scrum teams and another for *huge* development programmes [9]. LeSS is a formalisation and perhaps scaled-up version of scrum of scrums. They refer to *one team scrum* and use a single product owner and single product backlog with multiple teams. The teams contribute to a single potentially shippable product, with a common definition of done across the teams, at the end of a single sprint.

Scrum meetings or daily stand-ups are conducted separately within each team. Sprint reviews, in contrast, are conducted using a *bazaar* or *science fair* concept in a large room with multiple areas. In each area, team members show and discuss working code they have developed.

Emphasis in LeSS is placed on teams working together, at the sprint planning phase, to determine which teams will pick up which features. During the single sprint, team members are encouraged to talk, use open spaces, travel to other teams, communicate using code and develop communities to share ideas and interact across teams.

18.7.2 SAFe

Scaled agile framework (SAFe) is a framework for scaling agile across the enterprise [7]. SAFe operates at a team, programme, large solution and portfolio level and inherits principles from Scrum, XP and lean approaches as well as DevOps [7]. SAFe also adds layers for handling large-scale projects as well as techniques for managing a collection of products.

SAFe has a large set of training programmes, for roles in different levels of the organisation. Practitioners can become certified, to provide recognition for their skills and knowledge. Accredited consultants are available to help organisations adopt the approach.

In some ways, SAFe reminds me of the limitations faced by the Rational Unified Process (RUP). RUP, like SAFe, has many good ideas. But, the framework has become elaborate and burdensome to implement. SAFe attempts to cover every eventuality by providing advice and practices at every level of the organisation.

And anyway, the whole attempt to implement or impose an elaborate framework seems to undermine the whole philosophy of agile. Agile is supposed to be about empowering teams to find their own solutions. Implementing an elaborate set of rules or practices seems to go against that ethos, in my opinion.

18.8   Chapter Summary

In agile, small teams are desirable to encourage communication and collaboration. If, however, project scope is large and time scales are short, then multiple teams will be required. In this situation, self-organising agile teams must cooperate with each other to build a product. The scrum-of-scrums approach imposes onto scrum masters a significant burden for resolving impediments and dependencies.

In contrast, a matrix management approach has been employed at the Spotify music streaming service. At Spotify, everyone is simultaneously a member of a squad, chapter and tribe, as well as potentially several guilds. The squad is a self-organising team. The chapter is organised around a specialist skill set and focuses on professional development. The tribe is a group of squads working on the same product, while a guild is an informal community of practice with a specific focus.

Finally, large-scale agile frameworks like *LeSS* or *SAFe* give practitioners detailed advice and offer training and certification. These frameworks encapsulate many good ideas. But, somehow these frameworks run counter to the agile ethos in which teams develop their own process innovations.

References

1. Bass, J.M., Haxby, A.: Tailoring product ownership in large-scale agile projects: managing scale, distance, and governance. IEEE Softw. **36**(2), 58–63 (2019). https://doi.org/10.1109/MS.2018. 2885524
2. Bass, J.M., Beecham, S., Razzak, M.A., Canna, C.N., Noll, J.: An empirical study of the product owner role in scrum. In: Proceedings of the 40th International Conference on Software Engineering: Companion Proceedings, pp. 123–124. ICSE '18, ACM, New York (2018). https:// doi.org/10.1145/3183440.3195066
3. Kniberg, H., Ivarsson, A.: Scaling Agile @ Spotify with Tribes, Squads, Chapters & Guilds. Crisp AB (2012). https://blog.crisp.se/wp-content/uploads/2012/11/SpotifyScaling.pdf
4. Reis, E.: The Lean Startup: How Constant Innovation Creates Radically Successful Businesses. Portfolio Penguin, London (2011)
5. Salameh, A., Bass, J.: Influential factors of aligning spotify squads in mission-critical and offshore projects – a longitudinal embedded case study. In: Kuhrmann, M., Schneider, K., Pfahl, D., Amasaki, S., Ciolkowski, M., Hebig, R., Tell, P., Klünder, J., Küpper, S. (eds.) Product-Focused Software Process Improvement. Lecture Notes in Computer Science, vol. 11271, pp. 199–215. Springer International Publishing, New York City (2018). https://doi.org/10.1007/ 978-3-030-03673-7_15
6. Salameh, A., Bass, J.M.: An architecture governance approach for agile development by tailoring the spotify model. AI Soc (2021). https://doi.org/10.1007/s00146-021-01240-x
7. Scaled Agile Inc: Safe 5.0 framework (2021). https://www.scaledagileframework.com/
8. Smite, D., Moe, N.B., Levinta, G., Floryan, M.: Spotify guilds: how to succeed with knowledge sharing in large-scale agile organizations. IEEE Softw. **36**(2), 51–57 (2019). https://doi.org/10. 1109/MS.2018.2886178
9. The LeSS Company: Overview (2021). https://less.works/

Chapter 19
Cloud Deployment

Abstract Many software applications and services are now deployed on remote servers and accessed using internet technologies. We want to learn more about such routes to application deployment. We discuss some architectural issues that developers of cloud-hosted applications must face, including scalability, multi-tenancy, automated customer on-boarding and automated source code deployment.

19.1 Introduction

Cloud services are provided by remote servers accessed using internet technology. This is a rental model of hardware, storage and platforms. The cost of entry, the start-up cost, is significantly lower than in-house server provision. There is no need to create an air-conditioned server room with emergency backup power supply. There is no need to purchase racks of computers and create dedicated high-speed internet connections. Instead, an online dashboard is used to select and instantiate the compute or storage resources that you need.

Usually, cloud services are provided on a shared-resource pay-as-you-go basis. Multiple virtual machines, belonging to different clients, are executed on a single hardware processor. This *pay-as-you-go* model can be particularly attractive, if your compute or storage demands fluctuate significantly, the idea being you only pay for the services you use, when you use them.

However, over time, the cost of renting cloud-hosted servers will likely exceed the cost of in-house provision. For example, at the time of writing in August 2021, a small virtual machine from DigitalOcean costs US \$5 for 1 month [1]. You can purchase a hobbyist single-board computer, such as a Raspberry Pi Model 4b, for around US \$35 [12]. I've used both to experiment with installing and executing a small Jenkins server, for instance. For the first couple of months, renting a virtual machine from DigitalOcean would be cheaper. But if you plan to experiment over a longer period, say 6 months, then buying hardware might be a better option. Needless to say, if you need to build a commercial server room, with air conditioning and backup power, the DigitalOcean option is cheaper for much longer.

© Springer Nature Switzerland AG 2022
J. M. Bass, *Agile Software Engineering Skills*,
https://doi.org/10.1007/978-3-031-05469-3_19

But bear in mind, there could be other benefits to using DigitalOcean virtual machines, of course. The cloud-hosted virtual machines have the potential to be used in a production environment, which is not wise with a hobbyist setup. Also, many cloud vendors provide software tools to support production deployment. In addition, the skills acquired when you instantiate a service with cloud providers can be in demand from potential employers.

We are interested in cloud services from two standpoints. On the one hand, we are likely to be consumers of cloud-hosted services. On the other hand, we might be interested to deploy the software we create to cloud platforms. From both perspectives, it is useful to find out a bit more about these technologies.

19.2   Cloud Service Models

There are four main cloud service models: infrastructure-as-a-service, platform-as-a-service, software-as-a-service and serverless computing. We can think of these as providing increasing levels of support for application deployment. At one extreme, an infrastructure-as-a-service provider might offer bare processor and memory hardware, accessible through a network connection or perhaps with a standard operating system installed. At the other extreme, serverless computing solutions aim to remove all concerns about deployment from the application development team.

19.2.1   Infrastructure-as-a-Service

Many cloud providers offer raw virtual machines on a pay-as-you-go basis. Virtual machines can be started (and stopped) at short notice, often more or less instantaneously. Providers often offer virtual machines with a range of specifications in terms of processor power, memory and network traffic. This might range from simple single-core processors with modest memory allocations to much more powerful multi-core processors with significant allocations of working storage.

Persistent storage is usually available separately from the virtual machines used for computation. Connecting persistent storage to the processor is usually a (fairly) straightforward configuration step. Providers offer data archiving capabilities, for an extra cost.

19.2.2   Platform-as-a-Service

Platforms support software development by providing a database, business intelligence services, development tools or middleware services. This reduces development time and extends your capabilities. In the long run, the costs of such platforms might be higher. But initially, you can avoid the cost of integrating your own software systems to establish the platform capability. Instead, you can use the cloud platform whenever you need it.

For example, it is sometimes attractive to be able to deploy, configure and security harden a powerful production database server within an hour. This is a much quicker response than is possible if it is necessary to purchase, install and configure server hardware as well as operating system and database software.

19.2.3 Software-as-a-Service

Cloud-hosted software services, such as Dropbox [3], Google Drive [6], Office 365 [11] and Google Docs [7], have become very popular. Such services include social media, business services and entertainment platforms. Service consumers need not be concerned with application installation, deployment or maintenance since this is all performed (and charged for) by the service provider.

19.2.4 Serverless Computing

Serverless computing is a misnomer really, because the code still runs on a server, of course. However, the server (deployment, management and maintenance) is pretty much invisible to the developer. Essentially, all operational aspects of the service are outsourced to the serverless compute provider. The aim with this approach is to allow developers to focus on creating their application and not have to worry about deployment issues at all.

19.3 Cloud-Hosted Application Patterns

There are several issues we must consider if we design applications for cloud-hosted deployment. We learned about the concept of architectural styles in Chap. 8 and object-oriented design patterns in Chap. 9. We can now consider applying these pattern concepts to cloud-hosted software services [4].

19.3.1 Scalability

Cloud-hosted applications and services ideally adjust their resources depending upon current usage. As the number of users increases, then resources allocated to service provision are increased correspondingly. Conversely, as the number of users declines, resources can be released, reducing hosting rental costs. This is known as scalability or sometimes elasticity. Some cloud providers offer a range of services to support scalability. This might include measures to provide metrics for things like processor utilisation or number of incoming user requests. These metrics can be used to create thresholds that, in turn, trigger creation of new virtual machine instances. Increasing or decreasing the number of virtual machines supporting deployed services makes assumptions, for example, about state management. Certainly, scalability is much simpler for stateless services.

19.3.2   Multi-Tenancy

Cloud-hosted applications and services need to support multiple users sharing the same functionality. The data for each user needs to be kept separate, while the services provided are generally similar to each other. Several architectural styles are available providing different levels of tenant isolation. An authorisation system is usually implemented which identifies each user and provides access to their data (and no one else's).

19.3.3   Automated Customer On-Boarding

Cloud applications usually try to avoid manual operations when adding new users to the system. We aim to eliminate manual processes from the on-boarding activities that inhibit application scalability and increase costs. Hence, our emphasis is on patterns for *automated* customer on-boarding.

We try to reduce any sources of friction during the on-boarding process, initially collecting minimum information and making it easy for potential customers to get started. However, our automated processes will probably need to capture means of payment when we add new customers to the system. Our goal is to maximise the number of conversions from visitors to customers.

19.3.4   Revenue Generation

Cloud-hosted applications and services often implement a pay-as-you-go model. Providers must decide what user operations to measure and which to charge for. It is not easy for service providers to decide, in advance of launch, which will be premium features and will command higher value.

Often, a three-tier pricing model is used. The first *bronze* tier, often free of charge to users, provides useful but basic features. This tier is used to attract potential clients and gather user data. The second *silver* tier offers more advanced features at a higher price. Finally, there is often a more expensive enterprise-level *gold* tier for corporate clients.

19.3.5 'n'-Tier Architectures

For larger business information systems, we often use an 'n'-tier architectural style in which the presentation layer is separated from the business logic layer which in turn is distinct from the persistence layer. The layered architectural style was introduced in Sect. 8.3.4. The 'n'-tier architectural style is useful for reducing coupling between the layers of large-scale systems. For example, in principle, the storage technology can be replaced in the persistence layer, without affecting the rest of the system, assuming a good persistence layer interface has been defined.

In the cloud deployment context, we can take the 'n'-tier architectural style to another level of sophistication by deploying the different layers to separate virtual machines. Back-end persistence and business logic layers can be implemented behind the demilitarised zone, to improve data security. Hence, executing layers on different servers can offer improved resilience and allow us to more easily adjust compute resources to achieve performance targets.

19.4 Automated Deployment

I will explore automated continuous delivery in Chap. 21. To fully embrace a continuous integration/continuous deployment (CI/CD or DevOps) pipeline, build automation is used to test and deploy code that is integrated into the main source code trunk. There are various tool platforms, such as Jenkins [9], that can be used to implement CI/CD pipelines. Such a pipeline is used to trigger automated test, build and deployment activities.

For small teams or software start-ups, perhaps implementing a full CI/CD pipeline is too expensive. A simpler approach is to use git hooks to trigger a deployment, every time you commit to the repository [8]. Git hooks detect a repository commit and execute a script which might include copying an executable version of the software to the appropriate folder on a live web server [5].

19.5 Containerisation

Using a containerisation technology, such as Docker, simplifies deployment to multiple servers [2]. The container encapsulates configuration, software stacks such as frameworks, libraries and other dependencies, as well as the executable application. Containers support distinctive operating system and technology stack requirements for our different applications and services.

The container construction process itself can be version controlled. We automate container creation with scripts so the process is consistent and repeatable. Container libraries are available to get you started, comprising operating systems, databases and web servers installed and configured depending on your needs.

Containers have become widely used for application deployment, so much so, that container management itself is being automated. Kubernetes orchestrates container deployment, scaling, load balancing and roll-backs [10]. These features become more important if you are running a business-critical application or there are many users that depend on your service.

19.6   Chapter Summary

Cloud-hosted software services offer a low capital investment route to creating production applications. While well-suited to start-ups and those with fluctuating resource needs, outsourcing deployment and operations can be more expensive in the long run, compared with in-house operations.

However, products and services deployed in this way do not require installation by users and can support a worldwide audience. From a consumer perspective, we can focus on using services, while providers take care of resilience, maintenance and performance issues.

From another perspective, as developers of software services deployed in this way, we have learned a little about some new architectural concerns, such as multi-tenancy and scalability, which must addressed in application design.

References

1. DigitalOcean: Digitalocean—the developer cloud (2021). https://www.digitalocean.com/
2. Docker: Get started with docker (2019). https://www.docker.com/get-started
3. Dropbox: Dropbox (2021). https://www.dropbox.com/
4. Fehling, C., Leymann, F., Retter, R., Schupeck, W., Arbitter, P.: Cloud Computing Patterns: Fundamentals to Design, Build, and Manage Cloud Applications. Springer, Vienna (2014). https://doi.org/10.1007/978-3-7091-1568-8
5. Florence, R.: Deploying websites with a tiny git hook (2010). http://ryanflorence.com/deploying-websites-with-a-tiny-git-hook/
6. Google: Cloud storage for work and home—Google drive (2021). https://www.google.com/drive/
7. Google: Google docs: Free online document editor | google workspace (2021). https://www.facebook.com/GoogleDocs/
8. Hudson, M.: Learn how to improve your git skills. https://githooks.com/
9. Jenkins project: Jenkins. https://jenkins.io/index.html
10. Kubernetes: Production-grade container orchestration (2021). https://kubernetes.io/

11. Microsoft: Microsoft 365 | secure, integrated office 365 apps + teams (2022). https://www.microsoft.com/en-gb/microsoft-365
12. Raspberry Pi Foundation: Buy a raspberry pi 4 model b. https://www.raspberrypi.org/products/raspberry-pi-4-model-b/

Chapter 20
Technical Debt, Software Evolution and Legacy

Abstract Most of this book has been concerned with developing new systems or features. When students learn software development, it is usually on new projects starting afresh, without any previously existing source code. In contrast, most commercial software development effort is directed towards sustaining live systems that have existing user communities. Live systems already have paying customers. We need those customers to pay us for the development effort. In this chapter, we concentrate on the needs of live systems and how teams can support their evolution.

20.1 Introduction

Looking after a working software system is known as software maintenance. Software evolution is the process of making enhancements to a live system while at the same time supporting existing users. Maintenance and evolution costs are usually much higher than development costs.

When we build a new system, we should carefully consider these high maintenance and evolution costs, because future software engineers are going to perform various updates and improvements. If the structure of our software is shoddy or our code follows a convoluted logic, it will be clear for all to see that we have performed a poor-quality job. Our goal is to ensure that, when others read our code, it is clear, simple and straightforward to understand.

Hence, while we write programmes to control computers, we also write programmes for other software engineers to read and modify. These other software engineers are our friends and colleagues. We don't want to add misery to their lives. We aspire to write software that is as simple and elegant as possible, to perform the job.

When sustaining live systems, we must also balance the needs of current users against requirements to attract potential new customers. As we enhance a live product or service with new features, we usually try to avoid impairing the level of service we currently offer (unless, of course, there is a conscious decision to do that).

© Springer Nature Switzerland AG 2022
J. M. Bass, *Agile Software Engineering Skills*,
https://doi.org/10.1007/978-3-031-05469-3_20

In this chapter, I discuss several concepts and techniques useful for managing live systems. Legacy systems are an extreme form of live software services that have usually not benefited from sufficient investment in evolution or maintenance. I'll come on to discussing legacy systems shortly.

20.2   Technical Debt

In software projects, the phrase *technical debt* is a metaphor for monetary debt [2]. Small amounts of technical debt are not a bad thing and are actually a natural consequence of a healthy incremental software development process. Pressure to deliver new features quickly means deficiencies are introduced into our system design. Choosing a quick and easy solution now creates an implied cost of rework later, hence the monetary debt metaphor.

Over time, design rationalisation or tidying up becomes desirable to repay this debt. As development work continues, and more new features are added, the need for refactoring and even re-engineering becomes a high priority. Periodically, in a healthy project, the team will create opportunities to focus on significantly reducing technical debt.

Balancing investment in technical debt with the need for new features and functionality is important. Typically, projects do not have sufficient resources to deal with all technical debt as it arises. Indeed, a project with no technical debt is likely not creating enhancements quickly enough to satisfy customers. On the other hand, excessive technical debt impedes the prompt addition of new features and functionality.

20.2.1   Technical Debt and Agile

Iterative development processes lend themselves to transitioning from new feature development to maintenance and support, as a project evolves, as illustrated in Fig. 20.1. Early in the project, everyone contributes new features to create a new product or service. As the project matures, software defects will emerge and need repairing. When the system is deployed to customers, feature enhancements will be identified. Some agile teams include software defects in their normal iteration planning. Defects are added to backlogs and prioritised, and Kanban boards are used to monitor progress. Depending on the volume of defects, some teams devote an entire sprint to fixing defects and performing feature enhancements. This is sometime done as part of a quality improvement effort prior to a major release. As the system matures, focus shifts from creating new features to more emphasis on enhancement of existing features. During this phase of a product life, every second or third sprint might be devoted to enhancements and fixing defects. As time

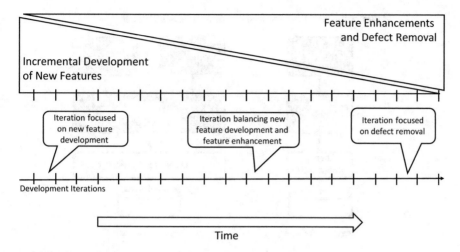

Fig. 20.1 Migration from new feature development to maintenance

goes on, teams increase the frequency of iterations focused on defects and feature enhancements.

20.2.2 Refactoring

Refactoring is the process of making changes to software that do not affect the external behaviour [1]. Refactoring is intended to simplify design, improving flexibility and maintainability without changing the behaviour of the software and repay technical debt previously accrued.

20.3 Software Evolution

Sometimes, modernisation of a software system is required. This goes beyond refactoring. Modernisation might mean replacing an outdated technology or re-developing the overall system architecture to support adding new features or services.

20.3.1 Wrappering

Wrappering is the processes of surrounded an existing system with new layers that can be more readily enhanced in the future. For example, a new user interface can

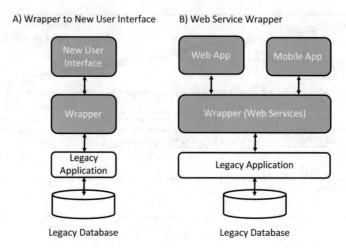

Fig. 20.2 Front-end wrappering approaches

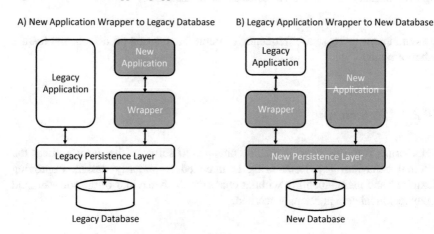

Fig. 20.3 Database wrapper approaches (Adapted from [4])

be added to a legacy application, as shown in Fig. 20.2a, while, using a web service wrapper, a thin-client (web-based) front-end and a mobile device application can be added to an existing installed application, as shown in Fig. 20.2b. This allows us to expose the application functionality and data without re-developing the core legacy system. This can reduce short-term costs and get the enhanced solution to clients sooner.

In other circumstances, with a problematic persistence layer, a new back-end storage infrastructure can be used to improve resilience or performance [4]. There are basically two approaches to wrappering data storage as shown in Fig. 20.3. We can either provide a wrapper to a legacy database and build new application on top of the wrapper, as shown in Fig. 20.3a. Or alternatively, we can build a new database, migrate legacy data and then create a wrapper for the legacy application to the modern database, as shown in Fig. 20.3b.

Wrappering can be cost-effective, compared to an entire re-development effort. The existing system is treated as a black-box, with minimum intervention. But new features are added using a more modern technology stack. A significant challenge is that legacy systems are often monolithic and hence difficult to decompose into logical subsystems. For example, the legacy persistence layer, shown in Fig. 20.3a, may not exist in a monolithic legacy system.

20.3.2 Re-engineering

Eventually, after many releases, a live software system will need a significant upgrade. The high-level architectural style may need to be reworked. A refresh of the entire implementation technology stack may be desirable. There may come a point where to a significant extent the system will have to be re-designed and re-implemented. This re-engineering effort is intended to deliver new, existing and enhanced services, but with a much improved internal structure and implementation.

20.4 Legacy Systems

Legacy systems provide important services, but are built using out-of-date technologies. It is important to emphasise that legacy systems fulfil significant needs. We rely on the services they provide. The drawback of legacy systems is that they are implemented using old technologies.

There are some technologies in computing that get old surprisingly quickly. I've spoken to practitioners working on a large-scale thin-client system, a database-driven web application for a big multinational enterprise. The web application is implemented using a framework and has just been deployed. The team is considering the next new application. A new and better web framework is now available. Consequently, the team choose not to employ the same web development framework used in their current system for their next application.

A less pejorative way of looking at legacy systems is to think of them as heritage. In the UK-built environment, we have lots of heritage sites. We have castles and palaces that are carefully preserved and maintained by large and well-funded institutions. Tourists from home and abroad (when we are not in the grip of a virulent pandemic) visit to enjoy the spectacle of such historical relics. Thinking of software as heritage helps us understand the need to nurture and evolve such systems. Rather than allowing them to decay into obsolescence. Investment is needed to support our heritage systems. Failure to invest will result in higher costs later.

We see legacy systems as a suffering from an extreme form of technical debt [3]. For historical reasons, the legacy system has not benefited from the (perhaps significant) investment required to bring it up to date. Successive management regimes prioritised investment in new short-term needs, rather than invest in updating existing systems. Organisations seem to lack awareness of the scale funding needed for ongoing evolution and maintenance existing systems.

20.5   Chapter Summary

Most commercial software development effort goes into sustaining live systems that have active users, rather than into creating new products. This chapter has focused on the evolution of live systems.

Technical debt is a useful way of thinking about investment decisions into software evolution. Technical debt builds up during incremental development when speed of delivery takes priority over elegant solutions. As new features are added, internal complexity builds up.

Periodic refactoring is used to reassert simple design. Refactoring is used to improve maintainability and flexibility without changing behaviour. Refactoring reorganises internal structure to facilitate future enhancement and is used to repay technical debt.

As systems age, the need for more far-reaching re-design arises. The implementation technology stack can become stale and needs to be modernised. Demand for substantial new functionality may impose the need for significant restructuring. Wrappering and re-engineering techniques can be used to address these needs.

References

1. Fowler, M., Beck, K., Brant, J., Opdyke, W., Roberts, D.: Refactoring: Improving the Design of Existing Code, 1st edn. Addison Wesley, Reading (1999)
2. Kruchten, P., Nord, R., Ozkaya, I.: Managing Technical Debt: Reducing Friction in Software Development, 1st edn. Addison-Wesley, Reading (2019)
3. Monaghan, B.D., Bass, J.M.: Redefining legacy: a technical debt perspective. In: Morisio, M., Torchiano, M., Jedlitschka, A. (eds.) Product-Focused Software Process Improvement, pp. 254–269. Lecture Notes in Computer Science. Springer, Berlin (2020). https://doi.org/10.1007/978-3-030-64148-1_16
4. Tripathy, P., Naik, K.: Software Evolution and Maintenance: A Practitioner's Approach, 1st edn. Wiley, London (2015)

Chapter 21
DevOps

Abstract We like to automate testing, because it makes it faster and repeatable for us to maintain high standards of quality. In a similar way, it makes sense to automate the build process. The idea is that we want to build an executable version of our code, run all our tests and, assuming all goes well, deposit the resulting release onto a server for execution. We want to get into the habit of making frequent improvements to our code, and doing all these steps by hand means we might forget or cut corners. So automating the build process means we remember to do all the steps needed, every time we release (which might be every 30 min or so, on some projects).

21.1 Introduction

One important idea emerging from the continuous integration, continuous delivery and DevOps communities is the benefit of automating build and deployment processes as much as possible [4]. Automation offers repeatable processes that can be evolved and refined over time. With automated processes, there is less pressure to take shortcuts, such as skipping certain testing and quality checks, when teams are under pressure of short deadlines.

However, build, test and deployment pipelines are an expression of an organisational commitment to high-quality efficient delivery processes. Significant organisational and cultural changes are needed to make these automated approaches a reality. DevOps is a compound of development (Dev) and operations (Ops) representing a set of practices, software tools and organisational culture to integrate product development and IT teams.

21.2 Build and Deployment Pipelines

First, let's look at a conventional build and deployment pipeline.

© Springer Nature Switzerland AG 2022

J. M. Bass, *Agile Software Engineering Skills*,

https://doi.org/10.1007/978-3-031-05469-3_21

21.2.1   Conventional Deployment Team Structures

In a conventional build and deployment pipeline, implementation, test and deployment of production software systems are performed sequentially, as shown in Fig. 21.1. First, software source code implementation is performed by a development team. Then, quality assurance evaluation is conducted by a test team. Finally, the completed application is deployed to servers or client workstations by an operations team.

One unpleasant side effect of this sequential process is that departmental structures become organised around specialist skills, as shown in Fig. 21.2a. Specialist skills can tend to be siloed in these conventional teams. Teams can become insular and isolated from the majority of developers working in software teams [6, 7].

Such sequential approaches can work well for some organisations, perhaps where software is interacting with custom-built hardware, in embedded systems, for example. But following lean principles, from Chap. 14, we want to reduce hand-offs between specialist teams. For example, the delays in hand-offs from development to

Fig. 21.1 Conventional deployment

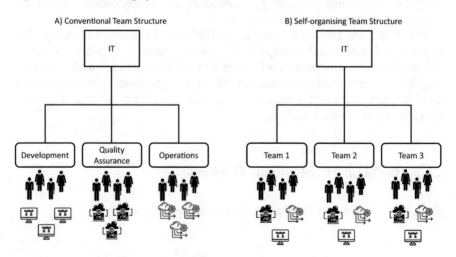

Fig. 21.2 Contrasting approaches to team structure

test and from test to operations can easily get out of control. In some organisations, these hand-offs can stretch to days or even weeks.

21.2.2 Self-Organising Deployment Team Structures

To overcome these shortcomings, self-organising teams, discussed in Chap. 2, are used to improve pipeline efficiency [9], as shown in Fig. 21.2b. In this arrangement, specialists from quality assurance and operations are assigned to development teams. As members of development teams, these specialists can support quality enhancement and operational processes without the need for departmental hand-offs.

21.3 Pipeline Automation

Automation is used to enhance build and deployment quality, repeatability and continuous improvement. Automated processes can be used consistently even when teams are under deadline pressure to ensure checks are completed promptly before code is released to clients.

In order to automate testing and deployment, we first need to automate the build process. Build automation is achieved using build tools which are controlled by configuration files. When a build is triggered, source code files are examined and build processes triggered for any files that have changed or for which compiled artefacts are missing.

You might imagine that build tools would be programming language independent, and yet build tools tend to exist around specific language ecosystems. Ant [1], Maven [2] and Gradle [3] are popular for Java language ecosystems. MSBuild [8] is used for the visual studio application lifecycle management and support the .NET Framework, C# and C++.

Build tool configuration files define dependencies within the source code and how the software is to be built. File locations and required components, libraries and subsystems can be specified. Some, such as Ant, Maven and MSBuild, use an XML-like syntax, whereas Gradle uses a Groovy- and Kotlin-based domain-specific language.

For further pipeline automation, source code commits in version control are used to initiate a test, review and deploy cycle, as shown in Fig. 21.3.

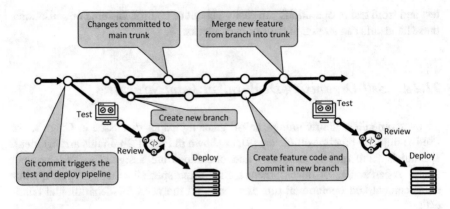

Fig. 21.3 Integrating a continuous deployment pipeline with version control

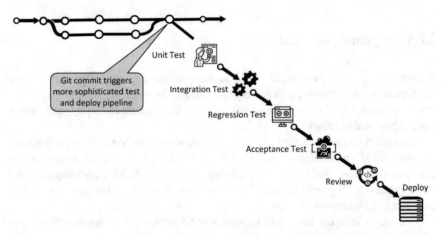

Fig. 21.4 More sophisticated test pipeline triggered from a version control commit

In more mature and stable development environments, the automated testing tasks triggered by a version control commit may be more sophisticated, as shown in Fig. 21.4. In this example, sets of unit, integration, regression and acceptance tests are executed on each commit to the main trunk.

The concept of a pipeline is coded directly into the Jenkins CI/CD software tool [5]. There are several ways of writing a *Jenkins File*, the file that configures the build process; one is shown below:

Illustrative Jenkins Pipeline

```
pipeline {
    stages {
      stage('Build') {
          steps {
              // steps for the build stage go here
          }
      }
      stage('Test') {
          steps {
              // steps for the test stage go here
          }
      }
      stage('Deploy') {
          steps {
              // steps for the deploy stage go here
          }
      }
    }
}
```

The *Jenkins File* distinguishes between *stages* and *steps*. A *stage* is a group of tasks that perform a conceptually distinct function. The *stages* in the *Jenkins File* shown are build, test and deploy, whereas a *step* is a single task telling Jenkins what to do.

21.4 Test Integration

I talked about testing and test automation in more detail in Chap. 16, of course. But the issue here is building automated testing into continuous integration and continuous delivery pipeline.

21.4.1 Testing New Features

The first stage is unit testing of new features under development. Initially, developers test their own code. Once the new features are merged into the main trunk, acceptance testing on the new features will need to be performed.

21.4.2   Regression Testing Legacy Features

The other aspect of testing is to ensure the new features have not introduced any problems with existing features. Hence, the need to test legacy features after new features have been integrated, this is regression testing, as discussed in Sect. 16.4.1.

21.5   Continuous Integration

Continuous integration is the practice of frequently merging new code into the main trunk of the project source code repository. Continuous integration encourages a different view on the branches discussed in Sect. 15.5.1. A conventional view of new feature development envisages long-lived feature branches. Feature branches are helpful because they keep the new feature code separate from the main trunk, while the feature is under development.

However, from a lean perspective, source code sitting in a feature branch is a form of waste; see Sect. 14.3. The feature branch code does not add value to the project until it is integrated into the main trunk. Delaying the integration of new code into the main trunk increases the likelihood of merge conflicts. Taking this view, feature branches are best avoided. Instead, features are developed on the main trunk.

21.6   DevOps and DevSecOps

As I said, DevOps is a set of practices, software tools and organisational culture to integrate product development and IT teams. Once the continuous integration and continuous delivery pipeline is in place, it becomes easier to enhance the process for security hardening. The DevSecOps community reminds us that including automated security into the build and deployment process is important. Security testing tools can be executed as part of the testing phase, prior to deployment as shown in Fig. 21.5.

21.7   Continuous Delivery and Deployment

The next step of automation after continuous integration is continuous delivery or continuous deployment. For continuous delivery, we automate the process of building a production version of the software system and moving this to an execution environment. Consequently, we have our latest product version ready to launch at all times. Following a review process, the latest production version can be released to customers.

In continuous deployment, we take this one step further. The idea is to automate the entire process and release the latest executable code into a production environment after each commit. This high level of automation is intended to accelerate the delivery of new features to customers and to attract feedback more quickly as a consequence.

21.8 Chapter Summary

In a conventional build and deployment pipeline, separate specialist teams perform software implementation, quality assurance and operational support for production applications. There is a sequential flow from development to test and on to operations. The hand-offs between specialist teams can introduce delays and inefficiencies into the deployment process.

Creating self-organising teams and automating this pipeline removes bottlenecks from the process, but requires significant organisational commitment. Specialist tools are used to support integration of new feature code into the main trunk and then automatically run selected tests and subsequently to move executable code into a production environment.

Once automated, the process is consistent, is repeatable and provides confidence in code quality prior to each new feature release. The approach avoids a large, time-consuming, integration phase towards the end of a project. The approach also avoids the risk of corner-cutting when teams are under pressure of short deadlines to release new features.

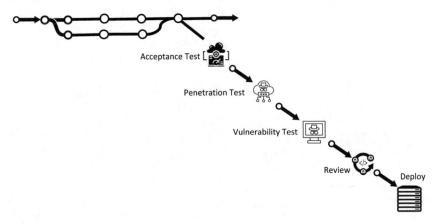

Fig. 21.5 Security testing triggered from a version control commit

References

1. Apache Software Foundation: Apache ant—welcome (2022). https://ant.apache.org/
2. Apache Software Foundation: Maven—welcome to apache maven (2022). https://maven.apache.org/
3. Gradle Inc.: Gradle build tool (2022). https://gradle.org/
4. Humble, J., Farley, D.: Continuous Delivery: Reliable Software Releases Through Build, Test, and Deployment Automation. Addison Wesley, Reading (2010)
5. Jenkins project: Jenkins. https://jenkins.io/index.html
6. Macarthy, R.W., Bass, J.M.: An empirical taxonomy of devops in practice. In: Euromicro 46th Conference on Software Engineering and Advanced Applications (SEAA), ppp. 221–228. IEEE, Piscataway (2020)
7. Macarthy, R.W., Bass, J.M.: The role of skillset in the determination of devops implementation strategy. In: Joint 15th International Conference on Software and System Processes (ICSSP) and 16th ACM/IEEE International Conference on Global Software Engineering (ICGSE), pp. 50 – 60. IEEE, Piscataway (2021)
8. Microsoft: Msbuild—msbuild (2022). https://docs.microsoft.com/en-us/visualstudio/msbuild/msbuild
9. Skelton, M., Pais, M., Malan, R.: Team Topologies: Organizing Business and Technology Teams for Fast Flow. It Revolution Press, illustrated edn. (2019)

Appendix A
Research Methods

The material, described in this book, has benefited from collaborations in commercial software development projects and original research in the software development sector. I benefited from an opportunity to work with Add Energy Ltd. (advising on their AimHi, AssetC and Asset Voice products), Invisible Systems Ltd. and Red Ocelot Ltd. and learned much from these activities.

Several of the chapters in this book have benefited from empirical research investigating the activities of practitioners engaged in software development projects. More specifically, Chap. 3 draws on [2–4, 11], while Chap. 7 benefits from [13]. In turn, Chap. 10 includes findings from [5]. Chapter 21 draws on evidence from [8, 9]. Chapter 18 benefits from [14, 15], and Chap. 20 includes findings from [10].

A.1 Research Sites

The research in [2–5] was conducted by investigating over 20 companies and UK government organisations. The companies, several of whom are multinationals, are based in the USA, Europe and South Asia.

The organisations in the study include well-known multinational internet and software service companies as well as government agencies and companies in the banking/finance, customer relationship management and retail sectors.

A.2 Data Collection

Respondents included over 100 practitioners with a wide range of responsibilities. They comprised product owners, senior executives (with job titles such as chief information officer, chief technology officer or head of engineering) as well as

© Springer Nature Switzerland AG 2022
J. M. Bass, *Agile Software Engineering Skills*,
https://doi.org/10.1007/978-3-031-05469-3

middle managers, agile coaches and development team members, such as software developers, testers and scrum masters.

A semi-structured interview guide was used during practitioner interviews. The interviews included open-ended questions to elicit topics from respondents not considered by the interviewer. Interviews, which typically lasted around 50 min, were recorded and transcribed.

A.3   Data Analysis

Data analysis was informed by grounded theory [7]. Interviews were analysed using a Glaserian grounded theory approach [6]. Open coding, memoing, constant comparison and saturation techniques were used to extract topics, concepts and themes from the interview transcript data [1].

A.3.1   Open Coding

Coding, in this context, does not mean writing software. But rather, coding is the research process of identifying the topics described in the source data. For this research, a sentence-by-sentence approach was adopted. The large volume of data made it attractive to use a qualitative analysis tool [12] to record and manage the coding process.

A.3.2   Memo Writing

Memos are short essays recoding the scope and content of topics and categories identified from the data. Memos include interview quotes and contrast the differing experiences and perspectives of respondents. Some memos build upon contemporaneous field notes taken during observations of practices or interviews. The memo writing is used to clarify, refine and sharpen categories. The memos are revised and enhanced as new transcript data is added.

A.3.3   Constant Comparison

Using the constant comparison technique, the researcher iterates back and forth between data collection and analysis. We use constant comparison to compare events or respondent perspectives that apply to each category we have identified.

We compared interview transcript codes with each other at two levels:

- within the same organisation or project team
- with outside organisations and teams.

In this way, the codes evolved and were refined over time using constant comparison.

A.3.4   Saturation

In the early stages of the research, interviews with each new company or project team cause reappraisal of the topics and categories which have previously been identified. New events, incidents, artefacts, development practices and stakeholders are discovered at each new research site.

As the study progresses and the number of interview respondents increases, the richness and detail of the grounded theory are enhanced as a consequence. Gradually, each new research site and practitioner interview results in fewer new discoveries and has less impact on the categorisation. The evidence from new interviews is increasingly consistent with the topics and categories previously identified.

Saturation has occurred when new research sites or interviews don't cause significant refinement to the topics and categories already identified.

References

1. Adolph, S., Hall, W., Kruchten, P.: Using grounded theory to study the experience of software development. Empirical Softw. Eng. **16**(4), 487–513 (2011). https://doi.org/10.1007/s10664-010-9152-6
2. Bass, J.M., Haxby, A.: Tailoring product ownership in large-scale agile projects: managing scale, distance, and governance. IEEE Softw. **36**(2), 58–63 (2019). https://doi.org/10.1109/MS.2018.2885524
3. Bass, J.: Scrum master activities: process tailoring in large enterprise projects. In: 2014 IEEE 9th International Conference on Global Software Engineering (ICGSE), pp. 6–15 (2014). https://doi.org/10.1109/ICGSE.2014.24
4. Bass, J.M.: How product owner teams scale agile methods to large distributed enterprises. Empirical Softw. Eng. **20**(6), 1525–1557 (2015). https://doi.org/10.1007/s10664-014-9322-z
5. Bass, J.M.: Artefacts and agile method tailoring in large-scale offshore software development programmes. Inform. Softw. Technol. **75**, 1–16 (2016). https://doi.org/10.1016/j.infsof.2016.03.001
6. Glaser, B.G.: Doing Grounded Theory: Issues and Discussions. Sociology Press, Mill Valley (1998)
7. Glaser, B., Strauss, A.L.: Discovery of Grounded Theory: Strategies for Qualitative Research. Aldine Transaction (1999)

8. Macarthy, R.W., Bass, J.M.: An empirical taxonomy of devops in practice. In: Euromicro 46th Conference on Software Engineering and Advanced Applications (SEAA), pp. 221–8. IEEE, Piscataway (2020)

9. Macarthy, R.W., Bass, J.M.: The role of skillset in the determination of devops implementation strategy. In: Joint 15th International Conference on Software and System Processes (ICSSP) and 16th ACM/IEEE International Conference on Global Software Engineering (ICGSE), pp. 50 – 60. IEEE, Piscataway (2021)

10. Monaghan, B.D., Bass, J.M.: Redefining legacy: A technical debt perspective. In: Morisio, M., Torchiano, M., Jedlitschka, A. (eds.) Product-Focused Software Process Improvement, pp. 254–269. Lecture Notes in Computer Science. Springer, Berlin (2020). https://doi.org/10.1007/978-3-030-64148-1_16

11. Noll, J., Razzak, M.A., Bass, J.M., Beecham, S.: A study of the scrum master's role. In: Product-Focused Software Process Improvement, pp. 307–323. Lecture Notes in Computer Science. Springer, Cham (2017)

12. QSR International: NVivo 11 for Windows Help—Welcome (2019). http://help-nv11.qsrinternational.com/desktop/welcome/welcome.htm

13. Rahy, S., Bass, J.M.: Managing non-functional requirements in agile software development. IET Softw. (2021). https://doi.org/10.1049/sfw2.12037

14. Salameh, A., Bass, J.: Influential factors of aligning spotify squads in mission-critical and offshore projects—a longitudinal embedded case study. In: Kuhrmann, M., Schneider, K., Pfahl, D., Amasaki, S., Ciolkowski, M., Hebig, R., Tell, P., Klünder, J., Küpper, S. (eds.) Product-Focused Software Process Improvement. Lecture Notes in Computer Science, vol. 11271, pp. 199–215. Springer, Berlin (2018). https://doi.org/10.1007/978-3-030-03673-7_15

15. Salameh, A., Bass, J.M.: An architecture governance approach for agile development by tailoring the spotify model. AI & Society (2021). https://doi.org/10.1007/s00146-021-01240-x

Appendix B
Further Reading

Having finished reading this book and working through all the exercises, there are some further books I think everyone should read. Here are my top 20(ish) agile software engineering books I think everyone should read.

B.1   Core Reading

For core software engineering books, my favourites include:

- Software engineering

    - Ian Sommerville's textbook on software engineering is widely used [23], or [17] is also good.

- Agile methods

    - Kent Beck's book on extreme programming [1] or one of Ken Schwaber's books on scrum [20] is worth reading.

- Software development (meaning code production)

    - Bob Martin's book on coding and standards has become popular with developers [14], or Steve McConnell's book on source code is also worth reading [24],
    - On *Design Patterns*, the most important book is from Gamma et al. [9],
    - For *refactoring*, you should read [8],
    - For *version control* with Git [13].

- User experience

    - For user experience, interface design and analysis, I suggest [21] and [11].

© Springer Nature Switzerland AG 2022
J. M. Bass, *Agile Software Engineering Skills*,
https://doi.org/10.1007/978-3-031-05469-3

B.2   More Specialist Topics

If you are interested to explore some of these more specialist topics in further detail, then I recommend:

- DevOps

  - *Accelerate* is interesting and based on analysis of a large practitioner survey [7].

- Security

  - Bell et al. place security in an agile development context [2]

- Requirements

  - A practical approach to requirements is in [3] and also for organising requirements [15].

- Large-scale agile

  - *Team Topologies* focuses on organising for flow [22].

- Legacy

  - Michael Feathers takes a practical approach to dealing with legacy code [6], or on *technical debt*, then [12].

B.3   Software Engineering Research

For those interested in pursuing research, for example, by doing a PhD in Software Engineering, I recommend:

- Research (in general)

  - Phillips and Pugh take a practical approach to advice for PhD students [16],
  - Mark Reed's book on *Research Impact* is good [18],
  - For *case study* research, try [26],
  - While for *mixed-method* research, [5] is good,
  - I've used a *grounded theory* approach; have a look at [10] or [4],
  - Zinsser's book on *non-fiction writing* will be useful for many [27].

- Software engineering research (specifically)

  - For *case study* research, check out Runeson et al. [19],
  - For *experimental methods*, try [25].

References

1. Beck, K., Andres, C.: Extreme Programming Explained, 2nd edn. Addison Wesley, Boston (2004)
2. Bell, L., Brunton-Spall, M., Smith, R., Bird, J.: Agile Application Security: Enabling Security in a Continuous Delivery Pipeline. O'Reilly (2017)
3. Cohn, M.: User Stories Applied: For Agile Software Development. Addison Wesley, Reading (2004)
4. Corbin, J.M., Strauss, A.C.: Basics of Qualitative Research: Techniques and Procedures for Developing Grounded Theory, 3rd edn. Sage Publications (2008)
5. Creswell, J.W., Creswell, J.D.: Research Design: Qualitative, Quantitative, and Mixed Methods Approaches, 5th edn. SAGE Publications (2018)
6. Feathers, M.: Working Effectively with Legacy Code, 1st edn. Prentice Hall, Englewood (2004)
7. Forsgren, N., Humble, J.: Accelerate: The Science of Lean Software and Devops: Building and Scaling High Performing Technology Organizations. Trade Select, illustrated edn. (2018)
8. Fowler, M., Beck, K., Brant, J., Opdyke, W., Roberts, D.: Refactoring: Improving the Design of Existing Code, 1st edn. Addison Wesley, Reading (1999)
9. Gamma, E., Helm, R., Johnson, R., Vlissides, J.: Design Patterns: Elements of Reusable Object-Oriented Software. Addison-Wesley, Harlow (2005)
10. Glaser, B., Strauss, A.L.: Discovery of Grounded Theory: Strategies for Qualitative Research. Aldine Transaction (1999)
11. Gothelf, J., Seden, J.: Lean UX: Designing Great Products with Agile Teams, 2nd revised edn. O'Reilly (2016)
12. Kruchten, P., Nord, R., Ozkaya, I.: Managing Technical Debt: Reducing Friction in Software Development, 1st edn. Addison-Wesley, Reading (2019)
13. Loeliger, J., McCullough, M.: Version Control with Git: Powerful tools and techniques for collaborative software development, 2nd edn. O'Reilly Media (2012)
14. Martin, R.: Clean Code: A Handbook of Agile Software Craftsmanship, 1st edn. Prentice Hall, Upper Saddle River (2008)
15. Patton, J.: User Story Mapping: Discover the Whole Story, Build the Right Product, 1st edn. O'Reilly Media, Sebastopol (2014)
16. Phillips, E., Pugh, D.S.: How To Get A Phd: A Handbook for Students and Their Supervisors, 6th edn. Open University Press (2015)
17. Pressman, R.S., Maxim, B.R.: Software Engineering: A Practitioner's Approach, 8th edn. McGraw-Hill Education, New York (2015)
18. Reed, M.S.: The Research Impact Handbook. Fast Track Impact (2016)
19. Runeson, P., Höst, M., Rainer, A., Regnell, B.: Case Study Research in Software Engineering: Guidelines and Examples. Wiley-Blackwell (2012)
20. Schwaber, K.: Agile Project Management with Scrum, 1st edn. Microsoft Press, Redmond (2004)
21. Sharp, H., Preece, J., Rogers, Y.: Interaction Design: Beyond Human-Computer Interaction, 5th edn. Wiley, London (2019)
22. Skelton, M., Pais, M., Malan, R.: Team Topologies: Organizing Business and Technology Teams for Fast Flow, illustrated edn. It Revolution Press (2019)
23. Sommerville, I.: Software Engineering, 10th edn. Pearson Education, Harlow (2015)
24. Steve McConnell: Code Complete: A Practical Handbook of Software Construction, 2nd edn. Microsoft Press, Redmond (2004)
25. Wohlin, C., Runeson, P., Höst, M., Ohlsson, M.C., Regnell, B., Wesslén, A.: Experimentation in Software Engineering. Springer, Berlin (2012)
26. Yin, R.K.: Case Study Research: Design and Methods, 4th edn. Sage Publications (2009)
27. Zinsser, W.: On Writing Well: The Classic Guide to Writing Nonfiction, 25th anniversary edn. HarperCollins Publishers, New York (2006)

Index

© Springer Nature Switzerland AG 2022
J. M. Bass, *Agile Software Engineering Skills*,
https://doi.org/10.1007/978-3-031-05469-3

Printed in the United States
by Baker & Taylor Publisher Services